WHAT MIKA KNOWS
and
WHY SHE AND THE MEDIA HATE TRUMP

*THE CONSPIRATORIAL PLANS
TO DESTROY OUR FREE CAPITALIST
DEMOCRATIC AND SOVEREIGN
AMERICA
plus
THE TRUTHS ABOUT AMERICA'S
CONTEMPORARY HISTORY IN TRADE,
EDUCATION, IMMIGRATION,
HEALTHCARE,
GUN CONTROL AND INTERNATIONAL
RELATIONS PRESIDENT TRUMP
IS ENDEAVORING TO REPAIR*

Donn W. Fletcher

ISBN 10: 0692155864
ISBN 13: 9780692155868
Library of Congress Control Number: 2018908335

*This book is dedicated to
President Donald J. Trump
and
enlightened "Deplorables"
who understand it was capitalist
ideas of working and producing,
not socialist welfare or illegal
immigration, that made
America great, and desire to
"Make America Great Again"
by taking back control of their
Government from
"the Establishment" members
like Barrack Obama, the Bush
family, the Clintons and its
founder Zbigniew Brzezinski
who have deliberately diminished
American wealth and productivity,
to benefit themselves and others
whose desire is to make America
just another has been member of
their New World Order,
One World Government.*

CONTENTS

FOREWORD

At end of the second decade of the Twenty-First Century, working, producing, taxpaying Americans who voted for President Donald Trump because they desire to maintain the faith, culture, values and Constitutional protections provided by those who gave birth to America are under attack.

They are under attack by elected and non-elected members of their Government controlled by *"the Establishment" New World Order* first announced publicly by charter member President G.H.W. Bush at the beginning of his Presidency in 1989.

These people are attacking not only the existence of America, but the idea of it, and those who nurtured and guided it and gave their lives for it for over two hundred and forty years.

For over forty years since July 1973 when Zbigniew Brzezinski and David Rockefeller created the formal organization of their *New World Order* and plans to achieve it many of their acolytes and members of their secretive, real conspiracy have been pursuing their dream of destroying the America President Trump and his supporters love.

They want it to be just another borderless, non-sovereign state member of their desired socialist One World Government under their control. Why? As usual, M-O-N-E-Y.

The Brzezinski/Rockefeller organization was based on a business plan to enrich global corporations and by extension, financial interests and the political class as well as further increasing their power at the expense of working Middle Class Americans. The quantified success of this plan can be viewed in *Chapter Six* of this book.

The most visible representation of these people 2016 to 2018 was Hillary Clinton who called patriotic Americans *"deplorables"* because she cared only about enriching herself at their expense, and by voting for Trump they would inhibit her ability to continue to do this.

But the criminal elements of the U.S. Justice Department and Federal Bureau of Investigation who broke laws endeavoring to ensure she would be the next President, so they could keep their good times rolling challenged even her prominence.

The enforcer for this group to keep anyone from outside their America destroying cabal being President was an ex FBI Director who was appointed to endeavor to remove President Trump.

In addition to his Government "pedigree," he was particularly qualified for this task by his checkered past of charging innocent citizens, ruining their careers, names and lives, and even trying to convince a parole board not to parole some of them locked up for twenty years for murder even though he knew they were innocent.

He is just one of the many working against the best interests of honest working Middle Class Americans, as have Brzezinski and the Bushes who came by their anti-Americans, anti-Trump views via similar paths of working for, then continuing to cater to the interests of the old money, Northeast Brahmin wealthiest one-percent.

His path was via his father's employment by one of the old richest one-percent families. Brzezinski's was satisfying the *"Internationalist"* desires of a Rockefeller, and the Bushes via a Bush working for John D. Rockefeller's brother over a hundred years prior to 2018.

In further pursuit of removal of President Trump these people are being assisted in this attack on our democratic process by members of *"the Establishment"* controlled, crooked Goebbels-like media who have also been working assiduously to rob our country of its sovereignty almost since the 1973 beginning of the Brzezinski organization.

In concert, these people are attacking the very fiber of America that made it great by supporting or proselytizing in favor of wars against concepts that cannot be defeated while, for political correctness, refusing to identify enemies they withhold truths about while allying with others who satisfy the criteria for enemies.

These effete so-called *"elite"* acolytes of the America destroying Rockefeller, Bush, Brzezinski *New World Order* One World Government concepts function solely for the benefit of themselves and other members of their *"Establishment"* who should only be referred to as "effete" because of their feeble conduct in refusing to uphold their sworn duties to provide for the safety of Americans, protect their borders, and maintain their Constitutional protections, but have chosen instead, through several administrations of both parties, to support only the interests of those whose objective is to deprive Americans of their culture, freedom, right of self-determination, and prosperity.

But they are also proactive in their deliberate destruction of all that has been America for almost a quarter of a millennium, as anyone paying attention to the words and actions of Hillary Clinton and Barrack Obama since 2008 or Presidents Bush, Clinton and Bush before them should be aware.

Hillary and Obama deliberately began importing thousands of members of the Islamic faith who verbally and demonstrably desire to displace American culture with the Islamic culture that provides only hopelessness and poverty to its followers. Then when campaigning for the Presidency Hillary deplorably stated she would increase the numbers of these people by one hundred thousand her first year in office. Can anyone interpret this as anything other than deliberately weakening America? If not, what?

To further empower *"the Establishment"* as did Obama and his three predecessors by following the lead of Carter who under the guidance of Brzezinski implemented the 1980 Refugee/Immigration Act to proactively increase the number of Government dependents to satisfy his *"Divide and Conquer"* immigration plan to offset the majority Eurocentric electorate of America via a socialist, dependent population, and in this case the added Government empowering probability of terrorism, all of which would weaken America.

But this was just a small part of the plan. The principal part is the years long illegal immigration of hordes of uneducated, mostly peasants from Mexico that as of 2018 had yet to accomplish the desired demographic changes. So, Hillary was going to be proactive in endeavoring to satisfy this need without waiting for procreation by aggressively promoting open borders and increased immigration… and thus, further destruction of America by turning it into a crime ridden Mexico Norte, thus providing America with a level of poverty and hopelessness beyond what Obama plotted for the future.

Good Americans are also under attack by the "education" system also implemented by President Carter under the guidance of Brzezinski that is, in reality, an indoctrination system not unlike those in totalitarian societies in Asia and Europe in the first half of the Twentieth Century that by the beginning of the Twenty-First Century had already failed.

This, as planned, is ensuring a hopeless future for America by indoctrinating its youth with what to think, rather than how to think, and depriving them of knowledge of the faith, culture, and values that produced the freest and most prosperous society in the history of humankind… all for the monetary and power benefit of the already most powerful in their quixotic quest for an homogenized, open borders world under one central government, or as George H.W. Bush declared in 1989; a *"New World Order."*

Beginning in 2016 we could witness this in the streets and college campuses being demonstrated by indoctrinated, uneducated socialist anarchists who are unwittingly ensuring a hopeless future for America just like that of the failed totalitarian societies.

But what has not been witnessed is Brzezinskite Obama, the most economically destructive and divisive President in American history, continuing to attack his political opponents as he did Conservative groups with the Internal Revenue Service.

This time, for the first time in history the ex-President is attacking his successor. With his multi-million dollar financed, thirty thousand strong, formal post-Presidential Organizing For Action, OFA, Obama has a new full-time position from which he is endeavoring to remove President Trump from Office.

Although we have been able to witness his underlings, the ex-Director of the National Security Agency, two ex-Directors of the Federal Bureau of Investigation and his ex-Director of the Central Intelligence Agency on television bloviating against President Trump with outrageous lies, and we have been witness to multiple communications between many of their underlings stating how they intended to prevent Trump being elected, and even after he was President stating how they were going to remove him from Office. But we have not been witness to Obama's direct involvement because, like *"the Establishment"* official organization, Obama's, the Clinton's, and Bushes involvement has always been concealed from the American public.

This is because it is a real conspiracy, a conspiracy against all that is America, a conspiracy against Protestant ethics and morality and its adherents who created America and have done so much good in the world, including abolishing African created slavery from everywhere in the world except where it was created; Africa where it is still practiced in the 21st Century.

Yet, many of these people who are American citizens and direct descendants of African culture that in its worst traditional tribal form permeates inner city America today, and whose members are the wealthiest people of African heritage anywhere in the world due solely to the generosity of those they are engaged in a campaign against, led by demonstrably racist Maxine Waters assiduously pursuing destruction of the country and culture that has provided this superior position for them.

Yes. Working, taxpaying, asset holding Americans are being seriously attacked from within their own country by many elements endeavoring to destroy it and their way of life for various non-sensible reasons of personal interest although they are beneficiaries of it who never before, and never will again if they are successful, had so much wealth, freedom or anything else.

Therefore, hopefully this book will inform productive Americans who their internal enemies are, and that President Trump is our last chance to regain control of America from these forces of evil promoting its national suicide and do everything within their power to ensure he has eight years to accomplish his difficult task of being America's Savior.

The Author
June 2018

TRUMP

AMERICA'S

SAVIOR

CHAPTER ONE
WHAT THE AUTHOR KNOWS

Knowledge is power, and depravation of knowledge empowers those in power. Thus it was with this knowledge the nefarious Zbigniew Brzezinski and his puppet, President Jimmy Carter, created the U.S. Department of Education in 1980 to ensure they and their co-conspirators in "the Establishment" like George H.W. Bush and many others to follow would have a less knowledgeable, increasingly placidly governable population to enable them to lead America into their desired non-sovereign state, borderless "New World Order" under control of their quixotically envisioned One World Government unopposed by an uninformed American population. - The Author

Much in this chapter is usually in About the Author in the back of the book but is in this chapter because it is hoped this will provide sufficient knowledge of the Author's background of experiences, education and knowledge to create a foundation on which the contents herein should be viewed with great concern by readers.

This includes the fact he knows what Mika and the rest of the President Trump hating, Goebbels-like *"Establishment"* media know, and why she and they hate and hypocritically, viciously attack him daily, **even to the extent of her outrageous, unsubstantiated, nationally broadcast accusation June 9, 2018 that the President abused his wife in the White House. This is unheard of outrageous media perpetuation of lies against an American President never seen before!**

Thus, it appears his daughter, Mika, is intent on perpetuating the incarnate evil perpetrated on Americans and their country by Brzezinski for half a century.

This is that Mika's father, Zbigniew Brzezinski, was unquestionably the single most damaging individual to Americans during the half-century prior to 2018. Yet, with full knowledge of his programs and America destroying intent thereof, she, her media co-conspirators, the *"Globalist"* heads of the top U.S. "security" agencies and many members of Congress on *"both sides of the aisle,"* as well as past Presidents Bush I and II, Clinton and Obama, through their actions and commentary demonstrate *de facto* support for his evil, immoral, destructive plans for America President Donald Trump is opposed to.

These plans, proven by Brzezinski's own words taken from his writings and comments presented in this book, include, in part: 1.) reducing, through immigration, the political power of the Eurocentric American electorate that created the country, and 2.) reducing American prosperity through trade deals and organizations to create *"equilibrium"* with other economies to create a *"New International Economic Order,"* i.e., *New World Order*... without consideration of cultural or other empirical differences.

His ultimate goal was elimination of the *"nation-state"* or sovereign countries like the U.S. with all people in a no borders world subjugated to rule by his desired One World Government and its quixotic attempt to achieve world-wide economic *"equilibrium."*

To facilitate these and many more anti-American plans he knew most Americans would not favor he needed to reduce the ability of average Americans to understand what he and his co-conspirators were planning for them. Thus, one of his first actions was to create the Department of Education under Government control by changing teaching to indoctrination, which he accomplished through his puppet President Jimmy Carter.

The daily attacks and lies about Trump by Mika, her effete sidekick and the rest of the anti-Trump media are an extension of the Government schools' indoctrination program wherein children are "taught" Republicans are bad and lies like Lyndon Johnson who incentivized the breakup up black families was the greatest President for Black America.

These *"Establishment"* political whores are tasked with extending these and other lies to the population as the Goebbels media did to enable Hitler and keep him in power by controlling what Germans of all ages knew and were supposed to think.

Therefore, all Americans watching, listening to or reading what the propaganda media purveys must be mindful what similar Goebbels' propaganda enabled Hitler to do in Germany because this was not much different from where Brzezinski's *"Establishment"* desires to take America, including war with Russia he possibly hated even more than his daughter hates Trump.

***

The Author was fortunate to have been born in a small town in the middle of the greatest country to ever inhabit the surface of the earth. The one that provided the most freedom, prosperity, peace, security and opportunity the human race ever experienced. That country was the United States of America that has since been changed dramatically by the so-called *elite"* to further enrich themselves at the expense of the rest of us by forsaking… actually deliberately adversely affecting… much of what made America great by endeavoring to enhance the rest of the world at our expense to further enhance their personal wealth.

This betrayal of America and Americans was perpetrated on us for over a century as of 2018. But was begun in a meaningfully big way about twenty-three months prior to the Author's birthday and has been being accelerated by these same people ever since.

That time was when President Franklin D. Roosevelt and his staff heinously lied to the American people to satisfy his promise to his third cousin, Winston Churchill, he would get the United States into World War II against their wishes.

This is a historically proven fact. But should anyone question this he or she can do their own research to verify it is what actually happened, or more appropriately, was done by the President to Americans and their country to ensure WWII would "happen."

In this undertaking a good place to start would be to ask the question; why was FDR inducting young Americans into the military over six months before Pearl Harbor was attacked? Also, why were bomb shelters being constructed in London two years before Hitler invaded Poland, supposedly causing the British to declare war on him?

But to demonstrate President Roosevelt and his staff probably committed treason because their actions were to start a war, consider; he deliberately failed to notify Pearl Harbor he knew the Japanese were on their way there, but ordered the two aircraft carriers that were at Pearl Harbor out of harm's way, out to sea, because he knew they would be needed in the South Pacific War he planned to declare after the attack.

Roosevelt and Officials in his Government deliberately used over three thousand Americans on December 7, 1941 as pawns, sacrificing them to start their planned war.

This was definitely a *"day of infamy,"* as FDR famously declared. But only superficially as a result of the Japanese attack. Had Americans who were vehemently opposed to U.S. involvement in the war before the attack known the facts of what their President and his Government did to cause so many of their sons, daughters, brothers, sisters and fathers to die they would have had a different view of the declared *"infamy."*

As terrible as this may seem to uninformed and unwary Americans in the 21st Century, this was not the first, or last, of such nefarious acts by members of the effete so-called *"elite"* families in control of the U.S. Government for two, three, even four generations during the one hundred and twenty-five years prior to this writing who are not dissimilar in their conduct to historic European royalty that married cousins to maintain generational, familial control of their countries' wealth and power.

The Author learned in his research; the U.S. has been under control of these people acting for the benefit of "them and theirs" aggressively on the world stage during this time, not to protect the country, but for greed, money and power. As Lord Acton said in the nineteenth century, *"Power tends to corrupt, absolute power corrupts absolutely."*

But the Roosevelt "family" is a particularly egregious American example of this. Endeavoring to follow the Roosevelt family tree is similar to the same task regarding the trees of many of the "hill people" in the "backwoods" of the Eastern United States. Both bring to mind the old country and western song, *"I'm My Own Grand Pa"*

For example; President Theodore Roosevelt, 1901 to 1909, a quarter century before FDR was a "distant" cousin of his. But it is not only the tops of the "trees" that constitute "control" of the Government. There is a multi-generational bureaucracy of families ensconced therein, also complicit in all the destruction the top has wreaked on Americans. Mika's father Zbigniew was a high-ranking member for over a half a century.

In the case of the Roosevelts one example stands out. Over three decades after FDR, his nephew Kermit was the top C.I.A. Officer in Tehran in1979 during the takeover of the U.S. Embassy doing what the C.I.A. does that often results in reactions like this one.

But "Teddy" Roosevelt's conduct before and during his Presidency seemed like a precursor to or actually a model for FDR's actions in 1941 and others that followed.

As Assistant Navy Secretary in 1897 he demanded President McKinley eject Spain from Cuba to get Americans behind a war effort against that country because he did not think Spain should be permitted to continue to control its territories in the Pacific or Caribbean, and a war against that country would give the U.S. Army and Navy what he called *"actual* [war] *practice."*

Although McKinley disagreed and desired to pursue a diplomatic solution, less than a year later, after the U.S. Navy, primarily under the direction of Roosevelt, had assets in place in the South Pacific, Atlantic and Caribbean the American Battleship Maine exploded in Havana Harbor under mysterious circumstances killing almost three hundred innocent American sailors.

There has been a wide consensus for years among those who have studied this that the explosion was generated internally, thus making this, as the circumstances of it also suggest, a U.S. perpetrated "false flag" event, or treasonous act to get Americans to support an unnecessary war by sacrificing three hundred American sailor pawns.

Roosevelt's argument loss of the Maine was the *"price"* the country *"must pay"* to assume its role as a *"great power"* seems to confirm the correctness of this consensus, as does the fact he already had Commodore Dewey in Hong Kong with forces ready for war, and had ordered him to begin offensive actions in the Philippines that was the primary strategic reason for that war because even then those in charge of the U.S. Government desired that country as a location for U.S. ground and naval forces in Asia.

Then there is Zbigniew Brzezinski's assessment: *"The Spanish American War in 1898 was America's first overseas war of conquest."* That seems definitive. Also, the fact the U.S. annexed and militarily occupied Hawaii in 1898 against the desires of that previously independent small country's people indicates the U.S. was on a campaign in which they were intent on securing under U.S. control any land mass in the Pacific.

Then in 1900 "Progressive" U.S. Senator Beveridge who was a strong advocate of *"American Empire"* presumptuously presented in a speech to Congress the aggressive U.S. posture in the world that still persisted in 2018: *"the Philippines are ours forever"* and the *"mission of our race, trustee, under God, of the civilization of the world..."* etc., etc. that should, along with Vietnam and other U.S. aggressions, explain why China, North Korea and other nations think they have a need to protect themselves from the U.S. God given right to *"civilize"* them via its superior military might.,

Also, pre-war propaganda, as later employed by FDR for WWII, Johnson for Vietnam and Bush II for Iraq, got the uninformed American public in favor of their wars.

It was thus Roosevelt got his unnecessary war. Then he charged up San Juan Hill three months later on the only horse in the battle, getting two hundred more young Americans on foot killed and a thousand wounded. But this was good for him.

Although he never spent over two years in any of his prior political offices this was the pivotal moment in his career. Two years later he was elected Vice President. Six months later peace-loving President McKinley was assassinated, and Roosevelt became the youngest U.S. President ever, as well as the model for subsequent lies and actions by other members of the effete so-called *"elite"* in pursuit of international power and wealth at the expense of the lives and wealth of Americans, and the future of their country.

Think of what happened sixty-two years later, November 22, 1963.

His actions and personal successes as a result were the example his cousin FDR and other families and generations of their America destroying cabal have followed over the subsequent hundred plus years. As President he was dictatorial, ruling through Executive Orders, was an ardent imperialist, and actively advocated the U.S. exercising *"International Police Power,"* which he pursued by doubling the size of the U.S. Navy.

Americans have since been victims of the so-called *"elite"* who have followed his example, perpetrating at least two more, maybe three, false flag events to start unnecessary wars, another assassination, and failed foreign and domestic policies.

These destructive results wrought by these people for personal power and wealth on their *Globalist"* alter of a *New World Order*, One World Government are a deliberate destruction of President Reagan's *"shining city on a hill"* that was a beacon for the world.

Thus, this Roosevelt history is important because it provides a historical context for what has been done to Americans and their country by the effete, who are not actually *"elite"* in any way, and their complicit bureaucracy for over a century that is not just continuing, but since election of Trump has viciously accelerated.

The fact Mika is a second-generation member of the "complicit bureaucracy" explains her vitriol of lies and vicious attacks on Trump. She is disturbed over the fact he is proactively destroying the legacy of her father who was a major player as co-founder of *"the Establishment"* formal organization, as well as its architect for the deliberate destruction of Reagan's America.

She and others in their *"Establishment swamp,"* like the "hill people," don't like "outsiders" like Trump intruding on what they consider their proprietary turf, especially as the "top dog" in a position to interrupt, or possibly terminate, their destructive programs…costing them a loss of power as well as billions of dollars each year.

***

The Author is not one of nor like any of these people. Although he attended an *"elite"* University graduate school with some of them and worked in their world for many years he was usually at odds with everything they espoused and apparently believed. At least ninety percent of them were so out of touch with reality he was incredulous.

He was raised by his blue-collar entrepreneur father who had only an eleventh-grade education, and his sixth-grade dropout mother, both of whom were born over a hundred years prior to this writing on small Texas farms during the time of WWI.

He attended public schools in a small Texas city, graduating from high school in 1958 with almost a year of extra credits.

During his school years he was introduced to the business world by his father at the age of six. He worked in one of his small stores until the age of thirteen when, after learning to drive at ten, his father gave his first car to him. Then at fourteen he worked for another store owner, selling products and driving his pickup for deliveries. This business experience resulted in his beginning to pay Social Security and Income taxes in 1954.

At fifteen he had his first business, generating a significant profit by exploiting his early years' business experiences at his father's side with which he bought his second car that was the cause of his first experience with the American "justice" system.

The balance of his public-school years he spent summers in the hot Texas heat as a laborer digging ditches and other manual tasks as a plumber's helper. During the school year he did building plans "take off" and bidding for his father's construction business.

The summer after graduation, at age eighteen he managed a large out of town excavation job with trucks and heavy equipment where he was responsible for all supervision, payroll, etc. Then fall of 1958 he began studying architectural engineering with a heavy six day a week schedule at a nearby junior college.

During the next four years he completed his only year of college, married, became a father, again worked as a laborer, designed a large home for a millionaire, another smaller one, as well as several small strip shopping centers. Also, seeing opportunity in President Kennedy's fear mongering about the possibility of nuclear war with Russia, he designed, received Government approval of his plans, and built several home fallout shelters, managed the shop and field crews for a home improvement company, was a union member backhoe operator, bought his first home, another automobile, was divorced, and as a result had his second experience with the U.S. "justice" system. Also, the IRS notified him it had discovered him, and began taking some of his meager funds.

Then, after a couple more experiences with police and the judicial system, he decided it was time to move out, onward and upward... time to, as is said, "Get out of Dodge."

So, in 1962 he bought a new Chevrolet Impala, put his last $500 in his pocket, his meager wardrobe in the trunk, and ventured west to Hollywood where he settled into an executive position with a steel building and manufactured housing company.

He was doing well, moving up socioeconomically like many

young Americans were able to do during the favorable economic climate of the time, until May 1963. Then, thanks to another generation of war mongers in the U.S. Government following the Roosevelt game plan, he was among hundreds of thousands of young Americans considered expendable pawns in another unnecessary war to enrich the effete non-*"elite Establishment"* and their military/industrial complex to stave another recession.

Recalling his parent's and their friends' commentary about this and the prior Korean disaster of only a decade and a half prior, wrought by these same people, he remembers wondering when would they ever stop creating chaos, death and destruction for no purpose whatsoever except money and power, or when would someone else stop them?

The reason given this time by the lying, pseudo-intellectual, inbred offspring of FDR's generation was problems with Russia in Germany they laid the groundwork for at the end of WWII. We should also note in 2018, thanks to Brzezinski, Russia was still the reason for all things bad because it was still the only credible state enemy they could use to generate needed fear, and target to keep the military/industrial complex growth going.

It is a rule: there must be an enemy for the people to fear. Without that; game over! Mika's father realized this and played it for well over half a century with his erudite, meaning strictly book knowledge - nothing else, detailed writings and upside-down maps.

So, we must not overlook the fact one of the major reasons for the continued targeting of *"Russia, Russia, Russia,"* even in 2018 by the Clintons and many other socialist, *New World Order "Establishment"* political whores, is to a great extent the influence of Mika's father on U.S. Government foreign policy as an avidly anti-Russia National Security Advisor to most Presidents since Lyndon Johnson fifty years before 2018.

NOTE: anyone offended by use of the term *"political whore(s)"* above, before and throughout the balance of this book must overlook his/her objection because *"whore"* is the only succinct English word to describe these people. According to <u>Webster's New World Dictionary</u> *"to seek or pursue ardently that which is immoral, idolatrous, etc."* as in whoring after their *New World Order* One World Government destruction of America, which is immoral conduct contrary to the moral code of the community of Americans. Thus *"political whore"* is the only proper appellation for these America destroying "w*hores"!*

***

Although touted as an intellectual expert in foreign policy, who received his Ph.D. at Harvard in 1953, Brzezinski was passed over for tenure, but continued writing, teaching and advising Government Officials on the subject until his death in May 2017.

The takeaway from this is; he was a smart guy with a subjective, not intellectual, hatred of Russia due to its treatment of his country of birth, Poland, who recognized he had a defined, less intellectually astute, ready audience for what he desired to peddle.

Thus, obviously understanding success results from giving the customer what he or she wants, he seemingly decided to satisfy the extant market for anti-Russia advice and whatever other desires the effete ones desired as the basis for his decades long successful career and pursuit of his desired, anti-American, *"globalist,"* socialist "Utopia."

However, Russia was not the real reason for the draft in 1963. That was the Vietnam War the effete ones were planning, and Brzezinski supported with LBJ, against that small, insignificant, strategically located country that was, in no way a threat to the U.S., its people, any U.S. allies, or anyone else. But the Author was not sent to Vietnam.

After basic infantry training he received advanced infantry training, was promoted to Sergeant E5, sent to Artillery Officer Candidate School, commissioned a Second Lieutenant in the Corps of Engineers, sent to three months of Engineer Officer training at Fort Belvoir Virginia, then, still with only one year of college, was the only one from his class of five hundred other, college graduate, Officers assigned to the staff of that prestigious military school where he remained, teaching, training and managing other Officers until he was discharged two years after the date he was inducted. This was just the beginning of a career of being selected and promoted without his asking.

We should also note Mika's father, Zbigniew Brzezinski, did well during Vietnam again by giving the customer what he desired with his support of President Johnson's treasonously criminal war during his tenure with him 1966 to 1968 even though he could not have failed to know Johnson committed treason in lying about the Gulf of Tonkin incident in 1964 that never happened to start the unnecessary war that cost 58,000 young Americans their lives, and rendered tens of thousands of others of them destroyed for life.

Therefore, Brzezinski had blood on his hands for suborning treason. Yet, with full knowledge of these facts, Mika lied about Trump and willfully falsely accused him almost daily for at least a year and a half prior to this writing, and will likely be continuing to do so as long as she is permitted to, thus continuing in her father's footsteps of complicity in aiding and abetting a criminally miscreant cabal of America destroying effete *"elites"* for money and fame, thus having the "blood" of a destroyed America on her hands if she, her morning sidekick and their media co-conspirators are successful in their efforts to depose President Trump.

It should also be noted she could not have been doing this if not for *"the Establishment"* conspirators in control of much of the U.S. Government and its complicit, co-conspiratorial, Goebbels-like media designed to indoctrinate, rather than inform, in order to deprive Americans of knowledge about her father's secret anti-two party system actions in 1973, and since, intended to convert America into the one party system of totalitarian government, according to his writings, he was seeking most of his life.

The media has never reported any of this, and studiously avoided ever mentioning Zbigniew Brzezinski, but the reader should now know Mika is fully aware of it, and is thus a supreme hypocrite, as well as willfully working to destroy the America most watching her on television desire to be enhanced, not destroyed.

Mika is likely not sharp enough to be fully cognizant what she is party to is simultaneous knowledge deprivation and indoctrination. While she and her effete sidekick are busy spreading falsehoods about Trump, indoctrinating the public dumb enough to watch them they are also depriving the public of knowledge they need to fix what needs fixing... as Trump began doing in 2017.

But her media bosses are because they know, as the Author's WWII veteran First Sergeant at Training Company M, Fort Polk, LA in May 1963 told him:

"First, you got to know you have a problem. But then, you got to know what the problem is before you can solve it!"

This fact is the basis of half the Goebbels-like program to deprive Americans of knowledge of what is being done to them, by whom, and why, to prevent their knowing problems created by Brzezinski's *"Establishment"* coordination of Government, media and corporations in a drive to change America into another, has been, non-sovereign state, member of his desired Utopian *New World Order,* One World Government, he described as, *"the trilateral relationship... as the basis for a new non-Eurocentric international system... central... to the development of the third world,"* or what British Authors Huxley and Orwell frighteningly called, *Brave New World* and *Nineteen Eighty Four,* that statements therein seem to be Brzezinski's guidance for his desired world.

Is this intellectually developed wickedness or real world applied wicked plagiarism?

Whichever, this academic ignorance of the vicissitudes inherent in treating people of different cultures like "one size fit all," expecting the same results is a big problem for America and the world created by Brzezinski and his *NWO* "academics."

The disastrous results of overlooking millennially proven differences and endeavoring to combine critical masses of three cultures with three different religions and languages under one American "roof" to weaken the country within to empower its Government via this *"Divide and Conquer"* plan to enable those in power to enhance the rest of the world solely for these conspirators' benefit should have been obvious long before 2018.

It obviously was, but these asses, like Mika, are so indoctrinated with their own inbred world view, incomprehensible to most of us in light of the daily proof of its failure, there is no way they are going to be derailed from their over insulated overcompensated short-term view short of blood in the streets, which is the likely not too distant result of their criminality... unless Trump is truly a Savior who can survive and create miracles.

***

After the military the Author spent three years expanding his father's small construction business into Corps of Engineers and HUD contracts from Texas to Alabama and Georgia, increasing its business volume ten times, signaling the IRS he seriously needed its attention again.

Then, still with only one year, plus one part time semester of college education he was accepted to the Harvard University Graduate School of Business where he was informed he was one of very few in the school's history to be accepted without an undergraduate degree, and one of only eight hundred out of many thousands of applicants accepted that year. Yet, even there the IRS dunned him for thousands in additional taxes.

Two years later, after graduation, he did not have to look for a position. He already had one as assistant to the President of the small, growing, publicly listed company where he did his first consulting job the summer between his first and second HBS years. He received compensation among the top of his class, plus a significant upfront cash bonus and stock options worth many multiples of that.

Shortly after commencing work at the company he received an invitation from the White House to interview for the newly named Office of Management and Budget. He did not respond because he was sure a Government job would not even begin to match his compensation, and he was not enamored by the idea of government employment. Unfortunately, this, probably his biggest, would not be his last big career mistake.

Then less than one year in his new position, his boss, still expanding his company, deciding to go international, sent him to Australia with side trips to meet business associates in Japan and Hong Kong. Three months later he was alone in a foreign country, twelve thousand miles from home starting a new business in an industry in which he had no operating experience.

But after less than two years he was married again and had a growing, profitable business in four Australian cities when his boss called him back to the U.S. and promoted him to Vice President International Operations, giving him responsibility, in addition to Australia, for European Operations that were started by several long-term company employees at the same time he was sent to Australia, but was failing and in desperate need of a turnaround.

He accomplished this, putting European Operations in the profit column in only one year while continuing to manage Australian operations. Then what he predicted during his summer of consulting for the company and the reason he accepted the position occurred. The now NYSE public company after only eight years in business reported its first large loss and was in need of a turnaround.

Because of this he achieved his objective. Four years after receiving his HBS graduate degree in business, at age thirty-four he was Chief Operating Officer of a New York Stock Exchange company, in charge of all its operations in the U.S., Canada, Australia, Mexico, Spain, France, Belgium, England, the Netherlands and Germany, and the company's business with many companies in over a dozen other countries, greatly expanding his international business experience and knowledge about other countries and their governments, as well as his own, about which much was not very positive.

In this position he interfaced with many high-level business and government people in many of these countries, not just purchasing, but making real estate deals and negotiating regarding interfaces between his company and government agencies, including what he calls non-elective, or more appropriately, given what they did to him: the most extreme form of non-consensual sex by two Government agencies, the FTC and FBI.

Some others were positive for him and his company, but he learned not so much so for the people of the other countries. The biggest positive was he was one of the first Americans permitted to do business in China twenty-five years after their revolution.

He continued to spend several weeks a year there for almost a decade. This gave him insight into how U.S. Government agencies operated outside the U.S. in ways that enhanced the wealth of the so-called "*elite*" in these countries, but not the people who suffered due to this, especially in the Philippines, and adversely affected companies like his.

Aside from the business and financial aspects of his experiences he gained knowledge about the people in his Government who thought very little of those in other countries or their laws. People who cared little about him or his company achieving success, only about forcing U.S. rules and regulations, and spying on the rest of the world, while enhancing the prospects of those supportive of U.S. "*Establishment*" policies, even if detrimental to their own people because they were rewarded immensely by the U.S.

***

Also, in this first foray into the corporate world he learned that, much like these highly placed foreign people, the focus and priority of most in mid management and executive offices was not enhancement of profits and the future of their company, but personal gain at any cost, especially to others or the company.

It was also when he learned the other side of the sexual harassment in the work place story from personal experience with three female employees. From 1974 onward, he refused to ever again have a meeting alone with a female employee.

He also learned what few Americans understand. That is the differences in cultural values and conduct between them and the rest of the world, and the indoctrinating lies being foisted upon their children in the U.S. public school system.

The vast majorities of immigrants are not as they are being presented. For example:

1.) The peasant class of Mexicans flowing into the U.S., since Jimmy Carter, under the guidance, actually as the puppet of Brzezinski, opened the U.S. gates with the 1980 Refugee/Immigration Act, and literally began paying them to come, are a burden, not contributory in any way to America or its future. The non-racist numbers prove this.

They are simply the major "*Divide and Conquer*" component of the Brzezinski plan to weaken the power of working middle class, asset owning Americans by growing the size of a foreign culture government dependent class of voters to create his desired one party, socialist political system, further empowering the Government over the people.

2.) Most of Africa is still a pre-Medieval, warring, backward tribal culture that produces not much of anything except menial items, tribal conflict and more poverty stricken, non-productive Africans whose culture has been expanded into most of inner-city America to deliberately create division, Government-empowering crime and conflict detrimental to black human *pawns* in the Brzezinski *"Establishment"* empowering plan.

3.) This is also complements of Carter's conversion of U.S. education into a dishonest indoctrination system with the creation in 1979 of the Department of Education under guidance of Brzezinski because it reduced the quality of education to the extent few graduates have the ability to contribute to society or enhance their futures. Many fewer blacks even graduate. This also, as planned, is non-contributory to a better America because it has wrought a massive decline in the quality and safety of life in inner cities.

But should anyone choose not to believe this please look at the black on black gang, i.e., "tribal" murder rates in Chicago, Baltimore, South Central Los Angeles and elsewhere with an objective, numbers do not lie point of view. That is proof.

4.) The Brzezinski *"Establishment"* controlled Government refused to admit Chinese seeking refuge here in 1997 because they are smart, organized, well-educated, incredibly productive people who would not be dependent on, nor enhance Government power.

Also, many Africans and African-Americans are followers of Islam, which is totally at odds with American cultural values, religion and judicial system.

Therefore, given religion and language are the two most important elements of cultures, especially those that thrive on ignorance of their populations, African and Latin cultures are irreconcilable with American culture and values, and serve only to enhance Government power, as is the central theme of the Brzezinski *"Establishment"* plan.

***

China was an incredibly expansive experience for the Author. This is important given what has been happening in the U.S., especially since the beginning of the 21st Century.

Mao was still alive at the beginning of his time there, as was his stringent form of communism. The people, especially the young, were so indoctrinated they could not be told anything.

They were born into communism and by 1974 vast numbers were firmly indoctrinated with its lies. They were even convinced buildings obviously built in the nineteenth century were built *"since the revolution"* only twenty-five years before, just as were beautiful hundred-year old trees lining a boulevard planted then.

Everything since the communist revolution was good, and everything that was good was a result of the revolution. Also, capitalism was something they were taught all their lives had to be stamped out, no matter what the cost. Sound familiar?

But it was not necessary to talk with the people to be frightened by all this. Mao's first communist party conference in 1921 was held in a house in the French sector where the Author, as an honored guest, got to sit in Mao's chair while he was served tea.

It was easy to tell this was a beautiful area before Mao and his followers because of the architecture of the homes constructed by the French. But the frightening part was these had numerous doors all around, in every wall, to accommodate the multiple families occupying them.

The fact seventy-two percent of indoctrinated, dumbed down *"Millennials"* and even the previous generation Americans in 2016 were followers of avowed communist Bernie Sanders, that they were indoctrinated to be anti-capitalist, shutting down free speech on university campuses, and violently demonstrating against President Trump because they are opposed to everything that really did make America great he and working, capitalistic Americans stand for should scare the hell out of every American.

If this is not turned around ASAP rather than later, people like Bernie and Hillary, or another Obama, will win the Presidency in very few years. This would be a terrible foreboding that what happened in Russia and China will likely be the future of America.

***

He gained tremendously, experiencing so much, particularly internationally in this position, experientially and economically, as did the company. Partially as a result of his internationally broadened offerings he returned it to profitability in one year.

In the next four years while eliminating or downsizing many non-profitable parts of the business, reducing the payroll, installing many lacking reporting, accounting and management control systems, changing its overall appearance and direction, improving its gross margins and return on invested capital, and doubling its revenues, he had time to do some personal investing.

During this time he bought lots in the best neighborhood in the city, built two luxury duplexes, bought beach front condos in California, assembled estate properties encompassing an entire large city block in the same part of the city for a condo development, bought a small apartment complex and a home on the Pacific in Mexico, as well as a large home for himself on the golf course, all of which more than doubled what he earned those four years, causing the IRS to spend time on him again.

Although he was not astute enough to recognize it, he could have stayed where he was and been comfortably set up for life by age thirty-nine. However, other challenges beckoned.

He purchased some real estate leases, to supplement his company where they were lacking market penetration, from a company in a similar business headquartered in Los Angeles. It had comparable volume to his company when he took it over and, although showing losses for five years and essentially bankrupt, in his opinion it had great potential. So, he thought combining the best of the two companies would result almost immediately in a company with much broader market appeal.

He convinced his boss of this and he engaged in negotiations with the Chairman of its NYSE parent. But shortly thereafter, his boss, lacking vision and seemingly becoming uncomfortable with the success of the turnaround of his company that was publicly known not a result of his management, and dealing with the management of the larger company he decided not to proceed. He also endeavored to enhance the public perception of himself and minimize the reality of who turned his failing company around.

This resulted in a parting. Then, strangely, a few months later the Author was summoned to the Securities Exchange Commission, in Washington at his expense, where he, attorney at his side, spent two hours being questioned by two SEC attorneys with a court reporter on either side of them, and microphones hanging above.

He had no idea why he was there and was not told because the SEC is not obligated to inform anyone they threaten with this conduct why they are doing this. So he still does not know anything except his ex-boss had recently announced, after he departed, he was selling the company for a lot of money, none of which the departed Chief Operating Officer would ever see.

However, the chairman of the Los Angeles parent agreed, after reading his comprehensive turnaround business plan, the company could be turned around, and made an attractive offer. So, over the next three and one-half years the Author succeeded in accomplishing this through some of the methods he previously employed, including his Chinese and other off shore experiences, as well as some financial gymnastics, selling off real estate, subdividing and leasing properties, buying out union employees, and instituting good management practices.

For this he earned as much in this shorter time as he did in nine years in his previous endeavor. But in retrospect he thinks the compensation aspect of this endeavor cost him in the long run.

Just as with the White House interview offer and mostly for the same economic reasons he rejected another political opportunity, the solicitation to run for Congress in Texas addressed later in this section of this book.

He and his wife were flown back to Texas two times, and treated, limos, etc., very well in an attempt to secure his commitment to this. He even received two calls from the White

House, not from the President (he would meet later for another reason) but from senior Republican aides.

But again, the compensation factor ruled. He was less than a year from finishing his current endeavor and getting paid, if he was correct in his assessment of success, which he turned out to be, a sum amounting to eight times the then Congressional compensation, and he would have to forgo the last year compensation and bonus if he left at that time, an amount that would have taken ten years of Congressional pay to recoup.

A seemingly no brainer decision, but he obviously could not foresee the potential for future gains had he been successful, as the big moneyed Texans tried to convince him he would. But, as is said: what is, is.

He already knew not to work for any of these people, his current or prior employer, or anyone without a good contract. He also learned he could not trust older executives like his previous and current bosses. Both resented a two decades younger manager who could accomplish what they could not.

The previous one chose to refuse to report the magnitude of the turnaround, saying *"it would not be believable,"* and manipulating the results downward, effectively costing him hundreds of thousands of dollars of compensation.

The current one was worse. In what he later learned typical Los Angles, if not California, unethical conduct, the Author had to pay an attorney thirty-thousand-dollars to collect five hundred thousand dollars of additional bonus he was owed under his contract because the SOB had his office files broken into and stole his contract, obviously thinking he would have been so insufficiently astute as to keep the original in his office.

But he was not. So, he collected his full compensation, and reasonably happily departed, proud of his accomplishment and increased bank account balances, to his spiffy new paid for contemporary in the Hollywood Hills to contemplate his future.

This experience and the prior one indicated to him the depth of dishonesty in corporate America as well as at the top in politics. This character was also in Los Angeles politics, holding a high profile public position, and close to the Senior Partner of his law firm that endeavored to ensure his crooked endeavor was successful.

He was a bona fide early member of Brzezinski's official America destroying *"Establishment"* organization, and personally involved in President Carter's most heinous act against the interests of the American people.

Under Brzezinski's guidance, allegedly to enhance the financial circumstances of David Rockefeller, his self-defined *"internationalist/globalist"* cofounder of their formal *"Establishment,"* Carter initiated proceedings that gave to the country of Panama the Panama Canal, the only access between the Atlantic and Pacific Oceans north of the tip of South America that America paid for and Americans died building.

***

At this point we must stop to note the demonstrated duplicity and total self-interest above all else, especially America, of Zbigniew Brzezinski, given this act was at his direction as National Security Advisor for the benefit of David Rockefeller - not for that of America for which he was being compensated by the American people to be advising actions and policies for their benefit - not that of his financier and power base, Rockefeller.

The proof of this is in his words in The Grand Chessboard; *"...America's alleged 'manifest destiny' -- were even further enhanced by the construction of the Panama Canal, which facilitated naval domination over both the Atlantic and Pacific Oceans."*

These words clearly state he knowingly, willfully potentially adversely affected America's interests for his personal benefit by placing the financial interests of his co-conspirator financier above that of Americans and their country.

But that was not the last of his deeds that were opposed to the best interest and benefit of his adopted country, or the world.

He had his hand in the U.S. severing ties with the Democratic Republic of China on Taiwan in favor of communist People's Republic of China at a time when the Chinese were still being oppressed, indoctrinated and impoverished by their government.

He also played a role, as Carter's Advisor in the transition of Iran from important U.S. ally to an anti-Western Republic. Then, as if all this was insufficient damage to the world, still as Advisor to Carter he admitted U.S. covert action got Russia to start the Afghan war in 1979 when he was also leading the U.S.in a new arms buildup.

He also admitted under him the U.S. supported radical Islamists to undermine Russia.

When asked if he had regrets about this, he responded, **"Regret what? That secret operation was an excellent idea. It had the effect of drawing the Russians into the Afghan trap and you want me to regret it? The day that the Soviets officially crossed the border, I wrote to President Carter: We now have the opportunity of giving to the USSR its Vietnam War."**

Asked if he regretted having given arms and advice to future terrorists he responded, **"What is most important to the history of the world? The Taliban or the collapse of the Soviet empire? Some** *stirred-up Muslims or the liberation of Central Europe and the end of the Cold War?"*

When he was told, "Islamic fundamentalism represents a world menace today." Brzezinski responded, **"Nonsense! It is said that the West had a global policy in regard to Islam. That is stupid. There isn't a global Islam...."** *[Le Nouvel Observateur (Paris), 1/15/1998]*

Really? This National Security Advisor to Carter and top national security advisor to other Presidents, including most recently, Obama, denied the existence of one of the world's three largest religions with over a billion adherents?

Should not this ignorance have denied him access to a U.S. President, let alone being a top national security advisor to several?

Guess not. In 2008 Democratic presidential front-runner and professed anti-war candidate Obama obtained the endorsement and foreign policy advice of Brzezinski who in 1979 endorsed the creation and support of militant Islamic forces in Afghanistan that were directed by accused "9/11" mastermind Osama bin Laden.

Ignoring that, Obama has since stated, *"I've learned an immense amount from Dr. Brzezinski who is one of our country's most outstanding scholars who has done a lot for our country."* He likely said this because Brzezinski was the one who chose and groomed him for four years to be the next *New World Order* America destroying President. He owed him. In fact, Michelle Obama should have given credit for Obama being President to Brzezinski, not Nelson Mandela to whom she publicly attributed this.

Well, the truth is, neither Brzezinski nor Obama did as much *"for our country"* as they both did to our country. In addition to the above there was much more damage by both.

In fact, Brzezinski groomed Obama to be his puppet just as he did Jimmy Carter, and Obama's actions prove he was very effective in doing this. Like Carter, Obama greatly increased illegal Latin immigration, even initiating massive immigration from Central America to satisfy Brzezinski's *"Divide and Conquer"* program to increase the power of *"the Establishment"* controlled Government by reducing the power of the Eurocentric majority of productive voters via increasing the population of predominantly uneducated, Spanish speaking Government welfare dependent potential voters.

But he went even further, obviously at Brzezinski's direction, by also deliberately importing multitudes of potential terrorists from Middle East countries to increase the fear factor of Americans, thereby also further empowering the Government.

He also was acting on Brzezinski's Russia hating and targeting plans of fifty years before when he took actions in the Ukraine to oust its popularly elected but Russia leaning President. This was an act consistent with Brzezinski's written instructions the U.S. must remove Russia as a contender on the world stage, but the first step toward this was to take the Ukraine.

It was for these reasons in 2016 Hillary Clinton went campaigning with Barrack Obama signifying she agreed with and would have represented a continuation of *"the* [Brzezinski] *Establishment"* policies of wars for purposes other than protection of America she and Obama demonstrated in Libya and the Ukraine, as well as the position, *"There isn't a global Islam,"* both agree with based on their refusal to acknowledge the fact of Radical Islamic Terrorism regardless of the continuing death toll of Americans and many others throughout the world.

These and other facts demonstrate Zbigniew Brzezinski was far, far from *"one of our country's most outstanding scholars."* For over fifty years he was the source of much of what is wrong with America and its place in the world in 2018.

It is his influence, especially via the non-publicly-disclosed Trilateral Commission he co-founded, that has attracted so many adherents/members who demonstrate the truth of the adage *"To expect bad men not to do wrong is madness."*

Objectively viewed, Brzezinski was little more than an overrated life-long anti-Russian academic based on his personal hatred of that country who was smart enough to maneuver himself into the confidence and good graces of one of America's wealthiest men whose *"Internationalist, Globalist"* policies and goals he shared, and then between them engineer the election of a not as bright as portrayed, but more grateful to them for being President, Jimmy Carter, who willfully let them pull his puppet strings to set America up for the destruction of its economy, education system and internal peace and harmony through their planned *"Divide and Conquer"* program to achieve their long term plans for increased wealth and control of the plutocracy we have witnessed since the election of good man Donald J. Trump to the Presidency of the United States.

The truth is Brzezinski's legacy in America based on what he and his followers have done to America since 1973 should be he was truly one of the *"bad men,"* actually evil incarnate because of all the damage he did to America that continues posthumously.

He and his followers are responsible for all the anti-Trump *"Establishment"* media, including his daughter's, and political strife the country has suffered since 2016 simply because Trump is an outsider they know will not follow in their footsteps or continue their America destroying programs as their co-conspirator Hillary would have.

This is What Mika Knows and the reason she hates Trump that if not disclosed to America will continue until the end of the America that was once an actually mostly good country, Reagan's *"Shining city on a hill,"* that will not survive unless the also mostly good folks at FOX NEWS do their duty to inform Americans of the facts of what is being done to them and by whom, rather than continuing to incessantly blame *"the Left!, the Left!"*

***

But back to the previously discussed early member of the Brzezinski *"Establishment"* organization, and the Author's also relatively inconsequential experiences:

He was also later a member of President Clinton's Cabinet involved internationally in Clinton's shenanigans. Not what we would call nice or even good Americans, especially since they even threatened to lie to the IRS about the Author... he guessed because of their Government contacts... attempting to get him nailed for tax evasion even though they knew nothing about his other income or taxes. All this by mega millionaires just to attempt to deprive him of the few hundred thousand dollars they owed him.

Also, during this time, he had another personal experience with some of the same-type morally and ethically corrupt denizens of the multi-millionaire West Los Angeles/Beverly Hills community that provided his first glimpse into the strong *"Leftist,"* anti-capitalist ties between "Hollywood" and the dishonest media most of America is still unaware of in 2018.

Two months before he assumed his position at the company in 1979, "Hollywood" released the movie "Norma Rae" starring Sally Fields who was given the Academy Award for Best Actress in it.

This was a total propaganda film full of untruths and sensationalism intended to enhance chances of the textile workers union unionizing the thirty-three thousand workers of J.P. Stevens, the biggest textile company in the country that was family owned and operated for one hundred sixty-seven years since 1812.

Since the Author's new company was the single largest retailer of J.P. Stevens' products in Southern California and he was recently named "President" of it in the Los Angeles Times his company and he personally became targets of the communists in "Hollywood" and the local *"Leftist,"* anti-capitalist media.

Please note his company did not sell as much of Stevens' products as the combined sales of the three department stores but was targeted specifically because it had multiple small stores throughout the area, giving it a higher profile to the average person in the area. Also, doubtful they would have gone after the department stores because their ownership and management were members of their rich community.

He began to receive phone calls and letters from members of the entertainment community who did not have a clue about the facts of what was going on. They just knew it was unions and media against a business, and they sided with their ilk.

He took a couple of calls from empty-headed "stars" who chastised him for selling the products of a company that was injuring and causing the deaths of its workers, which would shortly thereafter be proven lies for political purposes... not unlike the crooked media was doing to Donald Trump thirty-six years later.

The Author would also discover the total, all-consuming, "*Leftist*" mentality of the vast majority of all working in the entertainment business when he became a member of their management only six years later. He was frequently left totally and completely nonplussed after conversations with many of the high-ranking executives he dealt with.

Ditto, the big entertainment stars. The first; Steve Allen who was the biggest late night T.V. star like the three in 2018, but much bigger because he did not share much of the late- night audience with anyone else like the three effete little nerds in 2018.

Steve wrote an insulting letter to the Author that showed his complete ignorance of the entire matter, as the Author not too tactfully informed him in response.

The next was big black T.V. star of Caribbean heritage, Ester Rolle, who came with an entourage of her own demanding to see the Author, all of whom lay down in his sixth-floor elevator lobby blocking access to the elevators because he refused to meet with them. They were eventually removed by police who had to be called for this purpose.

Then a young black female reporter from a local T.V. station arrived. The Author naively agreed to meet with her for a few minutes. He answered her questions with facts and informed her of a few more, but she was not there for that.

That night he watched her report on T.V. when the only truth to depart her lips was she interviewed "*the President of the company.*" Everything else she said, except his name, was a stream of lies consistent with the lying media's dishonest misrepresentation of the entire ongoing attack on the company without ever reporting the extent to which the union was going in endeavoring to unionize it for the sole purpose of relieving its hopefully new thirty-three thousand members of thousands and thousands of dollars for them to pass on to their American Socialist Party, AKA Democrat, members of Congress to assist them in their decades long endeavor to turn America into a member of theirs, the Bushes and other members of "the *Establishment*" United Socialist States, or whatever they have decided to call it, *"New World Order."*

Then shortly thereafter in 1980 when Stevens company employees voted against the union, in favor of Stevens there was zero media coverage... sort of like the media treated President Trump when he accomplished something for the benefit of American citizens.

In 1983 the union ended its campaign against Stevens. Again, no news. Then in 1988 the company was bought by another textile giant for $1.2 billion. At that time, only seventeen percent of Stevens' employees were union members.

This entire episode almost forty years before Trump began his campaign for the Presidency was not unlike his experience. The same players, media and entertainment, still on the opposite side of capitalism and lying to support their ultimately failed position were on the wrong side just as in 2016 when they lost again.

But they are far from giving up. From 2016 until he became President they were continuing to join forces, lying about everything Trump in their endeavor to ensure anti-capitalist, communist since her times at Wellesley College, Hillary Clinton would be the next President. Then having failed at that, they continue to try to oust him from office.

***

He learned more from these experiences than he liked about people, politics and government: from the Roosevelts to Johnson, Carter, the Bushes, Clintons and Obama and all their complicit associates like Brzezinski. Every single one of them did more to harm Americans and their country than to enhance it while enhancing the wealth of themselves and their cronies in corporations and even foreign countries.

But his time in Los Angles yielded more disturbing facts about this area, especially West Los Angeles. There was plenty of money, but a tremendous dearth of knowledge about the real world, and a lack of common sense. It was like a big insulated bubble of rich ignorance with a very good climate, a lot of nice restaurants, bars, theaters, museums and great out-door space for exercise and enjoyment. So, what the hell?

After almost thirteen years of extensive travel, living in three countries, doing business in sixteen, and with another dozen, encompassing most of the religions and cultures on Earth, seeing and experiencing more of it than 99% of people ever will, including in his own country, he decided to take a Sabbatical.

He and his wife divided time between their Hollywood Hills cotemporary, their vacation home in Mexico on the Pacific and a condo they kept in Texas where they still owned other real estate, traveled some and just had a good time for two years and seven months until one day when the phone rang.

He had been reasonably comfortable with few worries, having a good time, and not even thought about looking for another position. In fact, he thought he would likely never have to work for someone else again. He was pretty sure there were many options he could pursue whenever he desired or needed, none of which were in corporate America. Never again!

However, he had not lost his drive, curiosity, or whatever resulted in his ending up in the diversity of places, situations and businesses he experienced. So, this call elicited another "What the hell?" moment in his mind.

On the other end of the line was an executive recruiter he knew with a really off the wall question that elicited his response. That was, *"How would you like to run a movie studio?"*

To make this short; one of the six major Hollywood studios lost a lot of money its prior fiscal year and was looking for someone to turn it around. He had two interviews, then he was the Senior Vice President of Studio Operations with a twelve hundred square foot executive suite including a private bath, two secretary positions, a conference room, an assistant, and even more important in "Hollywood," a primo parking space at the curb just outside his office that was on the first floor with all the senior executives.

Also, although even more of a neophyte here than in any of his previous endeavors, this one had a new twist. He was the only gentile on the entire floor, and the only one in the ranks at his level.

As usual, his area of responsibility was profitable again after the first year, and over the next three and one-half years he was given added responsibilities and bonuses... the first one after only three months... as well as several pay increases. It was another successful and reasonably financially rewarding endeavor, especially for the time and effort required. Also, only three and one-half years, but much more diverse and exciting.

Three months after he began he was reporting directly to the biggest media mogul in the world, involved in much more than studio operations, AND grossly underpaid for what he was accomplishing. But he thought this would be rectified. Wrong!

He was also responsible for the separate TV studio, real estate in New York, all non-creative business departments for movie and TV, as well as the financing and construction of the last fifty percent of a new $225 million, thirty-four story office building. Then green-lighting and controlling the filming of a major studio movie with approval of expenditures for the production, negotiating all kinds of deals with and for other studio executives, as well as those with other studios, handling all dealings with City of Los Angeles departments and politicians, some of the talent in the form of producers and directors, many with well-known names, as well as a few movie and T.V. stars, the U.S. State Department, some White House staff, President Reagan's "kitchen cabinet," the Secret Service, diplomats foreign and domestic, and many others.

He also sold the building without any real estate industry assistance... handled the entire transaction, including lawyers... for a U.S. record-dollars per square foot for the time, and a profit of $100 million for the company of which he was not paid one cent.

It was an exciting, and should have been even more financially rewarding, endeavor than his last, even though it wasn't. But he also did his usual business on the side.

He and his wife converted their Hollywood Hills Contemporary into a lovely, unique Art Deco property, and sold it for a one-hundred percent gain. Bought and remodeled a walled, gated small estate once owned by a big international star in one of the best neighborhoods in Beverly Hills and sold it at a fifty percent gain, and another larger one in Bel Air they rented to the German Government at a great rate.

He and his wife lived well, had a great time; movie premiers and parties, the Academy Awards... boring... and much more. But his most memorable part of the entire time was the few months spent working with the most powerful man in the industry, the Secret Service, other White House people and friends of President Reagan negotiating and planning his post Presidential Office on the top two floors of the building he played such a big role in bringing to fruition, especially when he was invited to meet the President who sat down with him for the best part of an hour talking about his early Hollywood days and thanking him for his office.

Reagan was a great, down to earth, totally different man from the arrogant political hacks in the position since, including George H. W. Bush with whom he attended a small, luncheon years before when he was running for President. Anyone who would not have known who he was would have never guessed Reagan was the President of the U.S.

This was a great way to leave the entertainment business, or anywhere, but he did not decide to leave his position, Los Angeles or "Hollywood."

It was "*deja vu all over again*" treatment of him in his Los Angeles experiences by more of the same people ubiquitous, not just in the entertainment business but in all of Los Angeles, of whose "club" he was not a member and could never be. (He should have followed the advice given to him before he left Texas those years before, *"Stay here where you belong."*)

Within two months of completion of the deal for the President's office, a short time after he completed sale of the building, and the movie he green-lighted and controlled the budget on was finished, AND just before bonus time, late one Friday a young executive who had not done anything at the studio except report to the Chairman of the company for a relatively short time walked into his office stating, *"We want you to look for something else to do."*

To avoid being arrested for assault, or worse, he just took his suit jacket, nothing else, and GTFO, rather than going up the hall and strangling the sorry little cowardly SOB who ordered this because he did not have the testicular fortitude to do it himself, or was actually afraid to do it, which was wise on his part. Then he never went back.

During the next two years he did a profitable consulting job for the producer of a new T.V. show starring a once big T.V. star that was failing where he recommended the problem was the star, and he was shortly thereafter removed.

Next, he did another very well-paid consulting job for a failing entertainment related technology division of a large well known East Coast headquartered conglomerate. He recommended termination of its CEO, which was done, and prepared a new business plan and organization restructuring.

These were implemented, and the business returned to profit the following year. But that was enough. He was fifty years old and wanted a new life or needed one before he had to deal with any more of these people who might cause him to end up in prison. This was found in a small Colorado ski town.

He moved there. Bought some properties, remodeled a hundred-year old historic building, built a few houses south of town and a large one in town for his home, but found the youthful mismanagement of the town communist and impossible to deal with, even though they did not know this was the political system they were practicing.

It was just what they were indoctrinated with in the U.S. Indoctrination system that should be attributed to Brzezinski, if anyone knew who he was. But, by plan, ninety-nine percent of Americans have never heard of Zbigniew Brzezinski, the principal architect of all Donald Trump undertook the fixing of in 2017.

That includes not just the indoctrination system and *"Divide and Conquer"* immigration, but also the moving of U.S. industries, capital, production and jobs to other countries to enhance corporate and financial institutions wealth at the expense of Americans to satisfy the *"Globalist"* and *"Internationalist"* goals of Brzezinski, his partner Rockefeller and all their insipid political and corporate crony co-conspirators.

"Insipid"? Yes! They would have to be stupid to think <u>destroying their own base of wealth and power to endeavor to create their *New World Order,* One World Government</u> they intended to control is a good idea. But this is exactly what Mika, her media allies and all the stupid anti-Trump politicians desire, obviously ignoring the fact; neither powerful and growing much more so, primarily thanks to this stupidity, Russia or China nor any of their allied billions of the world population would sit still for this.

<u>Destroying their power base, and impoverishing their people for power? Brilliant!</u>

These people, like those he found in his small-town America were all the same in the early days of the 21st century. They all remind the Author of dealing with the people in China all those years ago. They were definitely not capitalistic. Their main concerns were limiting business and providing subsidized housing for people who could not otherwise afford to live there.

But what really frightened him was the building inspector saying his home *"Is too big for two people. Three families should live here."* Shades of China and the 1966 movie *Doctor Zhivago* about the Russian communist revolution wherein communists moved multiple families into his home.

So, he picked up all his investment marbles and invested those in a small fast-growing city about a hundred miles away where the management was mature and capitalistic.

There he bought some lots and three small farms, built a couple of houses and sold his remaining lots to concentrate on developing the largest farm into a large upscale subdivision that is the nicest in the city of forty thousand.

While doing this he opened an account in Europe where he invested in Chinese companies, gold and silver, and did well even through the crash. But then picked up some of his marbles again and invested in real estate in Costa Rica.

During all this post corporate America time he did a few other small things, wrote four books, one of which published in 2003 resulted in a complaint letter from the Bush White House Counsel, and his response resulted in the Secret Service interviewing him in his Colorado "free country" living room for two hours asking him asinine questions.

He and his wife traveled to Europe several times, enjoying the architecture, food, and ambiance, as well as spending some time in Costa Rica. His "interfaces" with the IRS that began as soon as he was above the poverty level, even while he was in the military when the Government was paying him and calculating his taxes continued.

They still determined he needed to pay more at the end of each year, and over the years even took over forty thousand dollars out of his bank accounts he did not owe, would not give back, and told him, *"Sue us!"*

Bad people there and in much of the rest of the Government, like all those addressed and described above, because that is mostly the type Government attracts, plus its share of criminals, as has been proven since Trump announced his run for the Presidency.

And on that point, he thinks either Trump or someone in his campaign likely read the book he wrote on government and politics published in 2003 that resulted in his Bush II Secret Service interview because it contains chapters on every component of Trump's anti-*"Establishment"* campaign and Presidential agenda that was the cause of that interview.

***

This chapter has been a diverse read but given the subject matter of this book and its importance to the future of America it is important the reader have confidence in the veracity of what he or she is reading and that the Author has the breadth and depth of knowledge, experience and education for the reader to believe what is presented herein.

Hopefully, this confirms he has a sufficiently broad socioeconomic background, international and domestic business experience from blue collar worker to small business owner, to corporate America, and unique military and educational backgrounds, as well as interface with government officials from city to state, international, and the lowest levels in the U.S. Government to the highest possible, all as a result of the upward mobility afforded by American capitalism in the second half of the 20th Century.

We think you will find this book informative, thought provoking, even mind or position changing in some of the subject matter, and an overall important read because of disclosures like this:

"We don't care whether you're a Democrat or Republican as long as you are our Democrat or Republican"

- Important Republican Party member, 1982

This statement was made by the wife of a wealthy Texas industrialist to the Author during an interview with him in which he was being solicited to run for Congress in the 1982 mid-term elections by these two along with the chairman of the local branch of the Republican Party and four others, after which they promised him six hundred thousand dollars for his campaign and told him not to worry about income. *"We control several companies, and we will take care of you. If you don't win this time you will the next"*

This confirmed for him, as this book should for all who read it, The Big Lies of the *faux* "two party" system fifty percent of Americans who are Independents are aware has been perpetrated on the American electorate for decades by Brzezinski's *"Establishment"* and its complicit, controlled media that is little different from Hitler's Fascist, Goebbels media that functioned on the following guidance.

"If you tell a lie big enough and keep repeating it, people will eventually come to believe it. The lie can be maintained only for such time as the state can shield the political, economic and/or military consequences of the lie. It thus becomes vitally important for the state to use all of its powers to repress dissent, for the truth is the mortal enemy of the lie and thus by extension, the truth is the greatest enemy of the state." - Joseph Goebbels, Hitler's Propaganda Minister

This is exactly what CNN, MSNBC and other mainstream *"Establishment"* media began immediately after non-*"Establishment"* member Trump's election, and, as of this writing continued, endeavoring to turn the people against him to get him out of office, which was the sole plan for the *"Establishment"* appointed enforcer Special "Agent."

All media and both elected and non-elected members of *"the Establishment"* are working in concert to turn the deliberately uninformed American electorate against Trump with the specific intent of winning back Congress in the midterm elections, then impeaching him for no reason other than his destruction of their America destroying acts.

***

Here let's pause, or step aside again for a few minutes to take a look at the media, who they are, why those who are on camera are there, and who put them there to lie to you.

Let's begin with who put them there. That would be *"the Establishment"* members in charge of allocating media companies' money in a way they determine best to accomplish their objectives, which in this case is to turn you and other members of the American electorate against Trump to get him out of office - not to report any real news, just lies.

Thus, their mission, since the day he was elected, has been to create a climate of acceptance among the electorate of a coup to remove the President the people elected, but is opposed by "*the Establishment*" member media owner bosses.

They are working toward this objective in concert with the Special "Agent" appointed by the Assistant Attorney General who is a friend of his and the fired FBI Director, all three of whose sole objective even before his appointment was to prevent Trump from being elected, then after he was, to remove him from office.

He was not appointed to investigate collusion with Russia. If he was he would have already put Hillary Clinton and many of her people in prison because he had ample evidence to do that the day he was appointed, but has refused to even look at it, as have his previous employees in the FBI for which he was the Director for at least a decade.

So, hopefully, you and most working taxpaying Americans are beginning to see what the program to remove Trump actually is: a vast conspiracy on the part of the same effete "*elite*" people and their offspring who brought us the Kennedy assassination, the Vietnam War and the Bush II debacle in the Middle East that has cost trillions of dollars and was the genesis of the terrorism plaguing us in Western countries since.

The media's part in this is to precondition the public, per the Goebbels' guidance above, for acceptance of whatever lies are created to indict Trump and have him impeached. But its bosses who control the money are aware of at least two business decision making factors taught at the Harvard Graduate School of Business.

These are Probability Theory and the fact the most difficult and expensive form of advertising is to endeavor to stimulate primary demand. So how do they allocate their dollars to their "news" media in their endeavor to get rid of Trump?

First, let's look at probability theory. This is based entirely on numbers and facts that do not lie, nor are racist. But the media continues to endeavor to convince their audience via lies that they do or are. Otherwise their lies would not be accepted by even the least astute or otherwise inclined to believe them among us

This theory, based on historic facts stated in percentages of actual occurrences is used by gamblers to calculate the probability of drawing a winning hand before laying down their bets, or by business people to assess the probability of their intended investment turning out to be profitable.

Stimulating primary demand is simply endeavoring to interest people who have never seen or heard of a product or concept to buy it, or to change people's minds from what they have historically believed to believe something new or different.

Most people unwittingly apply both of these academic theories to reach conclusions or make decisions in their everyday lives. They just refer to it as common sense.

For example; when watching TV news, if they hear a tickler the next post advertisement news is about an armed robbery of a liquor store they would likely not bet their money the culprit is going to be a lawyer or corporate executive. Also, when a report or story containing any degree of subjectivity is presented the viewers are more likely to believe it if they have some predetermined favorable opinion or affinity for the news person presenting the story or the ethnic or socioeconomic status of the story's subject.

Politicians and political pundits use both theories for everything they do in endeavoring to either be elected or predict who will be, especially the politicians. But unlike the usually more knowledgeable business people they frequently subjectively misuse the information by misjudging their product as well as the customers for it.

Hillary Clinton is a good example, both in failing as a politician and as a pundit, which proved she would have been a lousy President for any Americans because the most important title of the President is Chief Executive of the Government of the United States, i.e., the business manager of the U.S. Government.

She proved she is a lousy business manager, and as she continues to demonstrate; she just thinks she is smarter than everyone else, which always results in failure in business.

She failed to campaign in some states Trump won because she made an incorrect subjective assumption about herself as a product vis-à-vis Obama, thus ignoring longer term, and more predictive of the probability of the outcome, historic voting patterns.

She wrongly determined she had a high probability of winning there based on the short-term results of one unique candidate with which she shared none of the winning attributes and all of his negatives. Thus, deciding not to spend either time or money there.

She chose to spend too much time and money where historic percentages of voting patterns based on ethnicity and socioeconomic status of the populations indicated she had a high probability of winning, totally ignoring the Electoral College, wisely established by our Founders to prevent exactly what Hillary did: pander to a majority of narrow interests to the exclusion of all others to become President of the United States.

She continued to state it herself even internationally over a year after the election: she appealed to inner city, and "brown," largely dependent Americans, single women and single interest voters to the exclusion of working, asset owning, taxpaying families, including married white women interested in the future of their children. Wrong, wrong!

But unfortunately, those in charge of the anti-Trump *"Establishment"* media are a hell of a lot smarter than Hillary, as well as astute business people who understand both Probability Theory, primary demand, and have a much better understanding of human nature in the same way Goebbels did. Thus, they apply all of this in their part of the depose Trump endeavor.

They are not endeavoring to stimulate primary demand, nor change the minds of Middle Class working Americans. They are simply endeavoring to increase the probability of more ant-Republican/Trump votes by increasing numbers of those already inclined to vote this way based on their historic voting patterns.

These are the Hillary defined "inner city," and "brown," largely dependent Americans, single women and single interest voters," as well as indoctrinated communist Bernie supporting *"Millennials,"* all of whom have little interest in the big picture of America, its economy, sovereignty and independence as a free capitalist nation, its military or economic strength, or anything else they cannot perceive benefits them immediately, personally.

They will vote for anyone who will give to them what they desire without having to work for it; free communist indoctrination, food, housing, healthcare, etc., and are susceptible to any lies that "fit" their view of the world, especially if those peddling them are people with whom they have some affinity.

This is the reason CNN and MSNBC do not have many primetime white males, or white males at any time unless they are among the morally lacking minority, willing to whore themselves out to *"the NWO Establishment"* for money. Most readers know who they are, so no point naming them here.

But this is where this media management shows its astuteness in utilizing probability theory as well as affinity appeal in its choice of lie peddlers.

Again, keeping in mind the numbers do not lie. They show all minorities whether black, Latino, homosexual, single females, or others have an extremely strong affinity for their own, and vote in the majority solely on this basis, frequently in numbers greater than eighty-five percent.

Therefore, both MSNBC and CNN have female, black and an effete *"elite"* adopted son of one of the richest women in America homosexuals as its primetime lie peddlers, and the rest of its programming is laden with many ethnic and effete commentators, some second generation, who have never worked at anything except talking down working Middle Class productive Americans and spreading as many lies as *"the Establishment"* media will reward them richly for peddling. Ditto much of the rest of the so-called *"Leftist, Liberal, Democrat"* network programming like *"The View"* and others.

Please keep in mind; neither what media management is doing or this description of it are racist, homophobic, anti-feminist, or anti-anything. What they are doing is simply good business, employing Probability Theory, advertising guidelines and known facts of human nature as taught at all universities in business, socioeconomic and human behavior classes, and the foregoing is only a description of this.

But it is dangerous to the future well-being of Americans and their country because it is in furtherance of the *"Diversity"* to *"Divide and Conquer"* program to further enhance the power of *"the Establishment"* at their expense.

***

They continue to lie about Trump twenty-four hours a day seven days a week because his truths are *"the greatest enemy of the* [deep] *state Establishment"* Brzezinski created to defeat the American people and turn America into a borderless, non-sovereign member of his perceived Utopian *New World Order*, One World Government, and they are frantic to get rid of him at any cost before he destroys four decades of their *"progressive"* movement of America to this end, and costs them dearly.

Please note: some members of *"the Establishment"* have co-opted the word *"progressive"* to portray their America destroying *"Liberal, Leftist"* ideas and programs as something good and moving forward when in reality they are the exact opposite of this. These are the people desiring to move America backward, into being just another failed socialist state under cover of falsely labeling their actions and goals that are metastasizing like a disease.

The fact this is not just a *"Leftist, Liberal,"* or *"Democrat"* endeavor should be readily apparent to most given the opposition and absolute determination on the part of so-called *"Right, Conservative, Republicans"* like Senators McCain, Flake, Corker, the entire Bush family, Romney, William Kristol and many others who are only superficially what they claim to be, and would have preferred Hillary Clinton be President because they are of the same America destroying... and let's not forget, Brzezinski... *"Establishment"* that has benefited enormously from open borders immigration, the America destroying trade deals, and the rest of their agenda Trump is against.

In fact, their conduct indicates the big money behind all of them told them at the beginning of their political careers the same as the *"We don't care..."* quote above, and they are only ostensibly *"Conservative Republicans"* because geography, family history or connections indicated they could more effectively accomplish *"Establishment* objectives with that title, like getting rid of a pro-America President Donald Trump.

"A fish rots from the head down."
- Old Chinese Proverb

This suggests when an organization, company or state fails it is the leadership that is the root cause, as in the case of the failing companies the Author was involved with during his time in corporate America.

Like those companies, the U.S., as he has been saying for three decades prior to Trump assuming the Presidency, has been failing by design of Government *"swamp"* dwellers enriching themselves through this decline at the expense of Americans.

The best example recently exposed to be one, if not the rankest, of all those comprising this dystrophic *"swamp,"* is the obviously criminally rotten at the top Federal Bureau of Investigation, the FBI.

It had been stinking up electronic communications and the "news" for a year at the time of this writing. So, although not planned, but so topical, let's begin our disclosure of the big lies about the festering problems of the U.S. Government with the FBI.

CHAPTER TWO
FEDERAL BUREAU OF INVESTIGATION

When this book was begun no thought was given to addressing individual Government agencies. The intent was to address the whole of the Government as the one monolithic, monster of growth and power detrimental to Americans and the future of their country it has become under forty years of control by the Brzezinski/Rockefeller *"Establishment"* some refer to as the *"Deep State"* determined to make America just another borderless, non-sovereign state member of their quixotically envisioned *New World Order*, One World Government world.

But since then actions of *"the Establishment"* members in control of the FBI demonstrated their determination to ensure achievement of their objectives by using the power of their agency to endeavor to determine the outcome of the Presidential election.

Attempting to prevent non-*"Establishment"* Trump being elected and ensure member Hillary Clinton would be the next President they illegally used the power of their agency for purely political means. In so doing they either turned the country's supposedly "principal law enforcement agency" into nothing but the enforcement arm of this cabal of America destroying for personal gain anti-American miscreants, or they just disclosed that is what it has been for years. Research indicates the latter is the sad truth.

This was demonstrated thru actions by those at the top of the agency. These supposed upholders of the nation's laws who have been on the agency or other Government payrolls for years demonstrated an almost incomprehensible lawlessness in attempting to affect the outcome of the 2016 Presidential Election by preventing Hillary from being indicted.

They schemed and plotted with one political party against the other, probably utilizing known falsified documents provided by one party to obtain court orders to the disadvantage of the other, obstructed justice, violated federal laws they are sworn to enforce, committed perjury, and proactively conducted, or not conducted, interviews to let those they know committed punishable crimes get away with them to enhance Hillary Clinton's chance to be elected. This is allegedly disclosed in texts between some of them.

Also, before Trump was elected President, during the campaign, the then FBI Director, Comey, in a televised statement, inappropriately assumed the position of the Attorney General, clearly laid out a case for Hillary to be indicted on criminal charges then stated that was not going to happen, likely because of direction from Obama's Attorney General to whom his position reports, probably with the concurrence of Obama himself.

It was later disclosed Comey determined this and wrote this statement before Hillary or anyone else was even interviewed, AND when she was it was not conducted in accord with FBI rules or any legitimate investigation. She was not put under oath, and reportedly not filmed or recorded. It was essentially a non-interview.

As if this was not sufficient demonstration of the corruption at the very top of the FBI, and that the Director was nothing if not a paid puppet member of *"the Establishment"* who was sure he could commit these corrupt acts with impunity, he went before Congress and lied about them, possibly committing perjury. He also violated the law by "leaking," actually providing, documents to a friend to leak to the press with the specific intent of getting a Special Prosecutor, or Counsel, appointed to pursue finding, if not creating, a case to, hopefully, get President Trump impeached. These are bad, corrupt people.

Although there was no known crime extant, which has historically been a prerequisite for creating a Special Prosecutor, "Agent" or Counsel, one was appointed to ostensibly pursue alleged Trump collusion with Russia. Not surprisingly, this person was an ex-Director of the FBI, buddy and longtime associate of Comey, and he was appointed by the Assistant Attorney General who was also a longtime friend and associate of both of these "fine" top Government law enforcement officials, at least one of whom has been a long time self-proclaimed, but *faux "Conservative Republican."*

If these three don't prove *"rots from the head down"* is a factual statement how about this?

After many, many months and millions of dollars trying to prove President Trump colluded with the Russians, which could not likely be proven illegal anyway, and failing, *"the Establishment"* phony *"Conservative Republican Special,"* let's call him *"Agent"* changed his focus to endeavoring to find the President guilty of "Obstruction of Justice" because he fired his friend Comey, the now proven corrupt FBI Director, to prevent him from proving the non-extant Russia collusion. *"Thicker than thieves"* comes to mind.

But what is amazing about this, in addition to the foregoing that likely not even Tom Clancy could conjure up, is this decades long U.S. Government employed legal whiz, now the *"Special Agent"* does not appear to be a very sharp knife in the drawer of many lawyers who are on the Government payroll for obvious reasons, rather than in highly paid private practice. Reason: the law states the

President is the one who appoints the FBI Director to serve in that capacity for a term of ten years, AND, still according to the law, *"can be removed by the President at his discretion."*

So, should not this character have been removed, or not been there to begin with, since he violated the law in even being the *"Special Agent"* because of his proven conflict of interest given his long term relationship with the Assistant Attorney General who appointed him and the corrupt FBI Director who was a principal in the case since before it was begun, or his proven incompetence, or simply because he should not have been permitted to continue spending millions of dollars of the people's money on a pro *"Establishment"* fishing expedition endeavoring to remove the President elected to get rid of Government *NWO* whores like these three rotting heads addressed above?

Or, how about this? In 2007 under the ex-Director, now *"Special Agent's"* leadership the FBI recommended prosecution of alleged Anthrax killer Bruce Ivins on, according to Democrat Congressman and scientist Rush Holt of New Jersey, *"Not definitive"* scientific findings that he was responsible for the Anthrax attacks at the beginning of this century. Other studies of this case also determined Ivins was not guilty. But because of the years long pursuit of him Ivins committed suicide in 2008.

So, on second thought; maybe Mr. *"Special Agent"* was picked to bring down President Trump because of his prior experience of convicting others who were likely not guilty.

But then, as you will see below, he was also FBI Director in 2003 to 2005 when the agency mailed 140 thousand harassment subpoenas to American citizens AND see below he was the Director who petitioned a parole board not to parole two prisoners he knew were wrongly convicted of murder in 1965, deliberately by the FBI on false testimony of agents to protect one of their informants.

All this indicates in addition to everything else, this guy is morally challenged, dishonest, a liar, unethical and totally corrupt. So, what we have is a career *"Establishment"* hit man, definitely *"Deep State,"* who was given a contract to bring down President Trump in any way possible, truth, honesty, facts or anything else that would get in the way of that be damned. Trump must be eliminated to protect all the criminals in the Department of "Justice" and elsewhere in the Government, and permit the America destroying plans that would have been continued by Hillary to get back on track.

***

With due respect to Sean Hannity of FOX NEWS who constantly qualifies disclosures of wrong doing by top officials in the FBI with the tag line about the *"rank and file"* agents and other employees of the agency being fine, hardworking people who risk their lives every day to protect the American people, we must explore the actual facts of an organization that could have survived over a hundred years in one configuration or another, have people at the top like these, some of whom were obviously promoted from the *"rank and file,"* and must do the bidding of people like these to keep their jobs.

Given the conduct addressed above one must ask; if they are so *"fine,"* why are they still there? Also, given the fact twenty years before these incidents and actions when different "management" and agents were employed, Hillary again lied to the FBI in 1997 during an investigation, but was also not charged then either.

Why does this conduct not demonstrate the agency has been a politically biased, pro *"the Establishment"* enforcement agency for a long time, especially given General Flynn was charged for lying to the FBI when they did everything in their power, including not even putting her under oath, to keep Hillary in the running for the Presidency?

Sounds like long term corruption and bias from top to bottom, but let's look at it.

***

The forerunner of the agency was established in 1908 under afore addressed President Teddy Roosevelt as a primarily domestic agency. J. Edgar Hoover became head of it in 1924, which given his history may not have been positive for the long term good of the organization. In fact, he could have laid a foundation for what we have seen more recently, in 1997, 2001, 2016, 2017 and 2018.

Hoover was an unlikely suspect to head a U.S. Government agency charged with domestic intelligence, security, and being its principal law enforcement agency. He demonstrated, mostly secretively, characteristics that, if known, at least during his time in the agency, forty-eight years from 1924 to 1972, would have caused him to be rejected for the position immediately.

He was a cross-dressing *"sex deviant,"* as he personally referred to homosexuals he unilaterally established programs to prevent being employed by the Government, which was made illegal in 1953, nineteen years before he ceased being head of the agency. So, he illegally headed the agency nineteen years, during which he broke many more laws than that one, possibly setting a precedent for Directors like Comey *et al.*

He consistently abused his power and had the agency abuse its. Under him the agency exceeded its jurisdiction, harassed political dissenters, used illegal means to collect evidence, and amassed secret files on politicians. Through these means he amassed great power to the extent he was even able to intimidate Presidents.

Nixon did not cross him because he was afraid of reprisals from him. But Truman, over seventy years prior to this writing, may have summed up, based on its actions in recent years, especially those pertaining to Hillary Clinton and other *bona fide* members of "*the Establishment*," and the proactive covert actions of top officials against non-"*Establishment*" Trump, the agency Americans have in the 21st Century.

Truman said in response to what he perceived Hoover was endeavoring to create all those years he was in charge, "*We want no Gestapo or Secret Police.*"

But today it appears the direction for years has been more communist KGB than fascist Gestapo. It is not openly abusive like that Nazi enforcement agency that policed a relatively small geographic area. It is clandestine in its operations, functioning on behalf of the more communist-like "*Establishment*" from sixty-five offices scattered around the world where its enforcers are not uniformed or accustomed to disclosing who they are.

Only domestically do some of them work uniformed, but only when pursuing an objective for which uniforms provide import, or limit injury to one of their own.

They function much more KGB-like, secretively and internationally, in a politicized way. But let's not let anyone conclude only its clandestine proactive, obviously political, pro-Hillary and anti-Trump actions lead us to this conclusion. Let's look at some of the agency history that should provide proof.

First: in the 1930s in no way could what they did be considered "law enforcement." They did not endeavor to arrest small-time bank robbers and others. They sent squads of machine gun armed men to sneak up on, surround and machine gun them to death.

Which raises the question: if they did this to these American citizens then, why are they not doing this to the murdering MS 13 illegal immigrant savages who are slaughtering Americans across the country in their own neighborhoods and homes?

Given this FBI history AND the facts these savages are only in the U.S. because "*the Establishment*" President Obama spent billions of taxpayer dollars collecting some of them from jails as post pubescent known delinquent "*children,*" putting them on air-conditioned buses in Honduras, shipping them two thousand miles across Mexico, and deliberately distributing them throughout America, everyone should be asking "**Why?**

But no one is because they are unaware "*the Establishment*" exists, who its members are, what their "*diversity*" goals for

America are, what is being done to achieve them, and even if they were they would not believe it because they think *"It can't happen here."*

So rather than *"Why"* how about some specific questions, the answers to which should present a clear picture of what is going on and who is doing it.

***

Are Americans so out of touch that when they saw on TV, before coverage was shut down, the busloads of thousands of unaccompanied pubescent minors coming across our southern border, they thought these *"children"* got together in Honduras, found all those buses, paid for them, arranged with the Mexican Government to cross their southern border and travel through that country, convinced their parents to permit them to travel to the U.S., got all the buses in a caravan, kissed their parents goodbye, got on and found their way to the U.S. border, negotiated their way across it, further paid their way to the many places across the U.S. to which they were scattered, and supported themselves until their parents could chain migrate here to be with them and begin collecting welfare?

Are Americans not aware **1.)** Honduras is the only country in Central America where the U.S. Government has a major military and bureaucratic presence, and forced reinstatement of their puppet President, after the people removed him, **2.)** Latin families are cohesive, and would never have permitted, or been able to pay for, their youngsters to get on buses, and travel alone two thousand miles across Mexico to the U.S., unless they had a deal wherein they would be permitted to follow ASAP, and they were sufficiently compensated or cared for, **3.)** Mexicans are very protective of their southern border because they don't want Central Americans to illegally enter their country, **4.)** thus, they would never have permitted these thousands of Hondurans, El Salvadorans, or others to enter Mexico unless the U.S. struck a deal with them to bring them across that country to the U.S. and ensure they would not end up in Mexico.

So, the answer to who is doing this is again, boringly true: the America destroying *"Establishment"* represented in this particular case by Obama who spoke admiringly of Brzezinski as his national security advisor, and members of his administration, including Hillary who said she would expand this type of immigration.

The purpose of this and other examples of the massive immigration push to get as many non-English speaking, non-contributory, Government dependent, preferably Spanish speaking, people into the country as possible, and give them voting status, is to get this segment of the population to a critical mass size, that combined with the black population, will create sufficient *"diversity"* to nullify the voting power of predominately European heritage, capitalistic, working, producing, taxpaying citizens, so these people dependent on the Government will greatly enhance the power of those within it, and those whose wealth would be enhanced via the desired new socialist America.

Hopefully this is a sufficiently clear picture of what is going on, who is doing it, and why they are doing it. But if it is not, there is no hope of a continuation of the America our founders created.

If this immigration is not stopped America is finished because it is people who create the cultures in which they live, and neither Africa nor Latin America, or parts of contemporary American cities wherein the populations replicate those of these two continents represent the American culture that created the success and prosperity achieved by those who worked, fought and died to "Make America Great."

But before anyone jumps to the conclusions Americans have been indoctrinated to believe regarding immigration and immigrants, he or she should use their noggins to connect the dots of all of this, and realize facts and figures are not racist. These are what intelligent, non-indoctrinated people throughout history and the world have used to make decisions about anything that affects them or their lives.

Population growth, prosperity, poverty, crime, health and welfare of the human condition, life expectancy, per capita incomes, productivity, and all the other important factors of human existence, where they predominate and the dominant cultures in which each exists must be viewed objectively, reality accepted, and those who refuse to accept these facts, and implement programs and laws that defy common sense, or break extant laws, must be overruled, fired or otherwise removed from positions that enable them, including voting *"the Establishment"* members behind this destruction out of decision making positions, if America is to survive.

***

This definitely includes everyone in these positions in the FBI and its controlling agency, the "Justice" Department, where there remain many holdovers of the most outrageously anti-America, destructive and criminal Administration in the history of the country still assiduously pursuing Obama mentor Saul Alinsky's communist inspired rules for creating a totalitarian socialist state in America.

Hillary Clinton is also an Alinsky acolyte and communist who wrote her college thesis on his communist teachings she has followed almost to the letter with regard to healthcare, welfare, gun control and class warfare throughout hers and her husband's political life.

Therefore, it is entirely reasonable to conclude anyone who would work so assiduously, as did those in top positions at both the FBI and "Justice" Department, endeavoring to ensure she would win out over Trump, including actively helping her and her staff get away with breaking multiple laws so she could stay in contention for the Presidency, rather than being charged with crimes, are, by extension, also assiduously pursuing the same anti-American goals as she and Obama.

The fact they presumably knowingly risked their careers by obstructing justice in shielding Hillary and her cronies from prosecution proves they actually desire a KGB-like agency, or they just desire to be able to function like agents of this type agency with impunity, or possibly they are of an age to have been indoctrinated to believe what they were doing was not bad.

Whichever, does not matter. Either is sufficient for them to be removed, possibly prosecuted, and for Americans to do whatever is required to prevent any more like these from ever again occupying positions with the authority they had. The following tidbits of FBI history and what its rogue officials and agents have been guilty of should convince any reader of the necessity of this if they desire to continue to be relatively free:

- In the 1960s, under Hoover, Martin Luther King was on the Agency's target list, continuously investigated, and even encouraged to commit suicide.

- During this time the Agency's list of covert operations under its official name, COINTELPRO, targets for attention reads like a list of any Americans choosing to exercise their right of free speech. At least twenty organizations on the list, seven Black, eight white, and others; Indians, Puerto Ricans, advocates of state's rights, and ALL protesting the criminal Vietnam War, clearly define the Agency as the anti-American citizens enforcement arm of support for *"the Establishment"* criminal actions. Are the actions of the Agency against Donald Trump in 2016 and since any different?

- In 1965 Agency Officials and Agents, utilizing false witness accounts, committing perjury, allowed four innocent Americans to be convicted and sentenced to death to protect an Agency informant. Over thirty years later, after two of the men died in prison, and the other two were released, the U.S. Government, i.e., U.S. taxpayers, had to pay one hundred million dollars because of the deeds of some of the Agency's *"fine"* Agents of that time.

- The agency continued to wiretap Americans without a warrant until 1967. After that they were supposed to get a warrant...

… emphasis on "supposed to."

- In 1971files taken from the FBI detailed its COINTELPRO investigations of private citizens and alleged assassinations of political activists.

- In the 1980s the practice of entrapment used by the Agency was supposedly "constrained." Tell that to General Flynn and President Trump's lawyers.

- In1992 after their murderous actions at Ruby Ridge where some of the Agency's *"finest,"* without provocation, perpetrated the long-range sniper killing of a woman on her front porch while holding her baby, the killing of her fourteen-year old son and his dog, and deliberately obstructed investigation of their actions, criminally obstructing justice.

- In 1993 they also obstructed investigation of their televised murder of over seventy American citizens with heavy weapons, a military tank and flame thrower after the local Sheriff previously said these people had not broken any laws, their guns were legal, and they had been living there peacefully over forty years. (Neither Bill nor Hillary ever justified this heinous crime on American soil during the President's first year in office.)

- In the 1996 bombing at the Atlantic Olympics the FBI improperly and wrongly leaked the name of innocent Richard Jewel as the suspect, again costing taxpayers dearly.

- In 2001 an Agent was sentenced to life for selling information to the Russians. The USA Patriots Act increased the FBI's power regarding wiretapping and Internet surveillance, AND to search citizens homes while they were away. Robert Mueller was also appointed FBI Director by President Bush II one week before "9/11" for a ten-year term that was extended two more years by Obama. (Possibly Mueller who was also appointed to investigate President Trump even though there was no known crime is a favored law enforcement, and cover-up Officer for both veneers of *"the Establishment."*)

In the same year, prior to "9/11," sentient adults may remember at least two FBI field Agents complaining about FBI headquarters "management" refusing to follow up on their reports of suspicious behavior of young Arabs taking flying lessons, but not desiring or receiving lessons about how to land.

That the FBI refused to follow up on this even in light of the fact the U.S. Government False Flag event planned in 1962, Operation Northwoods, to crash a plane into a high-rise building and blame it on "terrorists" came to light in April 2001, only four months prior to "9/11" is unbelievable. It raises serious questions about Agency involvement, as does the following.

- In 2004 the "9/11" Commission found the Agency guilty of not pursuing intelligence reports that could have prevented "9/11." They allegedly missed twenty-three chances to stop it. This provides even more reason to suspect "9/11" was not as reported, and further "*the Establishment*" FBI "management" was involved because it is just not credible the top "management" of the Agency could have consciously ignored all this information that made it to their desks.

Who could believe the heads of the top domestic intelligence agency ignoring all this intelligence? If true, this is the biggest example of ***"Rots from the head"*** yet. But the book *Spying Blind* published about the same time proffered the reasons for the Agency's "9/11" failings were 1.) a culture resistant to change or new ideas, as they still were a year later, which does not seem to wash with their prior failings, and 2.) inappropriate incentives for promotion, which doesn't make any sense either, given those failing were already occupying some of the highest posts in the Agency.

- Then in this same failure to follow up vein how about the 2018 Florida School shooting in which seventeen young Americans were murdered by a nineteen-year old the F.B.I. was specifically warned two times was an intended school shooter, as well as some of the still unanswered questions regarding perpetrators in other school shootings?

- Surely no one can accept an excuse of incompetence or unintended failure on the part of the highly trained, experienced personal of this agency in all the examples of failure to follow up in these serious matters, given the example below of the time they spent pursuing the Author without any indication of his involvement in anything, or what they did regarding Trump and Hillary Clinton.

- The intelligent mind must conclude; it is highly improbable highly trained personnel, including specially trained profilers for the types of people who commit these types of crimes could fail to follow up in any of these cases unless it was intentional.

- Given all their actions and inactions listed here and witnessed since 2016 against Trump and proactively in favor of Hillary and other proven *"Establishment"* members no one should accept any of their failures or criminality are accidental. There is too much evidence to the contrary, including the millions the Government spent on secret mind control programs to train psychic killers, as far back as Henry Kissinger's work in this field at Harvard in the 1950s at the same time Brzezinski was also there, as well as Government drugging of male students in the public-school system beginning around the time the Clinton Presidency began, before which there were very few school shootings.

All of this and the following must raise serious questions.

- In 2003 National Research Council publication addressed thirty years of *"deeply flawed"* FBI testimonies, misleading under the rules of evidence.

- 2003 to 2005 the Agency issued one hundred and forty thousand national security letters deemed by the Inspector General a form of Administrative Subpoena demanding records and data from citizens with zero connections to terrorism. This seems like a really big fishing expedition, raising the question; how many of its thirty-three thousand employees would have been engaged in handling these and the responses amounting to about six hundred letters and responses a day? Even seems more like harassment than fishing. But maybe they just wanted all this data to add to the information on tens of thousands of other U.S. citizens not guilty of any crimes in their Washington D.C. vault.

- In 2009, six years after 2003, the Agency agreed to release information on cases, and notify prosecutors about faulty testimonies given.

- Between 1993 and 2011 Agents wounded one hundred and fifty people, of which seventy died. All of these were deemed justified shootings. Given the years this would mean the seventy plus men women and children murdered in Waco were *"justified."*

- Then in 2017 all shootings since 2011 were also deemed *"justified,"* which means the FBI has not made a mistake when shooting anyone in a quarter of a century, including at least one proven innocent man who has to be just one of many.

This and the prior point causes one to think the agency's conduct has not changed much since the 1930s, as proven by all the *"justified"* killings of innocents at Ruby Ridge and Waco.

If these are insufficient to describe a rogue agency, consider the tactics proven employed against U.S. citizens by the Agency: psych warfare, smearing with false accusations and documents, planting false reports in the media, harassment and wrongful imprisonment.

In addition to all of the above, consider the actual crimes against individuals and the country so many at the top of the Agency committed to endeavor to prevent Trump being elected and ensure Hillary would be.

These are career members of the Agency like the one central to the investigation of Hillary and her co-conspirator's actual crimes, and the non-crimes of Trump who gave Hillary a walk in the face of incontrovertible evidence of her guilt while being instrumental in the appointment of the Special Prosecutor to investigate President Trump without any evidence of any crime or anything worthy of investigation. He testified he was with the Agency twenty-six years. Thus, presumably part of the time a member of the *"rank and file."*

This means he was promoted from this level within the Agency we hear so many excuses for, which are inexcusable given the number of these *NWO, "Deep State"* whores infesting this supposedly law enforcing agency who were obviously promoted from within that were exposed since Trump was elected.

This one testified before Congress under oath supported by FBI lawyers even though he was physically escorted out of the FBI building several days prior.

The fact that in his position of ostensible non-membership on the FBI team, whatever that means now, being a proven liar and on the official FBI electronic record with his intent to act to dislodge the newly elected President of the United States he still had the backing of the FBI is more evidence of how widely the anti-American *NWO "Establishment"* permeates this Agency and the entirety of the Government of the United States.

This one's demeanor and performance in his hearing demonstrated why he is an avid Hillary supporter.

He was arrogant, like he can't be touched, mean, nasty and snarling with words demonstrating his animus toward average Americans who have been paying his salary for twenty-six years just as Hillary demonstrated. But whereas Hillary referred to all of us as *"deplorables"* this condescending little f*** said he could actually *"smell"* us *"in a Walmart!"*

His demeanor also demonstrated why he likely favors the totalitarian form of government Hillary has quietly worked toward for forty years. He was straight out of central casting for a role as a member of the Fascist Gestapo, haircut and all, of which his conduct indicated he thought himself already a member.

This character is a frightening example of what the *NWO* is bringing to America. And it is frightening.

***

In fact, this frightens the Author, as it should any readers of this.

If there are so many permeating the FBI so confident of their *Untouchables* status they are willing to break laws to interfere in a U.S. Presidential Election what protection do average Americans have against attacks by them?

Might they decide to attack the Author or anyone else they desire for whatever reason they choose, like presenting these factual disclosures of their anti-American law-breaking conduct?

The Author has already experienced one long-term, unjustified interference in his life by this Agency. The documents referenced below are the ones he obtained after a two-year effort, a few thousand dollars and the assistance of a retired CIA Officer.

They demonstrate the time and money spent by this Agency to

investigate him, a citizen who had never committed a crime, and still hasn't. But given this, the history of the FBI, its conduct and that of its highly placed Officials disclosed since Trump announced his candidacy all bets are off where these criminals are concerned.

These documents are examples of some of the FBI's surveillance of the Author from November 1974 to January 1977 he obtained under the joke that is the Freedom of Information Act, ten months after he received a response from the Central Intelligence Agency stating, *"There are no documents available to you under either the FOIA, 5 U.S.C.§ 552, or the Privacy Act of 1974, 5 U.S.C. § 552a."*

This was also sort of a "joke" given it was C.I.A. covert personnel who made the arrangements for his first visit to China, provided documents for him in Hong Kong, including a clean second passport he could use to get into China on his first trip, which began October 14, 1974, precisely one month prior to the highly redacted FBI document dated "11/14/74."

But rather than a "joke," this proved the C.I.A. whose people he saw many times over the following years in Hong Kong, the Philippines and elsewhere, and were also surveilling him, did not want him to know any details about this.

He knows this for a couple of reasons: 1.) One time in the Philippines he had a meeting with the Russian Counsel General to the country who was also the business manager for the Russian/Philippines owned steamship company his company did business with. Then the minute he walked into his hotel room after the meeting the phone rang. When he answered, the response was *"Hello, comrade"* from a voice he recognized.

2.) He was visited unannounced at his U.S. home office one day by a gentleman who provided his C.I.A. "business" card, sort of obliquely thanked him for nothing mentioned, and asked him to do a fairly good-sized favor for him in Asia, which he agreed to. Then, as he got up to leave motioned to his card on the desk, saying, *"If you ever have any trouble with U.S. Customs or Immigration, or any other agency when you are out of the country tell them to give me a call."*

As interesting as this might seem to a reader, these factors should be kept in mind. The FBI did not have a clue what the C.I.A. was doing. Both were spending thousands of taxpayer dollars on someone as innocuous as a regular American businessman. The C.I.A. was aware of what they were doing and why, knew he knew them, and even deliberately disclosed this several times in Hong Kong and the Philippines like two business people just bumping into one another on a business trip.

48

But the FBI did not have any "business" reason to be doing what they were doing. They were just keeping tabs on an American businessman overseas, surveilling his U.S. home and his wife when he was away and even going into the neighborhood where he grew up asking questions about him. What for? Ridiculous!

So his opinion is the big difference between the two agencies is the C.I.A. is engaged in activities that can mostly be described as endeavoring to protect Americans, while the FBI seems to be functioning as the enemy of Americans, wasting taxpayer's money surveilling, collecting and storing vast amounts of information on them, and even endeavoring to deprive them of representatives they elect if they do not think they are appropriate servants of the America destroying "*Establishment*" for which they are the enforcement arm.

One example of each of these is: 1.) FBI actions regarding "9/11," in which it is difficult to see where they did anything for American citizens, or did anything to stop the terrorists, and 2.) their recent actions in doing everything within their power to prevent a man of the people being elected President while breaking the law trying to ensure *"the Establishment"* member Hillary Clinton became President.

Conclusions: Let those interested in acting against Americans worry about what the C.I.A. is doing. But American citizens should worry what the FBI is doing to them.

Don't agree with this? Read on.
***
The documents the Author finally received from the FBI, which were each addressed **"To The Director"** were so extensively redacted that when he presented them to the printer of this book he was told they could not be printed in a way they would be contributory to this work. So, all we can do is address them:
- the first dated "Hong Kong 11/14/74 that apparently was the genesis of the investigation of the Author is totally redacted to conceal whatever that was. Nothing but a big black area.
- then the one issued 1/8/75 indicated Washington was requesting Dallas investigate him, outlined his Sydney issued passport, that he lived there the prior year, his parents address, his description, birth certificate, American Express Card number, passport number, prior passport number, information on his travel plans six years prior the summer between his two HBS years, where he was born, his address and phone number six years prior, when he was first married and divorced sixteen and fourteen years before, and his TX Driver's License number, and photograph.

The last paragraph is instructions to those who would be doing the investigation not to disclose it was the FBI doing it. Instructions were to change the source of this information to "United States Government." (Question: if they already had all of this information, why would they need to investigate what they already had?)

- document from the Dallas office repeating all 1/8/75 information, requesting further investigation.

- this resulted in them going to where the following describes "AT FORT WORTH, TEXAS." Which yielded the amazing information of his telephone number, home address, office address and business based on "observation" at his office address. Then the agent reported that "operator 22, Credit Bureau Services advised" his SSC number, employer, dates employed, and two previous addresses.

Then, probably as was done regarding Trump, further pursued finding something to justify the time and money spent, i.e., looking for a crime or collusion with the Chinese because he was there two times by this time, the agent went to the Fort Worth police.

- there, "Detective Intelligence Section Fort Worth PD advised records negative." But, still refusing to accept there was nothing to investigate, pursued checking out if maybe he lied about where he resided when he moved back from Australia. But the Agent apparently went to the wrong place because he reported "advised records failed to reflect ever resided" there. So because of this, surely he must have lied about his current address.

- then now eight months into their investigation, 7/10/75 "observation" make and license of auto "parked in the driveway." Also, "Tarrant County Auto License Bureau confirmed car owned by" [Author]. Surprise!

Interestingly, however, the agent making this "observation" failed to indicate he spent three whole days making this, obviously expensive, "observation."

We know this because the Author was out of the country, which they probably knew, and his wife, being home alone, observed the Agent sitting in his car across the street from her home hours a day for three days. But before calling the police, on the third day she walked across the street and confronted him.

His excuse was he was a Texas Christian University art student who thought the Colonial home was pretty, and he was painting it.

He obviously also spent time planning his long "stake out" because he was able to show her an almost finished pretty good tempura painting of the house.

Still not satisfied much more time, and money, was spent completing a very detailed description of the Author's company, including products, how they were obtained from "throughout the world," etc. etc., really important information.

- still not satisfied, undated memo stated, "presumed his trip to China was legitimate," but "requested to check indices" and "due to commercial contracts with Communist China... interview in line with current intelligence criteria is requested."

- 7/23/75 instructions how to conduct interview. Then on and on until....

- 1/16/76 five pages of repeat of all before, summary of interview, lengthy details of interview and statement "his informant potentiality is not being considered at this time."

- 1/31/76 Totally redacted.

- 12/7/76 H.K. Over two years after beginning their fishing expedition, totally redacted.

So, bottom line; tens of thousands of dollars on fuel, Agents, management, office staff, overhead, and who knows what else, wasted investigating a citizen for nothing!

But they did likely do damage to the reputation of the one being investigated because much of the information collected could not have been obtained without disclosing he was being investigated by some Government Agency.

Consider all this in light of the absolute fact top people in this agency... who are not Russians... did everything within their power to attempt to illegally determine the outcome of the 2016 U.S. Presidential election. Then having failed in that criminal endeavor were still plotting some kind of, in their words, "*insurance policy*" to prevent Trump occupying the Oval Office.

Then, having failed in that endeavor, the recent FBI Director allegedly committed the crime of "leaking" confidential information to get his friend and predecessor Director of this agency appointed by another of their co-conspirators in the now obviously misnamed "Justice" Department, to find, or create something, anything, to find him guilty of, to cause him to be removed from Office while letting several people they were absolutely certain committed federal crimes go free, rather than getting them indicted.

Both, the actions against one party and non-action against the other, were for purely political purposes by an Agency that is supposed to be apolitical and nonpartisan.

If there is any doubt about this, consider: at the time of this writing over a year and a half after they were requested, the FBI was still refusing to submit to a Congressional oversight committee hundreds of thousands of subpoenaed documents related to their non-investigation of Hillary Clinton's Emails and other "*matters*," including probable obstruction of justice due to her and her staff destroying subpoenaed evidence.

If this conduct by these employees vociferously supported in the media and by others does not prove the criminal nature of many in high positions in our Government, as well as the truth of the adage below that bears repeating even for these "little" men, what does?

"Power tends to corrupt, and absolute power corrupts absolutely. Great men are almost always bad men."

- Lord Acton, 1887

Then there is the question of non-action, again, where there is real crime adversely affecting the lives of many Americans. What is the agency doing in the *"matter"* of the interstate functioning MS 13 illegal alien savages?

Does the Principal Law Enforcement Agency have them at the top of its "Most Wanted" list, and assiduously pursuing them?

This seems like something to put one of the six Assistant Directors, like the one sending Emails to his, also FBI employee, lover during the work day, in charge of.

Talk about a rogue Agency! History proves their anti-Trump actions are nothing new. If this is the country's "Principal Law Enforcement Agency" we are all in serious jeopardy! Might say, screwed! But it could be worse than that.

***

Some of us could be killed due to deliberate FBI actions alleged on FOX NEWS' Tucker Carlson show March 21, 2018 regarding the 2015 Islamist terrorist attack in Garland, Texas ostensibly resulting from cartoons about Mohammed.

The security guard shot and wounded in that attack appeared on the show with his attorney alleging they have proof the <u>FBI not only failed to stop the attack but was aware of it in advance because an agent accompanied one of the terrorists to the scene under direction of FBI top management. A Government agency creating terrorism in the U.S?</u>

This was not a rogue agent. He was allegedly acting under orders from the seventh floor of FBI headquarters while James Comey, previously Director and the *Special Agent's* buddy, was in charge. So, given Comey appears to be of the same ilk based on his leaking and lying to Congress, who knows what is possible?

This is frightening! If the guard prevails in his case it means the FBI was involved in endeavoring to create fear on behalf of *"the Establishment,"* the head of which at the time was Obama, which could explain a lot. As does the fact the father of the Florida Pulse nightclub terrorist shooter was an FBI informant.

It would substantiate the FBI is not only *"the Establishment"* enforcement agency, but also a participant in creation of fear to enhance Government power, which also could explain its failure to stop "9/11" on twenty-three occasions, the failure to follow up on warnings about the Florida school shooting and so much more.

It could also explain why FBI top management, including Comey, engaged in possible criminal activity to prevent Hillary being charged for all her crimes, which frighteningly raises more questions like; why was Obama literally importing "refugees" from terrorist country strongholds in the Middle East, and why Hillary stated she was not just going to continue this program, but increase the numbers to one hundred thousand a year.

All this proves the FBI hasn't changed its ways in over eighty-five years. It has just gotten worse by becoming more political. Neither citizens, nor Presidents, are safer, if as safe, today than Nixon and Truman indicated forty-five to seventy years ago.

And here is yet another example of just how bad the U.S. "Justice" Department and its FBI are for honest working American citizens as recently as 2017 under its Trump hating Director James Comey and Obama's Clinton consorting Attorney General.

This also further proves the Agency's real task is enforcement of *"the Establishment"* rules and goals with total disregard of citizen's rights, proving how crooked it and he were in their conduct against an innocent American Citizen.

In December 2017 a Federal Judge declared a mistrial in a conspiracy case against a seventy-one-year old Nevada rancher incarcerated by Feds after "Justice" Department prosecutors were caught withholding a *"massive amount"* of thirty-three hundred pages of "smoking gun" evidence undermining their charges against him, which was the criminal act of withholding exculpatory evidence that would have proven the rancher innocent. The judge accused the Feds of willful violation of his due process right.

This case supposedly arose from the Obama Bureau of Land Management acting against the rancher, as disclosed by a BLM chief investigator, *"in the most intrusive, oppressive, large scale and militaristic trespass cattle (seizure) possible"* after which the rancher summoned a militia to defend himself, his family and others from FBI snipers that had surrounded his ranch. But the fact he was publicly opposed to Federal Government over reach could have played a role, as it has in other instances.

So, here is another case wherein newly released, documents prove the FBI deployed numerous snipers around an American citizen's property for the obvious purpose of shooting whoever they were told or decided to shoot for whatever cause or not just as was done at Ruby Ridge to a mother, her fourteen-year old son and dog.

Later FBI analysis proved neither the rancher nor his family were violent and concluded the supposedly innocuous BLM was deliberately "*trying to provoke a conflict*" with the rancher and his family. Ergo the FBI "*snipers were in place*" to fire on American citizens who had not been proven guilty of any crime.

Given this case, Ruby Ridge, Waco, Garland, one hundred-fifty American citizens shot by the FBI between 1993 and 2011, seventy of whom died, and the others shot between 2011 and 2017, were all deemed "*justified,*" it seems "*the rank and file*" of the Agency are definitely the enforcement arm of a miscreant "*Establishment*" controlled Government who can never be found wrong in shooting a couple hundred American citizens in a quarter century, just as their unprosecuted superiors in charge who are proven criminals under Federal laws can also get away with their criminality.

Therefore, given all the foregoing information in this chapter, it is past time Sean Hannity of FOX NEWS cease nauseatingly qualifying disclosures of wrong doing by FBI officials with the tag line about the "*rank and file*" agents being fine, hardworking people who risk their lives every day to protect the American people. It is the American people's lives that are at risk!

Who the hell does he think shot all these people and manned the tanks at Waco, FBI top ranks like Mueller, Comey, and McCabe?

Why does he think they, including all the snipers, are trained at Quantico where U.S. Marines are trained how to kill their enemy?

Answer: because the FBI "*rank and file*" are also being trained how to kill their enemy, which appears more and more to be American citizens when they are told to, just as the Marines do without questioning their orders.

But the big problem with all this is the Federal Bureau of Investigation is a just a microcosm of the entire humongous beast that is the overgrown, *New World Order,* "*Establishment*" controlled, doomed to fail Government that functions, not for the benefit of working, taxpaying Americans, but for itself by governing for the benefit of illegal alien immigrants it desires to be citizen supporters, and major global corporations.

It is as Zbigniew Brzezinski and David, "*Americans have too much democracy,*" Rockefeller planned back in 1973, and the know-nothing souls in Hollywood, most of the rest of the entertainment world and "*the Establishment*" media political whores like Mika Brzezinski and her effete media sidekick seem to love.

Like those in failing businesses, inbred and causing the failure as in the FBI, all those in the Federal Government adversely affecting the lives of citizens must be replaced with new "blood" from outside their failing America destroying culture... or else!

All the above proves America is on a fast track to totalitarianism, pure and simple, like the Bushes, Carter, Obama, Clintons, their minions and Brzezinski have been planning for and moving America toward most of their adult lives.

So, there really is no "or else" because if they defeat Trump and stay in control the destruction of America as we have known it will be *Fait Accompli*. America; *Kaput! Fini!*

Consider: if they spent the time investigating Hillary they did the Author, would not her fat you know what be in prison today? <u>If not, all of us should be very afraid!</u>

If anyone still wonders what we should be afraid of please reread this chapter, paying close attention to the FBI abuses, even killing, of Americans, and its supposed failures regarding "9/11" and the many shootings it had advance notice of.

Then, finally, consider what we have on our hands in the form of this major domestic law enforcement agency wherein it is known well over a dozen of its top officials worked assiduously, employing all the power of the Agency, endeavoring to prevent Trump becoming President. Then since he is they continue to endeavor to remove him.

We have all heard of the *"Deep State."* Well, it doesn't get much deeper than this the Soviet Union would be envious of.

Combine this with the "deeply" stupid Americans, including members of Congress campaigning to abolish the only law enforcement agency protecting us from being overrun by people who desire to replace our Government and way of life with theirs they are coming to America to get away from.

We are being attacked from outside and inside by many endeavoring to destroy everything good about America. So, maybe the few of us remaining who desire to save it should become as proactive as those bent on destroying us.

Possibly a good place to begin would be this one truly anti-American Agency and all the anti-American law arrogance its top people have demonstrated before Congress.

If nothing else this would be a good counter to those in Congress endeavoring to abolish Immigration and Customs Enforcement, an agency that actually protects us.

CHAPTER THREE
GOVERNMENT

CREATING AN ORGANIZATION DELIBERATELY INTENDED TO PLACE CONTROL OF AMERICA IN THE HANDS OF AN INSTUTIONALIZED CORPORATE/GOVERNMENT PLUTROCRACY

"These men, largely private, were functioning on a level different from the public policy of the United States, and years later when New York times reporter Neil Sheehan read through the entire document [the history of the Vietnam war] *he would come away with one impression above all, which was that the Government of the United Sates was not what he had thought it was; it was as if there were an inner U.S. Government, what he called 'a centralized state, far more powerful than anything else, for whom the enemy is not simply the Communists but everything else, its own press, its own judiciary, its own Congress, foreign and friendly governments - all these are potentially antagonistic. It had survived and perpetuated itself, often using the issue of anti-Communism as a weapon against the other branches of government and the press, and finally, it does not function necessarily for the benefit of the Republic but rather for its own ends, its own perpetuation: it has its own codes which are quite different from public codes. Secrecy was a way of protecting itself, not so much from threats from foreign governments, but from detection from its own population on charges of its own competence and wisdom.' Each succeeding Administration was careful, once in office not to expose the weaknesses of its predecessor. After all, essentially the same people were running the governments, they had continuity to each other... Thus, the national security apparatus kept its continuity, and every outgoing President tended to rally to the side of each incumbent President."* - David Halberstam, THE BEST AND THE BRIGHTEST, 1973

This ironically published the year Brzezinski and Rockefeller formalized "*the Establishment*" organization confirms there has long been a cabal of continuity... "*Shadow Government, Deep*

State" or whatever one chooses to call it... in charge of the U.S. Government regardless who the people elect to represent them.

In 2016 to 2018, this Government was, and still is, represented by the people in the "Justice" Department, FBI, Federal Judiciary, Supreme Court, State Department, many so-called Republican members of Congress like McCain, others like the entire Bush family, and the Clintons, Senator Feinstein, Obama and all the holdovers from his Administration, etc., etc., who have demonstrated, but not disclosed, their membership in **"an inner U.S. Government... a centralized state"** via their anti-Trump words and deeds.

Reread the quote. It describes why they continue to pursue ousting Trump from the Presidency: he does not represent the continuity of control of America Hillary, Bill, both Bushes, the Clintons and Obama have abided by their entire political careers.

The only difference between the 2018 *"Establishment"* and that described in the quote is the media, judiciary and others described as enemies of the **"inner U.S. Government"** in the 1970s were long ago coopted to become full-fledged members of the America destroying Government Brzezinski *"New Economic World Order"* even though many of them are probably not fully aware of exactly what it is they have bought into and represent, especially the media..

Amazing what money and power can buy, isn't it?

Not to Brzezinski and Rockefeller. They knew exactly what they were doing and what a fertile plowing field for what they planned was already prepped for them.

***

In 2018 except for President Donald Trump and literally a handful of his compatriots, America still no longer has a Government *"of the people, by the people, for the people."*

Control of the U.S. Government was still largely in the hands of Obama holdovers and other members of *"the Establishment"* whose desire is to promote an even larger, more powerful, institution wherein more decisions are made, and more taxpayer dollars spent, for the interests of themselves and their co-conspirators, people who are fighting the President daily to prevent him from doing what he was elected to do.

The wrong kind of people, who as Thomas Sowell said, *"pay no price for being wrong,"* are still fighting figuratively *"tooth and nail"* to maintain the Government as the America destroying institution in which they have found refuge from capitalism for at least four decades at the expense of the much lesser paid American citizenry whose interests have suffered because of what these people have been doing.

The just discussed FBI is only one relatively small example of the kind of people the Government has attracted and put in positions where they are "working" against the interest of working Americans from which they are going to be difficult to extract.

Just think; if the people at the top of that organization and those yet to be found out in America's "Justice" Department, our top law enforcement agencies responsible for the enforcement of the law and administration of *justice* in the *United States,* are willing to break the nation's laws to prevent Trump from being elected and then continue to break laws to endeavor to remove him from office, what are the others likely to do?

They are all aware Trump's actions to enhance the entire country and the lives of its working productive citizens will render much of what many of them do obsolete because he is a businessman. Unlike his predecessors who were mostly political hacks concerned only with doing the bidding of large corporations, and raising money to endeavor to stay in office, he will likely do as successful business people do, and continue to look at results versus cost and act accordingly, hopefully, to the detriment of these people.

The opportunities for this are boundless. But here is one example that should have been at the top of his list: he has yet to take any of the horribly needed action to turn around the failing for decades Department of Education.

The quality of education in America, and the future of the country, has been declining since May 1980 when this abortion of America's future was performed by Jimmy Carter under the guidance of Doctor Zbigniew Brzezinski to stop real education so he could begin indoctrinating America's young minds for his nefarious reason of creating the anti-capitalistic, uninformed, pliable population we saw rioting in the streets and on university campuses in 2018 for all the wrong, destructive reasons implanted in their heads by Brzezinski's indoctrination system.

Again, non-racist numbers tell the story. In 2018 test scores in all subjects achieved by America's indoctrinated youth are, and have been for years, significantly below those achieved in most western industrialized nations and many third world countries. This in spite of the fact the per capita dollar cost of "education" in America greatly exceeds what any of these other countries are spending.

So, how long is it going to take Trump to realize his mistake in this part of the Government, and get rid of the entire Department and its staff of 3,900 totally non-productive, destructive, employees who are spending sixty-eight billion dollars, or $17,382,413 per employee, per year to continue destroying our country's future?

Think these employees, Democrats, *"the Establishment"* Republicans or any others benefitting from the way their Government has been for years will placidly accept this?

Doubtful! American Socialist "Democrats" who controlled the U.S. Congress for all but four of the seventy years prior to 1994 and many years since, and their superficially Republican *"Establishment"* cohorts, such as the two Presidents Bush who only masqueraded as Conservative Republicans, were just as assiduous enablers of this big Government and its continuing growth as Clinton and Obama.

These enablers and the people who are drawn to the form of government they engender are not the type of people who provided much of the greatness of America. They are the opposite in their mindset and conduct.

Rather than being of the mindset of achieving through work and accomplishment and engendering an environment in which others can do the same, they choose government because of the security, healthcare, retirement, and, especially in the case of the enablers, MONEY and POWER.

Thus, the culture of the U.S. Government is defined not by those whose mindset would continue to provide Americans with the prosperity, freedom and upward mobility of the past President Trump is endeavoring to reinstate, but by those like Obama whose mindset is to inhibit the ability of Americans to work and achieve through the imposition of authoritarian government rules and restrictions Trump is striving to remove, and by enablers of these whose desire is to use the prosperity of the country to the benefit of themselves and their cronies on the global stage. Although possibly worse today, this is not a new development.

As stated by General Motors Chairman Thomas Murphy in 1962, *"Success is now sufficient evidence to invite scrutiny by the government to determine how success can be 'remedied,' as if it were a disease. To win is to lose; and the losers are not just the companies found 'guilty' of success. The real losers are the consumers."*

This statement had even more merit in 2018. The *"consumers"* are, of course, the American people for whom those in government have blatant disregard. This is evidenced by many government actions, but some are more salient than others.

American Telephone and Telegraph, AT&T, was a roaring success for over ninety years in 1983, both for itself and American consumers. It continued to improve service and profits while reducing the real cost to consumers during all those years.

This was apparently too much success for the American Socialist Democrat controlled Congress that *"remedied"* this success by breaking up the company that year to provide American consumers with the multiplicity of companies, higher prices, less service, losses and bankruptcies experienced over the next decade.

Those successful but do not pay the price desired by those in Government will suffer the wrath of the Government while those who are well connected and financially support the Government's parasitic *"seekers of refuge from capitalism"* employees and enablers can do little wrong in the eyes of their government". The best, recent examples of this are Microsoft and Enron.

Microsoft was a successful outsider that did not bring offerings to those in Government and suffered the consequences by having the "Democrats" endeavor to do to it what they did to AT&T.

Enron was a disaster that cost Americans, including the Author, financially, even more than the attack on the World Trade Center, but its executives, while enriching themselves also enriched both Republican and Democrat branches of *"the Establishment."*

The only consequences suffered by any of the Enron executives is one of them was rewarded with a high-ranking position in the Bush II Administration, and even though some of his conduct in this position was questionable Bush continued to support him. Gives new meaning to *"it's not what you know, but who you know"* doesn't it?

But after the Bush Administration was in power the Government eased up on Microsoft, as its Chairman, Bill Gates found a new religion. He became a big financial supporter of the religion of which Bush was an adherent. No. Not Christianity.

Gates may be a Christian, but the substantial financial contributions referred to here were to the United Nations, *"New World Order,"* One World Government causes that are, privately, so dear to the long-term Government dependent Bush family.

Gates also pledged millions of dollars to failed African causes at about the same time Bush announced a trip and an additional seven hundred million American taxpayer dollars to Africa. Gee! Could there be a connection?

Surely there was, and it was appropriately consistent. The entire U.S. Government is firmly under the control of those whose allegiance is not to the American people who pay their salaries, but those like the Bush family that for over a hundred years, since II's grandfather was high up in the U.S. Government in charge of weapons procurement during WWI.

They function entirely for the advancement of the Bush I (who was a charter member of Brzezinski's formal *"Establishment"* organization) *"New World Order"* One World Government agenda, and only ostensibly cater to American voters.

All the enablers, like the Bushes, Republicans and Democrats alike, assiduously pursue a big business, non-American, pro-One World Government strategy of let's level the playing field by moving American production, jobs and dollars to the Third World for the benefit of big corporate profits and political power to the detriment of Americans.

And they ensure they will continue to have willing accomplices in the form of U.S. Government employees through Government hiring practices and appointments.

These practices and policies, such as the quiet FBI policy during the Clinton Administration of not hiring Protestant white males, ensure the Government's Third World mentality. As long ago as 2002, the thirty percent of U.S. Government employees of Third World ethnicity was double their percentage of the U.S. population.

This makeup, and agenda, of the more highly paid Government employees ensure it will not function in the manner, or with the efficiency of the American private sector.

Average Americans are literally dumbfounded at Government policies and decisions, the stupidity of which eludes common sense.

It seems even when there is a simple answer, which is usually the best one, the Government solution is always convoluted and not in the best interest of the country or its citizens, much like we have witnessed in Third World African and Latin countries for decades.

There is an incredible degree of both stupidity and arrogance demonstrated in Washington, and there is a complete disconnect with taxpaying citizens. The situation seems to be, as *The American Sentinel* put it: *"Washington versus America."*

The U.S. government is, and has been for years, the institution most detrimental, even destructive to the future of a free, democratic and capitalistic America. Reason: a big, powerful, central government is diametrically opposed to these concepts. The larger the government in relation to the private sector the less prosperous Americans will become.

According to the study "The Size and Functions of Government and Economic Growth," an increase in the size of government by four percent, from twenty-five percent of Gross Domestic Product to twenty-nine percent, would result in a reduction of real annual economic growth of two percent, a decline in the rate of growth of more than one-third... as happened to the country during Obama's time in office... as planned, it would seem to anyone familiar with Obama's idol, communist Saul Alinsky's *"Rules for Radicals"* on how to establish a socialist totalitarian society. Don't believe this?

Read it!

***

The road to continued prosperity is that the U.S. historically was on before the gates were opened to comport with the Rockefeller/Brzezinski 1974 *"Globalist"* agenda via the Brzezinski/Carter 1980 Refugee/Immigration Act that spurred massive immigration of Third World denizens. That road is: **economic growth must exceed population growth**.

The primary reason for Third World poverty is they are much more productive of humans than they are of goods and services. In fact, as the non-racist numbers prove, as their populations increase the percentage of production of goods like food actually decline relative to the percentages of population increases.

To the extent the population of those of Third World culture and mentality increase in the U.S., especially in government; the more demand there will be on the non-Third World, non-government, capitalistic private sector and average working Americans to produce more to keep up with the growth in humans and pay more taxes to support them.

The annual population growth in the U.S. between 1990 and 2000 was less than two percent, but it was greater at the end of the decade than at the beginning and increased dramatically under the *"brothers of another mother,"* Bush II and Obama, 2001 to 2016.

There really was little difference between them even ostensibly. Both were little but proactive implementers of the father Bush I proclaimed *"New World Order"* agenda that was definitely the *"mother"* of all both did as President.

But few Americans are aware of this; thanks to the same dishonest U.S. media trying to remove Trump from the Presidency fifty years later. If not for both being members of families with multiple generations of membership in the America destroying *"Establishment"* neither would have ever been President.

We have previously discussed the Bush family Government involvement that dates back to WWI, but we have not had cause previously to address the fact of Obama being a third generation U.S. Government employee. In fact, the reason for his schooling in a Muslim school in Indonesia in the 1960s has not been factually disclosed by the media.

He was there because his mother was a C.I.A. employee when William Casey was there in charge of the activities of that organization to oust the socialist government and union management of resource companies in that country referred to as the *"Jewel of the Pacific"* because it is the most resource rich country in the South Pacific.

In some quarters what Casey did there was referred to as *"the second greatest genocide of the 20th century."* But even though that and the rest of Casey's C.I.A. history is interesting reading, it is beyond the scope of this writing, except for Casey's ending, and how that might relate to the warning Senator Schumer gave Trump in early 2017: he should avoid crossing U.S. Intelligence.

The Obama first generation Government connection was his mother's parents. These grandparents also happened to be U.S. Government employees for some time and were responsible for raising Obama after his time in Indonesia.

Bush, like Obama, refused to say, *"Radical Islamist Terrorists"* due to the same above referenced *"mother,"* and both increased the Government spending and American's expense of living dramatically, including the cost of American healthcare; Bush the cost of pharmaceuticals, Obama insurance.

But regarding Third World population growth; in just one year, 2005, *faux "Conservative Republican"* Bush II permitted the population of illegal Mexican immigrants he referred to as, *"Just good folks looking for a better life,"* to expand, lying to the American public as he was willfully implementing the effete *NWO "Divide and Conquer"* plan to enhance Government power due to the propensity of those with a Third World mentality to be more Government dependent, and require more interventions due to their lifestyles inconsistent with Western norms.

Obama, for his part in this specific *NWO* endeavor, had to be more proactive. Due to the decline in the U.S. economy under his tutelage the numbers of illegals crossing the southern U.S. border began to decline.

Since this was increasing the time before this population would reach the critical mass percentage of the population sufficient to exceed the primarily European heritage population and ensure the Brzezinski *"Establishment"* desired one-party Government, like the USSR, would be in power without challenge forever, short of armed revolution, he had to do something.

This "short of armed revolution" comment should cause you to think about the years long efforts to get rid of the Second Amendment, and the mass marches in 2018 of hundreds of thousands of indoctrinated students ignorantly marching in support of elimination of yours and their Constitutional right to bear arms to protect yourselves, primarily from an oppressive government like the one Brzezinski envisioned, and is represented by the actions of top FBI and "Justice" Department officials in 2017 and 2018.

But Obama's "something" was to make a deal with the Mexican Government to permit him to bring untold tens of thousands of *"unaccompanied children"* from the worst parts of Central America, including jails and prisons, across Mexico from its southern border to the U.S. in air-conditioned buses, and spend untold billions of U.S. taxpayer dollars to spread them, and shortly thereafter their families, their crime, poverty and American impoverishing economic dependency throughout the country, and *voila!*

Like *"two birds with one stone,"* more of the above, plus countrywide MS 13 gangs and crime, the DACA issue/problem and larger future generations of non-assimilating, divisive, Government empowering, Spanish speaking under educated, wages lowering *"Diversity."* Great *NWO* job, Barrack!

***

All this is not unlike what Jimmy Carter did with Castro to empty his prisons onto the streets of America over thirty years prior, destroying the beautiful park and high end commercial east end of the Wilshire Blvd. "Miracle Mile," a tremendously economically successful part of Los Angeles for decades, turning it into the most crime ridden and violent "Rampart" section of the city in less than a year, and bringing crime into the beautiful Hancock Park residential area, as well as reducing wages and employment of the American citizen population of southern Florida by over thirty percent.

Contrary to all the lies told in favor of Mexican immigrants this is what they do in their own country. That is why parks in Mexico are mostly paved or dirt, and all nice large homes have walls and guards. Even large retail stores have police or military guards with automatic weapons slung over their shoulders because, as one Mexican businessman said when questioned about this, *"If not for the guards they would just go in and take whatever they want."* The truth is; this is what has happened here also.

The similarity of these actions by Carter and Obama is suspicious. So, we should not forget 1.) Brzezinski once bragged he was primarily responsible for Carter being President, was officially his National Security Advisor, but given his influence in immigration, education and other areas was actually in reality his puppeteer, 2.) he was also an advisor to Obama who touted his brilliance and how he valued his advice, and 3.) both were out of Brzezinski's deliberately America destroying playbook.

The demographics of the increase in population growth since 2000 show it was attributable almost entirely to the minority part of the existing population and immigrants of a Third World ethnicity.

Historical empirical evidence indicates continuance of this trend will result in population growth gaining on the growth in productivity, resulting in America becoming less wealthy on a per capita basis that... if Third World population growth continues...

will eventually result in U.S. wealth continuing to decline versus the rest of the advanced, industrialized world. We should all realize this is not positive for our future.

**

During the Clinton years, taxes as a percentage of GDP were three percent higher than during previous peace times at twenty-two percent of all goods and services produced.

Since Federal Government expenditures usually exceed Government revenues, resulting in deficit spending, the U.S. Government was consuming more than twenty-five percent of all the wealth created by America's citizens during the Clinton years. But this increased after Clinton, and dramatically so during Obama's time in office.

It was estimated the Federal Government would increase in size, and expenditures, by at least twenty-two percent in the years between 1999 and 2003, mostly under a Republican, Bush II Administration. This was over five percent per year, exceeding the growth in Gross Domestic Product, or production of the entire economy by a factor of two times.

This projection would have resulted in the size of the Government, or the amount of the wealth produced by the economy consumed by the Government, increasing by an absolute amount of over six percent during those four years, seventy-five percent of which were under a veneer "Republican" President.

According to this "Size and Source" study, government of this size would result in growth of the U.S. economy being no more than one-half of that experienced during previous good years, which is exactly what happened during Obama's two terms.

Given the recent population growth rate as of 2016, population growth and economic growth would have been at parity in 2017, or on the precipice of Third World inverse proportionality of population growth to economic growth, which is what real statistics... if they were available... would have shown was going to happen if Trump had not reversed most of Obama's economically destructive rules and restrictions.

Therefore, had Hillary been elected and continued Obama's deliberate destruction as his and her guide post to a socialist America, Saul Alinsky's *"Rules for Radicals"* specified: Hello, Third World America!

This would have been entirely attributable to a pro-Third World, multifarious, *"diversity,"* New World Order One World Government orientation by the effete *"elites'* in control of the U.S. Government that will cause it to become larger and ever more intrusive, Third World style, reducing economic growth in the U.S. while wasting

U.S. prestige, and taxpayer dollars, on failed programs to enhance Third World economies unless President Trump is successful in *"draining the swamp"* and staying in office for two terms. If not, we will be back to the salutation at the end of the last paragraph above.

The Government will intervene more and more in the business and lives of Americans, becoming more oppressive, and squeezing more and more out of the tax paying, productive sector of the population to support Third World populations.

As Murray N. Rothbard demonstrated in *America's Great Depression*, the root cause of economic collapse has historically been government intervention. The great depression and the stock market collapse were not a result of capitalism, but of government attempts of Soviet-like central "planning" and intervention, as is continuing by the Federal Reserve in 2018 even though it has proven a failure since its beginning in 1913.

Rest assured nothing was learned from experience that could cause those in government to change their *modus operandi,* as proven by Clinton, Bush II and Obama.

***

Having planned the invasion of Iraq and destruction of its government, as stated in writing over the signatures of Jeb Bush, Dick Cheney, William Kristol and other Bush Neocons in <u>The Project for the New American Century</u> in August 2000, to either take over its oil or deliberately destabilize the Middle East on behalf of the U.S. military/industrial complex in its need for perpetual war, before walking into the Oval Office, Bush II needed a quick fix to the then declining U.S. economy.

He needed to appease the American electorate, so they would not raise too much hell over another unnecessary war, as happened with that "complex" fiasco, Vietnam, thirty-six years before.

To endeavor to enhance U.S. industrial production, historically the primary engine of U.S. growth because investment in plant and equipment creates economy enhancing jobs, was not an option. For the economy already in decline since implementation of Clinton's NAFTA less than ten years before that would have taken too much valuable time... possibly years. So that was a no go. Then, how to get a quick fix?

In home building, also one of America's biggest industries, when people have jobs and thus, the ability to purchase homes construction can begin within days, not years.

Problem was; given the slowing economy there were insufficient numbers of people able to purchase homes, or get them financed, to cause a quick recovery via new home building. Thus, another dilemma: how to get home building up and running quickly?

No problemo! All the Bush II regime had to do to satisfy its salivating, warmongering *"Conservative Establishment"* membership that had been promoting the unnecessary war against Iraq for years was quickly create millions of people who could "afford" to buy homes, or inversely make the buying "affordable" for them. Then promote this in a way sufficiently attractive to the target market segment to cause them to buy it.

How about literally free money and new homes at practically no cost to as many people as possible who had no discernable means to pay for them? That should do it... and it did. But it also did much more than that. As sure as hell, everyone in the Bush regime...being the geniuses they obviously were... must have been able to foresee what this might cause, at least to some extent, if not fully.

***

Government intervention and policy can be, and has been, disastrous for American interests on a micro as well as a macro basis. U.S. Government policies and actions have been solely responsible for wiping out, or having substantial negative impact, on companies, and even entire segments of American industry, and on the American people, even the entire world.

It was the Bush II Administration warmongering appetite and solution to make it palatable to the American electorate that created one of the greatest economic disasters the world has ever experienced... even greater than his $7 trillion and still counting in 2018, Iraq disaster.

Given housing had always been a stable U.S. industry and the mortgages working Americans used to purchase their homes were previously provided only to buyers who were economically qualified as financially capable of servicing the debt they undertook for their home purchases these mortgages were always considered one of the most solid and safest investments possible... until Bush II and Iraq.

To get economy enhancing housing construction going ASAP they not only removed the usual financial qualifying of buyers and appraisals of properties to ensure the proper match of these two very important and normal economic prerequisites, but they, extremely irresponsibly, even did more to expedite the buying, financing and building. They gave cash up front to those they knew could not afford the mortgages they were being given and added this to the amount they owed.

There is no question this Bush Administration knew exactly what it was doing, as well as the economic damage it could do to the U.S. economy and the lives of so many Americans that would be adversely affected by its actions.

The only part of this "*the Establishment*" effete political whores who should never have been in charge of our country, or even employed in its Government, could possibly not have foreseen was the disastrous world-wide economic disaster it would create.

That is attributable solely to the greedy criminal element on Wall Street who multiplied the effect multiple times through their extremely profitable business of creating "derivatives" they knew were worthless, but peddled as AAA with the assistance of the crooked rating agencies the uninitiated were not aware would lie and misrepresent for money, thereby creating a world full of crap paper products they had to know were worthless, as well as what eventually happens to holders of worthless paper: they lose!

But the treasonous Bush war criminals... which committing the treasonous act of lying to start a war and even murdering Iraqi citizens before commencing it qualifies them as... who could not permit their "*Establishment*" co-conspirators suffering, had to get back in this game to save them.

Thus, was created so much new money to bail out the criminals on Wall Street the U.S. economy and primarily American citizens were still suffering mightily even eight years after they left office, which was further exacerbated by "*brother*" Obama in continuing and expanding the Bush warmongering and expanding his Socialist programs in so many ways it would take another book to elaborate them. So, moving on......

***

The Food and Drug Administration with the complicity of ostensibly "*Democrat*" Congresses is a disaster for the American people. Over a half century before 2018 Congress added a proof of efficacy requirement for drugs. At the same time, the time restraints on the FDA for the approval process were removed. The result: prior to 1962, the average number of new medicines introduced annually was forty-one. Since then, the number has been sixteen, and drugs already in use in Europe are not approved for use.

Also, prior to 1962, the average approval time for new medicines was seven months. In 2002, it was eight years. Don't know how long it is since, except probably more important is the fact Americans have been deprived by this agency, through its approval process, of drugs already in use in Europe for some time. Yet, Washington politicians of both parties continue to lie to Americans about the quality of U.S. healthcare versus that in Europe... again proving where their loyalties lie.

Worse yet, Americans are being deprived of healthcare by Government policies. Because the FDA process costs eight hundred million dollars per drug, many drugs that could help Americans are not even put into the approval process, and smaller companies that might otherwise contribute to the healthcare of Americans have been deliberately priced out of the market, leaving only larger, more slowly moving, less innovative companies in the game.

In past years, FDA policies resulted in a national shortage of eight critical medicines, including those to combat chicken pox, diphtheria and tetanus. According to the *WALL STREET JOURNAL*, the number of vaccine manufactures declined from thirty-seven to only fifteen by 2003 as a direct result of Government intervention and policies, and only one maker of some vaccines remains.

Thus, a larger Government agency, spending more taxpayer dollars, resulted in an increase in the cost of healthcare, while quality and service declined. This is a replication of the Department of Education. The reason for all this decline for more money is, per Mr. Sowell; *"decisions in the hands of people who pay no price for being wrong."*

These are but two examples of many somewhat hidden from the taxpaying public wherein Government inefficiency is even more detrimental to the American public than in the examples of which most everyone is aware: the U.S. Postal Service that has increased the basic price of postage about fifteen times in fifty years operates more like the Third World than Switzerland or the Netherlands, and Amtrak, which is always requesting additional funding is even way behind most of the Third World.

Also, few, if any, of the thousands of cargo containers stacked up in American ports containing goods for American consumers or sitting empty because their goods have been unloaded and there aren't any American exports to fill them, are imprinted with names of American companies. Nor were they transported to the U.S. on ships owned by American companies or built in America.

The reason for this: again, U.S. Government anti-American policies, especially trade wherein, since Brzezinski/Rockefeller, it has been entirely one sided. Products from other countries come into the U.S. duty free, but U.S. products have stiff duties imposed on them by these same *"allies."*

In absolute contradiction to *"free market"* capitalistic, competitive pricing, and business, labor negotiation practices, the supposedly *"Democrat"* U.S. Congress imposed policies for years that eventually destroyed the U.S. flag carrier fleets and the commercial ship building industry in the U.S. that took with them tens of thousands of American jobs.

They forced unionized wages on U.S. carriers and set rates U.S. carriers were required to charge for products being off loaded at U.S. ports, but competing foreign carriers could not be bound by these wages or rates. They also imposed upon U.S. companies the rule of U.S. law prevailing over that of the host country in which a company was doing business.

The problem with this that could be ascertained by anyone smart enough not to be a U.S. Government job seeker of refuge from capitalism is U.S. law does not apply to non-U.S. companies, or ships carrying other nation's flags competing in the same markets.

The result: U.S. carriers were forced to pay higher, congressionally imposed wages, and charge higher rates, but their competition was operating on a free market basis, able to determine their own expenses and revenues based on competition with other flag carriers. This made the competition more profitable. But wait. It was even worse.

The rates set by the Government were higher than companies needed to earn a fair profit. So, the companies were willing to rebate money from their freight charges to their customers. Since these rebates were legal in other countries from whence shipments originated, the foreign companies were even able to be more competitive by rebating money, causing the cost of freight to shippers to be less than that set by the U.S., but the U.S. companies could not do this without breaking U.S. law imposed upon them. And the U.S. Government pursued those companies that did not abide by this.

The result of these U.S. Government policies: billions of dollars of goods shipped to the U.S. every year are shipped on vessels owned by Russian, Japanese, German, Philippine or other nationalities, that were built in Japan, South Korea, Scandinavia, Germany or other countries, but not in the U.S., and tens of thousands of American jobs were not lost to competitive disadvantage, but were taken away by the U.S. Government through non-competitive policies forcibly imposed only upon American companies.

Given it is just not possible those "brilliant" people in the U.S. Congress were not aware of what they were doing, especially since the U.S. flag carriers lobbied for years for a change of these policies, every American should be asking those "*Establishment Democrats*" again why they deliberately destroyed two U.S. industries and the jobs of tens of thousands of Americans. What other interest were they serving? Brzezinski's?

Was there a U.S. business or banking interest they gave preference over interests of working Americans, such as David Rockefeller's Chase Manhattan Bank's bad Panama loans Jimmy Carter possibly saved by giving the canal to Panama to collateralize the loans with asset backing? Americans should want to know.

But if not for the Brzezinski/Rockefeller official *"Establishment"* organization so many members of Congress are members of none of this destruction of American industries would have occurred.

Does any intelligent reader now really think whether majority or not, either veneer party could have accomplished this economic destruction of America without the complicity of the other, and the media? Hopefully not!

Surely by now readers are fully cognizant that for over forty years when all of this non-American working taxpayer legislation was rolling out of Congress without a fight or ever being reported by the media, as the Government was growing there was a lobbying establishment also growing and throwing millions of dollars a year at Congress to BUY legislation that favored certain industries, especially the financial establishment that benefits as a result of corporate and industry profits whether American or elsewhere, AND wages, costs and taxes are much lower in most other countries than in America even though prices in the U.S. do not frequently reflect that, autos for one big example.

All these years it has been the financial industry banker, David Rockefeller's *"International/Globalist Establishment"* agenda, but with many... let's be kind just this one time... "members" for which Brzezinski was the non-public, inside Government operative who worked through Carter, Clinton, the Bushes, Obama and others to wreak all this destruction in pursuit of his and the other conspirators objective to achieve their anti-American goals of a Utopian, unrealistic homogenized world with *"income equality"* for all, regardless of productivity or contribution, <u>under one government, much like the European Union that is part of this larger plan.</u>

In fact, Brzezinski was a highly respected member, and attended annual meetings of the also non-publicized international European organization cabal with the same goals as his, also at the expense of American jobs and the country's economy. One might also call this treason because of the <u>intentional damage</u> done to America in favoring others.

So-called *"elites"* like Kissinger, the Clintons and so many more America destroying members of *"the Establishment"* are also members of this organization. Hillary has been a frequent annual attendee of these meetings for years.

<u>Bottom line; none of this is *"Conspiracy Theory."* When so many highly placed Government employees and other connected people are conspiring to do what they have been doing to America it is an actual international anti-American conspiracy.</u>

So, let's dispense with *"it's the Democrats, Leftists"* or whatever.

It is, as stated in this book; *"the Establishment"* of Government employees like those in the FBI, big corporate management, elected officials, educators, and media.

***

And thanks again to "*the Establishment*" U.S Congress there are only two major civil aviation aircraft manufacturers providing aircraft to the world's airlines remaining in the entire world; Boeing in America and European Airbus Industries, a company founded and owned by five European countries.

Before Airbus there were three American companies dominating the worldwide industry. What happened?

Answer: the U.S. Congress. That's what "happened." Its members used their same, insipid, pesky rule U.S. law, rather than host country law, governs the conduct of American companies, thereby rendering the U.S. companies non-competitive in the world market place.

They accomplished this by placing some U.S. aircraft-manufacturing executives in prison for paying agent's fees to people who provided access and influence to government decision makers regarding the purchase of aircraft in some countries.

That these agents and their fees were legal, standard operating procedure necessary to the consummation of sales contracts in many countries was seemingly not a concern to the dolts in the U.S. Congress, or they were otherwise influenced.

This was not legal under U.S. law, but this is interesting given there are thousands of lobbyists in Washington D.C. doing exactly the same thing the agents were doing in the other countries: giving money to representatives in Congress for access and contacts.

And Americans wonder why some other people strongly dislike the American Government and by extension Americans. Leaving aside for the minute the U.S. is the only country in the world that has been starting illegal, unnecessary wars, and bombing and killing innocent men, women and children while supporting with U.S. taxpayer's money some of the most brutal dictators in the world even when their citizens desire they be removed for half a century. How about hypocrisy?

Thus, it was this international war criminal "*Establishment*" controlled U.S. Congress was responsible for loss of additional thousands of American aircraft manufacturing jobs AND paving the way for Airbus Industries competition to Boeing, resulting in the American company having to compete with the governments of some of the companies to which it endeavors to sell aircraft.

Since it has previously been established it is just not possible for them to be so dumb as to not know what they were doing, Americans should, also in this case, be asking "*the Establishment*" political whores what masters they are serving at the expense of the taxpayers who pay their salaries... even though they should now know it is Brzezinski's *NWO* plan.

As is not unusual with the many incompetent parasitic seekers of refuge from capitalism populating the U.S. Government wasting billions of dollars of America's wealth every year, when they make a mess through their incompetence, or because they are serving some interest other than American taxpayers, they use even more taxpayer dollars to attempt to fix their creations.

In this case, to attempt to restore some of the competitive edge of which they relieved Boeing, they provided three and one-half billion dollars of taxpayers' money to Boeing in 2001, and many, many more billions since, even though Boeing has shipped a lot of its manufacturing to China further adversely affecting U.S. jobs.

This money is in the form of "loans" through the Government agency known as the Export Import Bank. It is provided to permit Boeing to produce aircraft for foreign governments and companies by financing the aircraft shipped to the foreign customers who then owe American taxpayers, through Boeing. But it is doubtful the foreign customers are the European countries that own Airbus.

Most likely, these customers are less creditworthy, even Third World countries, some with U.S. *"Establishment"* backed dictators. Anyway, American taxpayers are left holding paper showing multiple foreign interests owe Americans billions of dollars simply because of either the stupidity or corruption of their elected representatives.

The jobs for Americans would probably still have been there without the "loans" if not for prior actions of the U.S. Congress.

So, while discussing the subject of airplane manufacturing we should note most who fly have probably noticed many U.S. airlines are using Airbus planes rather than equipment from Boeing. This could be because they prefer the Airbus product, or the price was better, or Airbus and its governments provided better loan packages than Boeing and the U.S. Government. Whichever the case, this is just another example wherein the U.S. Government has not been helpful to American interests when and where it should have been.

***

Around 1981 the Government established a tax credit, a direct offset of taxes owed of ten percent of the value of new equipment purchased and put into service by U.S. entities. It was intended to encourage economic expansion to provide jobs and enhance the economy. This was a good idea except for one little flaw.

The credit was not limited to equipment produced in the U.S. It applied to all equipment purchased and put into service. As a result, the tax credit was helpful to taxpayers who employed it to reduce their taxes. But it was not helpful to the economy, and it was not accretive to Government income because it reduced tax revenues.

If the credit had been intelligently structured to apply only to American produced equipment it would have provided the economic impetus desired and, in cases such as this one, would have given American manufacturers a ten percent price advantage over foreign products. That would have been helpful.

In four years between 1998 and 2002, eighteen U.S. steel companies filed for bankruptcy, twenty thousand steel workers lost their jobs, Pittsburg and the U.S. economy were further adversely affected, and Bush II did something he had to do many times. He took action that was diametrically opposed to his previous polices.

Contrary to his oft-stated *"Establishment free trade nonsense"* he sought tariff protection for the U.S. steel industry just as President Trump did in 2018. But does anyone remember Bush receiving all the negative media coverage Trump received? No?

Well that would be because Bush II, like his father, Clinton and Obama, was a construct of and *bona fide* member of the Trump hating *"Establishment,"* of which we should not forget his father was a charter member.

But this time we can and should blame the *"Democrats."* Why?

Because before Brzezinski even made it to the U.S., in the decades following World War II, while the Japanese and others were installing new, electric blast furnaces in their steel industries, the U.S. industry continued to rely on turn of the century, outdated technology. But U.S. steel industry executives did not willfully do this because they wanted to fall behind and become non-competitive with the rest of the world.

They were forced into this position by the *"Democrat"* controlled U.S. Congress of the time which, despite years of assiduous lobbying by the industry, refused to permit the industry sufficient amortization and depreciation to provide the cash flow required for U.S. makers to upgrade their furnaces to become competitive.

Even then, as in 2018 and for years before, just like Pelosi and Schumer, these people, also like the contemporary *"Establishment"* were anti-capitalist socialists only interested in dividing up the U.S. economic "pie" and parceling it out to their dependent constituency they have since 1980 been assiduously endeavoring to enlarge through illegal immigration.

The result of this Government policy was the decimation of the U.S. steel industry. But job losses between 1998 and 2002 and bankruptcies were almost meaningless compared to prior plant closures and job losses over thirty years prior to that time.

A quick trip to Pittsburgh and the surrounding area would provide, even in 2018, a good idea of the negative financial impact upon a small segment of the U.S. economy by U.S. Government anti-business tax greed policies that have not abated since, but have just changed to moving this, like the auto industry, off shore to shore up *"the Establishment"* member's finances at the expense of those of average Americans and their economy. But what cannot be seen is the impact upon the total macro U.S. economy.

In the mid1960s when the Government was gearing up for another massive *"Establishment"* failure, the Vietnam War, it had a *"Buy America"* policy for Government financed projects. But even then, the U.S. steel industry was so decimated the Government had to forego this policy because the U.S. steel industry could not satisfy the Government's needs for its Vietnam quagmire.

As a result, much of the steel used in the Vietnam buildup was made in Japan where the U.S. was instrumental in rebuilding its steel industry post WWII as it has been in other industries in other countries since. Thus, the potential positive financial impact of the war buildup on segments of the American economy was lessened.

This is ironic since indications then, and historically viewed, were enhancement of the slipping U.S. economy at that time, its worst since WWII, was the major reason for this illegal war.

Also, given all these historical, empirical facts should we not ask in 2018 whether the Rockefeller/Brzezinski *"Establishment"* in control of Congress and its media for at least forty years are not anti-American in attacking Trump's steel tariff actions for his stated purpose of ensuring the U.S. remains a viable sovereign nation?

This is only possible if we are self-sufficient in critical basic industries like steel.

It's impossible they are not cognizant of these facts, yet so determined to maintain control even to the detriment of their own power base. Are they simply so shortsighted and stupid they ~~think~~ believe America and they will survive if they and all their indoctrinated little nit wit *"Millennials"* have their way, and turn America into the socialist, actually communist, non-sovereign, open border Utopian *New World Order*, One World Government haven for denizens of every failing Third World country on earth desiring refuge and free everything they desire?

Well, whichever it is, here is a fact of real life that if they are not aware of will soon become sorely cognizant of if they get their way:

"The economy that does not produce the things it uses and consumes will not survive."

                             - Harvard Business School Professor, 1970

***

Their 1986 tax law changes they forced on the only other non-*"Establishment"* President since they gained control of the Government, President Reagan, proved they had not learned much, if anything, from history.

With this action they "tanked" the U.S. real estate industry and the construction and savings and loan industries "serving" it much as their Bush II would almost twenty years later.

Both times the loss of jobs, foreclosures and savings and loan and other bankruptcies rippled through the entire economy affecting every aspect of it, but not as badly as the Bush II action for his insane, unnecessary war did to the worldwide economy.

Again, *"the Establishment"* action which at least in some part seems to have been fueled by their usual anti-wealth, pro-tax revenues, posture resulting from taxpayer investments in real estate and the tax shelter aspects of these investments amounted to shooting the U.S. economy in its foot via subsequent savings and loan bailouts, covering depositors' losses, and sale of properties at losses by the Government agency created to dispose of the problems cost the taxpayers dearly for several years.

***

The anti-business posture of the mostly pre-formalized *"Establishment"* controlled Government that caused the problems encountered by U.S. shipping, shipbuilding, steel, aircraft manufacturing and other industries during the decades after World War II also caused the U.S. to look like anti-capitalistic, socialists on a global scale.

The USSR communists were global capitalists on a relative basis, as their contemporary Russian heirs continued before Trump.

It can be argued the *"New World Order"* One World Government concept supported by *"the Establishment"* veneer *"Republicans"* and *"Democrats,"* including both Presidents Bush, Presidents Clinton, Carter and Obama, plus the many powerful people behind them, had as its impetus and model the anti-business posture of the *"Democrat"* controlled Government that for decades hamstrung Americans endeavoring to conduct business on an actual *"free market"* basis.

While other governments, including even the Russians, were actively pursuing global business opportunities for themselves and their companies, American companies had to fight the U.S. Government to compete.

The events of 1973 spurred big business, old, East Coast *"establishment,"* money into action. These events were: the Nixon Administration quit the gold standard. Tariffs were proposed against imports into the U.S. because the country faced its first trade deficit in over eighty years. And legislators suggested legislation to lift import tax exemptions for U.S. global businesses because it was perceived their trade practices were already costing American jobs.

But these U.S. Government actions were too unilateralist for the *"Establishment"* old, Northeast one-percent money. So, their *"New World Order"* One World Government pro-multilateral, Rockefeller/Brzezinski takeover of the U.S. Government was organized in the interest of large global businesses, and their plans were begun to be implemented in earnest. The misnamed *"free trade"* programs, legislation such as NAFTA, and that five of the last seven U.S. Presidents represented their interests are evidence of their success.

However, the cover story in past years of Americans benefiting from associated *"free trade"* had begun to unravel under Obama as more and more highly paying jobs were shipped off shore only to be replaced by low paying service jobs, more and more business suffocating regulations were implemented, and the economy began to suffer as a result.

But *"Thank God."* If not for this at this time *"the Establishment's"* next in line ...excuse the non-euphemistic but not intended literally term... whore would have been put in the Oval Office, meaning Hillary Clinton would have been the next President. With that the possibility of a free and independent, capitalist America after eight years of her Presidency would have been nil.

It would have been *fini, kaput,* over because she would have been nothing but a continuation of *"the Establishment's"* Obama failed destructive policies. But she wasn't. Encore *"Thank God!"*

Donald Trump appeared on the scene at just the right time. Although fifty percent of the electorate are unaware of this or refuse to accept it, and the media is working overtime lying and doing whatever it can to save its America destroying *"Establishment"* bosses from extinction, Trump is our savior. If not for him the near-term course for America was into the dustbin of history among all the other failed socialist, impoverished states like the USSR. So again: *"Thank God"* for President Trump.

***

But let's not settle into a state of euphoria over this. Big international corporations and the financial industry have tasted the short-term profit increases and increased capitalization benefits of off shore production for over three decades, and as usual, will not deal with long-term problems until they arise, or are somehow pushed or economically rewarded for taking actions that could enhance Americans or their country.

More importantly, unscrupulous politicians have reaped the power and money benefits of the program and will continue to promote the various *New World Order* One World Government profit enhancing schemes like NAFTA to the detriment of all Americans. But this is nothing new.

Policies and actions of the U.S. Government have caused economic declines for decades. Then, the same people responsible for the policies causing these economic declines are responsible for the actions or lack thereof, responsible for bailing the economy out of the declines.

Some historical examples of resolution of U.S. economic declines are as follows:

- The Great Depression came to an end with the U.S. entry into World War II after Pearl Harbor and the massive military buildup accompanying it.

- The late 1950's recession that followed the playing out of the post-World War II expansion was solved with the Vietnam military buildup and the expansion of NASA.

- The Mid 1970's recession that began with winding down and pullout from Vietnam was stymied by the Reagan Cold War buildup.

- The post-Cold War recession was stymied by the Gulf War and through expansion of communications and technology industries, to some extent, by Government programs.

Many economists, academicians and government theoreticians will argue theories of competitive advantage, monetary policy, interest rates, money supply, etc. as having great influence on the economy.

However, these are like the proverbial gnat's ass when compared to government policies, treaties and blunders such as those mentioned above that have had long term, lasting effect on the steel, healthcare, real estate, aircraft manufacturing and other industries, and weigh heavily on the economy due to the unnecessary costs generated and thousands of jobs involved.

Japan, which lacks natural resources, save those they import, mostly from Australia, has no competitive advantage over the American automobile or steel industries except the policies of the U.S. Government. And it has the disadvantage of lack of proximity to its product's markets.

Also, Japan, Germany, Sweden nor any other country has an actual competitive advantage of any kind over the U.S. in aircraft manufacturing, shipbuilding or shipping other than the policies of the U.S. Government providing them the upper hand. In fact, the country with the advantage of being able to control the origin, shipping and importation to the U.S. is the U.S.

Thus, the only competitive advantage involved in these cases is the American business disadvantage created by *"the Establishment"* controlled U.S. Government and its anti-American policies favoring a *New World Order* One World Government.

The only true competitive advantages in the world today, other than select abundant natural resources others may not possess, are brains, cheap labor, educated work forces and proximity to end user markets. The other, created, competitive advantage is government policy. Companies availing themselves of all of these will perform very well at the expense of those in the U.S. if the Government continues to impose policies disadvantageous to America, favoring big global businesses and Third World economies at the expense of average working Americans.

General Motors, like other American companies, has shipped much assembly to Mexico to take advantage of the cheap labor made available to it under NAFTA, and for the advantage of less stringent pollution controls in that country. As a result, GM can have lower production costs. But has anyone noticed a reduction in the price of GM products, or has the difference gone into GM's pockets as increased profits?

The only real advantage American consumers have been recipients of as a result of U.S. Government *"faux free trade"* policies is the flood of products from mainland China.

The low cost of these products coupled with low-cost mass distribution systems and low profit margins of companies, principally Wal-Mart, had an anti-inflationary effect on the U.S. economy.

The principal cause of this is the one and one-half billion population of China whose labor the Chinese Government pretty much throws in for free when they price products for export because of their desire for foreign exchange.

But the potential, long term, deleterious effects of the U.S. providing China that is not really a friend, with so much spending power far outweighs the anti-inflationary benefits being derived. We have been seeing this for at least two decades as China has become wealthier, and militarily and economically more powerful.

They, along with Russia, have become sort of a "parallel universe" to the U.S. and Western Europe that will eventually result in it surpassing the U.S. in influence

Examples presented above should be enough to convince skeptics that <u>government policies and spending have far more influence on the economy than any other factors</u>. But if there is any doubt, consider the reason for the usually greater strength of the economy resulting from the consumer's ability to spend when the Government is spending for military buildups, or other large Government programs. The Government is larger than any other industries or companies and has vastly more economic power.

Although it seems to never be mentioned because it would refute the claim of benefits to America, policies and <u>agreements such as NAFTA that resulted in shipping eight hundred thousand manufacturing jobs out of the U.S. to Mexico during its first decade have had a tremendous detrimental effect on the U.S. economy.</u>

By moving production of so much consumed or used by Americans including tires, shoes, autos, clothes, electronics, plumbing fixtures, sections of Boeing airplanes, steel, toys, bicycles, fabrics, furniture, tools, etc. out of the U.S., <u>jobs and purchasing power of Americans were sacrificed</u> to a slow but certain *"Establishment"* rendered U.S. suicide.

Ten-dollar per hour service industry jobs replacing twenty-five-dollar per hour manufacturing jobs represents a reduction in purchasing power that is not going to be replaced as long as jobs continue to leave the U.S. and Third World immigration provides an overabundance of people willing to work for lower wages.

This will be more and more disastrous to the American somewhat "consumer" driven economy. Period! No question! It represents a Government, self-imposed suicidal, demise of the U.S. economy, and eventually, as a result, the entire country.

Remember: ***the economy that does not produce the "things" it consumes and uses,*** whether computers, shoes, or autos, ***will not survive,*** regardless of what Washington politicians and their paid for economists continue to tell the American public.

Any short term "bounce" resulting from increased military spending will serve only to cover up the longer term endemic problems of Government policies being continued under the veneers of the Republican and Democrat parties of the America destroying Brzezinski engendered Bush, Clinton, Obama *"Establishment."*

These policies are pro-big global business, pro-Third World, *New World Order* policies, enhancing profits of large global companies and supposedly leveling the economic playing field in favor of the Third World at the expense of Americans.

And, if these were not enough, Washington and its "education" industry co-conspirators continue the long-term destruction of the "giant engine of prosperity," the American economy, through destruction of the U.S. education system.

This is being done through endeavors to accommodate, rather than educate, the members of the U.S. population of Third World ethnicities and illegal immigrants by leveling the academic playing field and indoctrinating rather than educating. This is detrimental to all Americans and to the future prosperity of the country.

This misguided Brzezinski *"Establishment"* Government policy at one time resulted in the Irish economy being the fastest growing in Europe because American companies unable to find qualified personnel within the American, LBJ *"Great Society"* had been "pushed" offshore to countries like Ireland that have well educated populations actually able to read and write because their education systems have not been denigrated through government policies and political complicity.

Most American economic problems are, again, the result of these policies and actions on the part of Washington *"Establishment"* politicians uninterested in the best interests of American taxpayers. They have... *"God help us!"*...even ceased teaching children to write in cursive or longhand, teaching only printing, which slows the thought process due to its manual requirements. Don't believe this, test it yourself.

So, we are going to, in a very short time, have a population that will be called only half-illiterate in most of the world because of the half-wits populating *"The Swamp"* that is America destroying Washington, D.C., which is probably revenge on the rest of America because Washington, D.C. was long ago destroyed, intellectually, ethically, morally and even physically by the ***"inner U.S. Government, centralized state"*** President Trump is pursuing removing from control to *"Make* [and keep] *America Great Again!"*.

CHAPTER FOUR
ONE WORLD GOVERNMENT

THE OPPOSITION TO TRUMP AND HIS "*MAKE AMERICA GREAT AGAIN*" PLANS

In 2018 there were two *New World Order* One World Government movements plaguing the Western world, particularly America. One is common knowledge. The other is a secretive, stealthy cabal. Both have the objective of relieving the U.S. of its national sovereignty, and its citizens of their democracy and protection of the U.S. Constitution.

The first is the United Nations, which has the goal of subjecting the entire world to its Socialist rule solely for the benefit of the Third World. The second is the Trilateral Commission cabal of political, financial and big business interests, a large part of which is the very large military/industrial complex, who desire to redefine the world in terms of Brzezinski's "*New International Economic Order*" to enhance their profits and power.

Both are detrimental to the future of taxpaying Americans who are the backbone of America's economy because both desire to diminish America's prosperity. But the latter in favor of a Third World enhancing, leveling of the worldwide economic playing field through redistribution of that prosperity, as represented by Obama, is the real threat.

The purpose of the business and financial elements of this is increased profits through use of the Third World by moving American capital and jobs there to increase the difference between costs and revenues, and hopefully increase the number of consumers for their products, therefore even more profits.

But the interest of the political class, and the broader military/industrial complex that is the real constituency of large numbers of them, and thus of the also "stealthy" Zbigniew Brzezinski, is much more than profits. It is stark power and control over the world, as he described it "*American Global Supremacy*," which it was his opinion "*the Establishment*" of the U.S. Government should exercise over all with little regard for costs or collateral damages.

This element is represented by, as most should be able to determine from their words and actions, especially their anti-Trump vitriol because of his potential diminution of their political control of the U.S. Government and its media, in addition to Obama, the Clintons, the Bushes, McCain, Rockefellers, members of Congress including Dianne Feinstein, others like David Gergen, Henry Kissinger and many, many more.,

That Americans are aware of the United Nations, but not of its nature and agenda, and are not even aware of Brzezinski or his Trilateral Commission is not surprising. Most of the major media in the U.S. support both and are either connected to or owned by corporations whose Officers are members of the Commission, as are vast numbers of those masquerading as representatives of the people, and those who control the components of the vast public and private Indoctrination System.

Also, many top controlled "news" anchors and commentators are actively pro-United Nations, pro-*New World Order*, AND proactive in suppressing any honest "news" about either. They do not report much about the U.N., but have never reported on, or mentioned the existence of the Commission because they either share its member's anti-democracy ideas or are paid so much they would not dare risk their careers or income.

The proof of this is the lack of answers to these questions: *"Why have you [media] never reported anything on something as important as the Commission, and why have you not reported the content of any United Nations conferences like that in Monterrey, Mexico regarding imposition of U.N. taxes on U.S. citizens? Do you not think the U.N., anti-private property position, or its taxing U.S. citizens newsworthy to Americans?"*

In fact, the main media has become so biased in favor of non-American, pro-U.N., pro-Third World, pro-*New World Order*, anti-America agendas the only truly informative, free press, source of news and information is that which can be obtained through subscription that is totally non-reliant on advertising.

The reason for this is the power and influence of the big global business advertisers that support the media. Their officers, executives, management and ownership are either supporters or members of the *New World Order* One World Government schemes because of their typically shortsighted business management vision of short term increased profits, stock option gains and bonuses they believe will result from Third World production and the greater ease of sales, trade and exchange they experience under expanded *faux* *"free trade,"* multilateralism and limited national sovereignty.

What they envisage is an entire world structured like their desired ultimate configuration of the European Union, one currency, no border controls, no trade restrictions and one unelected, non-representative government responsible to only those who enhance the power and wealth of those in control of it.

Two real world factors seem beyond their comprehension: 1.)

European countries have similar cultures and standards of living as North America, but the Third World, like Mexico, is vastly different, culturally and economically, and this *"Diversity"* will be the ultimate disrupter of their "brilliant" *New World Order* plans, as we are seeing in the streets of America in 2018 the failure of their forty-year endeavor to force *"Diversity"* on this country. 2.) Although, they understand the need for a credible external fear threat to cause people to complacently accept their economically and culturally destructive ways they arrogantly pursue this without regard for world realities.

Here is where the wheels really come off their entire scheme. They, following Polish bred Brzezinski's inbred hatred of Russia advice since the 1960s, continue to use *"Russia, Russia, Russia"* to satisfy that external threat need without consideration of the real-world situation of which Brzezinski also obliquely informed them.

Russia is not actually a threat to the U.S. The Brzezinski created *"Establishment"* in the U.S. Government is the threat to Russia because of its widely known, at the top levels of governments worldwide, U.S. military and economic pursuit of Brzezinski's *"**American Global Supremacy**,"* or actual world domination via control of its desired *New World Order* One World Government, as has been clearly stated in many places should those who are indoctrinated yet curious desire to ameliorate their ignorance.

Russia, as Brzezinski has clearly shown in his writings has zero need or desire to attack or take over the U.S. because of its *"catbird seat"* on the Eurasia chessboard wherein seventy-five percent of the world's population reside in possession of most of the world's physical wealth, including seventy-five percent of its known energy resources and produce thirty-four trillion dollars, or seventy-five percent of world Gross National Product, versus only eight trillion or twenty-five percent for North America.

Given these facts why would anyone think Putin or eighty percent of Russians who favorably rate him and have seventy-five percent of the world's wealth and population at their doorstep, or anyone else, desire to go a third of the way around the top of the world to endeavor to militarily take control of the worst educated, most racially and culturally divided, non-cohesive, least healthy, most Government dependent, spoiled people in the Western world?

They wouldn't if they were not constantly lied to about this and almost everything else by their Government and its controlled media. They would understand President Trump is correct in his view the U.S. Government should, for the benefit of Americans and the rest of the world, be friendly with Russia, rather than targeting it for their next war.

But since U.S. media, the Government, and "education" system, desire to keep knowledge of policies of the UN, and even the existence of the Trilateral Commission, from Americans, it is incumbent upon them to inform themselves about these interests before it is too late to save America's freedom and sovereignty.

***

For over forty-four years U.S. Government national and foreign policies have been guided by Brzezinski and members of his Trilateral Commission because of the highly placed officials, including all U.S. Presidents since Carter, except Reagan and Trump, have been members and that, my friends, is the sole reason for the crooked endeavor to oust President Trump from office.

The U.S. jobs destroying, *"free trade"* treaties such as NAFTA, American culture destroying immigration policies, billions of dollars to Mexico, Africa and others, and the appeasement of Arab regimes are all a result of the Trilateral, *New World Order* and U.N. influences within the U.S. Government endeavoring to oust Trump.

Also, as Ross Perot pointed out in 1992 *"the* [U.S.] *standard of living doubled every generation and a half"* in the 1960s, but the growth rate at the time of his comment indicated it would thence *"take twelve generations for our standard of living to double."*

Perot, an independent adamantly opposed to NAFTA, was at about 25% favorability until he dropped out of the race because, as he said, his family was threatened, which is likely because the other two candidates were *bona fide* members of the Brzezinski Trilateral Commission that has as its main goal a stealth one-party Government wherein the President of the United States is theirs. Whether *"Republican or Democrat,"* they don't care if he or she is "theirs," which Trump is not.

Therefore, all we can do is hope Trump did not sign the Government financing Omnibus Bill that did not include sufficient financing for "the Wall" the Bushes and the rest of their *NWO* gang, including *"Republican"* leaders in the House and Senate, were opposed to, as well as appointing as National Security Advisor the same week Bush acolyte and war monger John Bolton, who tried to get Clinton to invade Iraq in 1997, six years before Bush II did it, for the same reason Perot dropped out.

But that aside, in the intervening quarter century since Perot, it has become obvious the U.S. standard of living will likely never double... or even rise again for average working Americans because it has been declining for them since Perot's 1992 comment.

This decline in the rate of increase amounts to real decline for the majority of Americans in their standard of living that can be laid directly at the doorstep of those who have imposed their pro-U.N., Socialist, *New World Order,* globalist policies on America.

It is these policies that have resulted in; the shipment of production, AND JOBS, out of the United States in the interest of corporate profits, the cultural and prosperity denigrating immigration and welfare that have caused social unrest, friction, the massive increase in crime and the associated, annual, multi-billion-dollar costs thereof.

Also, their thinly veiled, *socialist,* pro-governmental control of land, especially by Obama, and the means of production of natural resources, under the pretense of environmental protection, have been inflationary, particularly to the cost of housing, and, thus, contributory to decline in the standard of living.

Under Clinton, Bush II and Obama these aspects of Government exerting a negative influence on the standard of living got worse at an accelerated rate. There were rapid increases in the size of Government and its spending, overreaching Government controls, crime, and even activist environmentalism within the veneer *"Republican"* Party under Bush, just as under the two Democrats.

In fact, given the extent of Bush II increases in size and spending of Government, not known at the time of Perot's prediction, there is not anything evident within the halls of the Government, corporate America, or academia that could provide any indication of a change of direction, until President Trump took Office.

But new crops of *New World Order* globalists are still being produced every year by effete *"elite"* American institutions of higher "learning" like Harvard University where in 2016 its President echoed President Obama's ridiculous statement, *"Global Warming"* is the greatest threat America faces. No! You, Obama, Bush and your *NWO* cronies are!

The increase in size of the *socialist...* actually communist... indoctrinated population of those from which future government and corporate... as H.G. Wells said in his <u>Outline of History, Volume II</u>...*"voluptuaries and incapables"* will be selected, does not bode well for the future of a democratic, or prosperous America.

According to the 1993 publication <u>Members of the Club</u> many universities, even then, had professors or Officers who were members of the Trilateral cabal of American destruction. Ivy League Harvard even held as many as four (five percent) of the total of eighty membership seats available to the entire U.S.

Any wonder <u>Harvard has degenerated from its pre-eminent academic position to the socialist production mill that has made it the pre-eminent center of the destruction of the America that was a beacon of freedom for the world?</u>

If there is any wonderment about this all anyone has to do is consider the position of its President concurring with Barrack Obama on global warming, or look at wild-eyed, radical, *leftist* Professor Elizabeth Warren who rages against everything conservative and common sense, or see the amazingly anti-conservative, anti-Republican, pro-Democrat writing of a Professor at... *God help us*! the Harvard Graduate School of Business.

The new globalist, Harvard indoctrinated socialists will, just like those in power the quarter century before 2018, continue to promote their America destroying *"New World Order"* the First President Bush proudly trumpeted thirty years prior to 2018.

Why? Because they will be the *"voluptuaries and incapables"* selected to benefit *a' la* the Clintons and Bushes, while America suffers. This is the way of totalitarian, socialist societies, as evidenced by the model for the United Nations, the Soviet Union.

But these people are terribly myopic.

***

There were about seven and one-half billion people in the world in 2016. Of these, one billion, or thirteen percent were within the Trilateralist defined First World encompassing only North America, Western Europe and Japan... the three legs of the Trilateral "stool" that is the world they think they control.

Of the other six and one-half billion, about one and one-half billion could be found in the People's Republic of China, and over one billion in Islamic countries. Thus, the combined Chinese and Islamic countries represented about thirty-three percent of world population, leaving almost four billion, or fifty-three percent as members of the relatively non-productive, poverty stricken, non-Islamic, Third World.

The twenty percent Chinese Communist and thirteen percent Islamic, or total thirty-three percent populations are at some odds with the thirteen percent of the above defined First World in obviously different ways. This has been adequately demonstrated by radical elements of Islam through terrorism.

The political and economic power aspirations and gains of the Chinese have been sufficiently well demonstrated in Asia and elsewhere to anyone watching. Additionally, the Chinese have reportedly been providing weapons and technology to Islamic countries that are providers of natural resources China needs, and others on the West's enemies list.

Should this make the Chinese an enemy of the West?

When the Soviets were doing the same, they were the designated enemy of the West. Seems the Chinese have displaced them, at least to some extent, in this regard. But there is reluctance of the U.S.

"*Establishment*" to consider doing anything about this because China plays such a significant role in the creation of their wealth.

So although "*the Establishment,*" for their benefit in keeping the wool pulled over the eyes of the U.S. voting Proletariat, verbally attacks China for its misdeeds in having so much production and jobs moved to its shores by American corporations and for "*currency manipulation*" with the cooperation of the U.S. that it and most other countries also engage in, there is no way in hell these America destroying bastards are going to upset their financial applecart with any significant adverse actions toward China.

Thus, this will likely be a long lasting symbiotic relationship until the Chinese who are holding the best cards in this relationship decide differently. But Russia is "*a whole nother story.*"

It does not play a part in the wealth creation of "*the Establishment*" except in one other indirect way: it is a credible enemy when it is defined as such by the U.S. media under direction of our *NWO* Government.

In 2016 with the U.S. economy sliding, sliding away via fewer jobs and declining S&P 500 companies reporting lower and lower earnings for several quarters, thanks to the anti-American taxpayer Obama Administration, the U.S. was in dire need of an economic boost that could be provided over a relatively long term financial horizon via the return of capital, production and jobs to the U.S., as candidate Donald Trump proposed.

But there was not a quick fix as employed by Bush II in quickly cranking up residential construction. That bridge was burned.

In a tough situation like this in the past there was only one solution. Roosevelt, Truman, Johnson and lastly Bush II did it. But 2016 being an election year this was not an option.

If Trump was elected and did what he said he would Russia nor anyone else credible would be a concern, and the U.S. could be put back on a proper, successful economic track of reducing Government and rebuilding the economy without distractions.

But if Hillary Clinton was elected, it would also be "*a whole nother story*" because she already indicated the War on Terror was not a sufficient threat for her to even name, and warring against a concept was proven by Bush II to be a losing proposition with no real economic benefits, anyway.

Therefore, Russia was the only credible game for "*the Establishment*" warmongers in need of a credible enemy to keep the U.S. military/industrial complex ginning along, providing some jobs and economic growth. Therefore, a new, hopefully, Cold War could ostensibly require sufficient investment and jobs creation to have a short term positive effect on the economy. But this was dicey.

Hillary being another long term *bona fide* member of the proven America destroying Brzezinski organization, and her stated policies a definitive promise America would continue its downward spiral, it was certain she and others of her ilk in the West would not forego Russia as the actively defined threat to be dealt with.

This was true due to its resource wealth and guidance from anti-Russia Brzezinski that they could not realize their desired *New World Order* world domination unless mother Russia was removed from the position in world power it holds.

So, although unknown to most uninformed members of the U.S. electorate, the outcome of the 2016 Presidential election could have had consequences that had they known could have changed the way many of them voted... destroying the "*ignorance is bliss*" theory.

But the election of Trump did not seriously deter "*the Establishment*" still in *de facto* control of much of the U.S. Government and its *New World Order* One World Government accomplice Trilateralists in Europe.

They elected to continue pursuing policies weakening America and increasing the numbers of potential enemies with two hundred and sixty percent greater numbers, greater rates of population growth, and economic and political influence, particularly in the growing Eurasian part of the world, and who possess nuclear power. They decided to continue to define Russia as the great threat it is not for obvious reasons.

And, they elected to do this solely for profits and political power, as well as continuing to bring as many of the fifty-three percent of the populations of the Third World to the U.S. as possible for the same purpose.

Therefore, does not the egocentric stupidity of these "leaders" of thirteen percent of world population to unilaterally deplete their own means of production, and weaken their own prosperity, in pursuit of increased power in the face of potentially growing enemies over two and one-half times their size, that control eighty percent of the world's known fossil fuel reserves, upon which their productivity and prosperity are, at least somewhat, dependent for the foreseeable future, shine with brilliance?

Throw in the fact the fifty-three percent they pay lip service to endeavoring to "help" largely hate the West, are mostly anti-American, and collectively, plus the Chinese, represent seventy-five percent of world population, possessing a significant percentage of essential natural resources and means of production, including whole sections of Boeing aircraft, and tools and equipment, including military equipment.

Then the true "brilliance" of the effete "*elite*" brains continuing to pursue their pro-Third World *New World Order* One World Government at the expense of the West, and the policies of the U.S. Government really shine.

The United Nations

The United Nations is the Soviet Union *redux* on a worldwide basis!

It is not democratic. Its policy devising bureaucrats are not elected by any people. Its bureaucracy is inbred, and its "leaders" are appointed from within. They are not accountable to anyone outside of the organization. It functions just as the Soviet Communist *Politburo* functioned prior to the breakup of the Union of Soviet Socialist Republics. It functions solely for the perpetuation, increase in power, and benefit of its bureaucracy. It is not unlike the Vatican, a government unto itself by those who have spent their entire "working" lives within the organization.

Just like those in the U.S. Government working for increased power of their bureaucracy, who are using the plight of America's Third World populations, United Nations bureaucrats are preying upon the media induced ignorance of American and European citizens to increase its power and further its programs toward world dominance by pillaging the power and prosperity of the West through use of the plight of the real Third World, primarily Africa and some smaller poverty-stricken areas like Haiti.

Americans need know only the following, anti-democracy policies of the United Nations to demand a U.S. Government withdrawal of American taxpayer support of it:

- Its intent to disarm the entire world, except itself, especially Americans.

- Opposition to private property, and intent to deprive everyone, including Americans, of this basic building block of freedom.

- Its intent to tax all productive citizens of the world, including Americans, through a global income tax, and a tax on international currency transactions.

- U.N. bureaucrats perceive armed citizens a real threat to their plans for world domination. They perceive armed Americans to be their primary stumbling block because of the American desire for freedom of thought, action, and self-determination.

- Their true nature is identical to that of those Americans who hypocritically desire to deprive all other Americans of the means to protect themselves while they possess weapons for their own protection, as does Hillary Clinton.

Like anti-gun ownership activists Rosie O'Donnell, Sara Brady and others who possess guns for their family's protection, the

Secretary General of the United Nations, while behind disarmament of the world, does not buy that program for himself.

Even though unable to obtain U.S. permission to arm his body guards with assault rifles, illegal in the U.S., the U.N. Secretary General ignores U.S. law. He and his bodyguards course the streets of New York City armed with assault weapons illegal for American citizens who provide much of the financial support for his organization.

Any doubt this is being done with a wink from U.S. Government authorities? If not, the U.N. could not get away with breaking this U.S. law that apparently applies only to U.S. citizens, much like laws illegal Mexicans are permitted to violate with impunity.

The United Nations determined at its 1994 conference in Cairo, Egypt the ownership of private property it is not beneficial to, or in the best interest of, all the people of the world, especially those in Africa and other like places wherein democracy is uncommon.

What this means is private ownership of property deprives U.N. bureaucrats of the ability to control the disposition of property for purposes of supporting and enhancing their power at the expense of the rest of the world, primarily the western world.

Given the opportunity, they would use the concept of "land reform" wherein those in power in totalitarian states buy the support of the people by giving to them the assets of production, primarily land they seize from those who provide prosperity.

This was demonstrated in the African country of Zimbabwe where its government seized white owned productive farm land and redistributed it racially among those who were instrumental in helping the government take and remain in power.

It should have been obvious this redistribution would be destructive to the productivity, and prosperity of all Zimbabweans, and the net result in Zimbabwe would be a need for more foreign aid provided by Americans and Europeans, of course.

Because much of it is funneled through U.N. channels, the United Nations bureaucrats use it to strengthen their support among those in the Third World they are using as their power base, again at the expense of Western Capitalists.

Such is the nature of humans in possession of power, or in pursuit of it. Therefore, we must never forget Lord Acton's 1887 warning: *"Power tends to corrupt, and absolute power corrupts absolutely."* To do so is, as proven by history, always suicidal.

The application of this policy of taking private property, if applied within the prosperous nations, as desired by U.N. bureaucrats, could destroy these nations' prosperity, and could result in a diminution of world prosperity similar, on a relative basis, to what happened after the decline of the Roman Empire.

But these thoughts of proven human nature and history are beyond the capability of the minds of the so-called "intellectual" and political ruling class, half-wit effete *"elite"* who have been leading America and the rest of the world down the path to decline and destruction for decades. Here is a good example:

"In this respect those antagonists were precisely like the enemies and friends of world federation in 1948, now when it is obvious that no difficulty in the way of a world government can match the danger of a world without it."
- Carl Van Doren, 1948

This comment by so-called "intellectual" Pulitzer Prize winner Mr. Van Doren is in his Introduction to his book *The Great Rehearsal* which is a comparison of the founding of the United Nations, he refers to as "*world federation,*" to the "*framing and adoption*" of the U.S. Constitution over a century and three quarters before.

Obviously, he is saying a world without a One World Government is a much more dangerous place than a world of sovereign nations, thus overlooking most of the proven facts of history and human nature, including the empirical evidence *"diversity,"* as in differences in language, religion, culture and race, are so divisive it is impossible to bring them collectively, peacefully *"under one roof,"* or government.

He demonstrates a total disregard of the old factual adage *"birds of a feather flock together,"* and demonstrates a total ignorance of the fact of basic homogeneity of culture... same language, race and religion... of the populations of the thirteen states, ignoring the *"now,"* his word, of the real world he obviously had little experience with. Also, as within the U.N., his stated vision was not favorable to wealth or private property.

He was a typical pseudo so-called "intellectual" so admired by others of his ilk, sheltered, at least intellectually, whether self-imposed or otherwise, like so many of the effete *"elite"* in control in the U.S., as were David Rockefeller and Zbigniew Brzezinski.

The same, power-based myopia afflicting these and many more U.S. globalists also afflicts U.N. bureaucrats. They are not concerned about world prosperity, or the future of the world. They demonstrate an inability to "think" that far into the future. Their only concern is their power. This is demonstrated in their anti-capitalistic policies regarding private property and taxation.

***

To provide "independent" financing for their *NWO* One World

Government, the United Nations conference in Monterrey, Mexico in March 2002, attended by President Bush II whose father was a big supporter of the *New World Order* he proudly announced to the world in 1989, was held for the specific purpose of developing plans to tax the productive citizens of the world, especially Americans, Bush and the media, based on their non-disclosure, seemed to demonstrate *de facto* concurrence with.

But is it possible they had not considered their plans to eliminate private property would adversely affect their proposed tax revenues by reducing income potential of those they proposed to tax?

Certainly, the Bushes either were not capable, given their One World and Government dependent proclivities, or never considered this before supporting this democracy and prosperity destroyer.

The United Nations has clearly demonstrated it is without doubt a global, Socialist organization bent on world domination that has as its operating concept the Marxist Communist theory of *"from each according to his ability, to each according to his need."* As such, it is hostile to American liberty, ideas, democracy and sovereignty.

Why then, does the United States Government, after having expended so many dollars and so many American lives for over seventy years, as of 2016, following World War II, ostensibly, in the interest of eliminating the Soviet, Socialist, Marxist threat to Americans, and in preventing World War III, continue to support this U.N. worldwide, Marxist threat with American taxpayer dollars and the U.S. military?

Given it is known Soviet Communism resulted in a Russian per capita Gross National Product of only twenty-seven hundred dollars per year, versus twenty-two thousand in the free, non-Marxist, countries of the West in 2002, why would those in the U.S. Government, or anyone, desire to impose this type of government on Americans and the rest of the Western free world?

Answer: M-O-N-E-Y and P-O-W-E-R for themselves.

Should not President Bush's attendance at the United Nations conference where the taxation of Americans and others in the West was the central topic, and his choosing to keep Americans uninformed about it, be of concern? After all, his central theme presented to the American people as the reason for electing him was reduced taxation, was it not? Yes. Just like his father. But, also like his father; he willfully lied.

Also, why did President Bush decide to support the U.N. position on *"global warming"* after his sojourn with their bureaucracy in Mexico, when it was diametrically opposed to his campaign position?

The answer: Like his father, he ~~was~~ is a liar. But more importantly both of these so-called *"Conservative Republicans"* are no more than closet replications of Carter, the Clintons and Obama in ninety percent of what they did as President and since.

This would be obvious to anyone who takes time to consider what they did to healthcare, insurance, immigration and more. Shy of that effort all anyone must do to know what they really are is be aware of their negative words and actions toward Trump.

But still; why would any President of the United States, who is sworn to protect the Constitutional rights of Americans and enforce the laws of America, even attend the conferences of, let alone support, an anti-American organization that explicitly states it is *"not bound by the laws and the judicial pronouncements of any state,"* meaning it does not recognize the Constitutionally legal protections of American citizens?

Sorry, but as the WWII Sergeant said, ***"First, you got to know you have a problem. Then, you got to know what the problem is before you can solve it."***

So what everyone needs to know is: 1.) we have a really big problem, and 2.) that problem is the Brzezinski one governing political party *a la* communism or Fascism in the form of *"the Establishment"* in control of the U.S. Government for almost four decades, excepting only Reagan and Trump, AND the only way to solve it is to ensure Trump has two terms to save us.

Then ensure that never again do we elect anymore *New World Order* whores like Jeb Bush or any of the others who ran against Trump in 2016 or anyone running as a Democrat because anyone who would do this has to really be an adherent to the communist party doctrine and the destruction of a free, capitalist America.

The only way to save ourselves is to elect only *"bona fide outsider"* business people whose orientation is to treat the U.S. Government like a business... no more inexperienced political hacks like the Bushes, Clintons or Obama who don't know how to do a damned thing except the bidding of the America destroying *"Establishment."*

That would be a reinstatement of the slow national suicide Americans experienced since Jimmy Carter, except for the "spring" of Reagan and the "summer" of Trump.

Surely none of us working, contributing, assets owning, taxpaying, freedom loving capitalistic Americans desire to endure another multi-decade "winter" of decline like that.

***

Given all the foregoing information about the U.N. why does the U.S. Government continue to provide financial and military support for the U.N. bureaucracy power enhancing *"divide and conquer,"* so-called *"independence movement,"* which amounts to the "Balkanization" of the world?

This breaking up countries into smaller, weaker, non-self-sustainable entities incapable of defending themselves against oppressive, U.N. World Government military forces known as *"peace keepers"* as has been the case in the Balkans, East Timor and other places is obviously for enforcing U.N. power on a broader scale. Why support this?

It should be noted the Clinton and Bush II Administrations were very much in favor of this in the Balkans, and Bush even sent Clinton as the U.S. representative to little two hundred and fifty thousand population East Timor for its independence celebration. Why?

However, when much larger Crimea did the same without cooperation of the U.N. or the U.S., the Obama Administration refused to recognize Crimea as an independent state, which is still the position of the U.S. and its European allies. Why?

Americans should desire to know answers to these questions from the U.S. Government and their Presidents. But since they will not be forthcoming and *"the Establishment"* media is sure as hell not going to report any of the facts about these actions selectively supported or not supported by their Government, here are the answers:

The Crimea action was untruthfully reported as an invasion by Russia to make it "fit" *"the Establishment"* anti-Russia continuing commentary to substantiate its credible enemy status in the eyes of the American electorate.

The Balkan outcome was also an anti-Russian move against one of its allies. But East Timor was supported by the U.S. because it is a U.S. enhancing, physically anti-China move due to the location of East Timor on alternative sea lanes used by oil tankers transporting fuel from the Middle East to East Asia in the event of hostilities.

Therefore, the answer to the first two questions is the U.N. provides cover for the U.S. by doing much of what it desires without this ever being disclosed to the public, and *"the Establishment"* shares the U.N. goal of breaking up countries to make them non-self-sustainable if they are a threat their *New World Order* like, say Russia, if it were possible.

It is understandable the United Nations, due to its need for support of four billion souls residing in the non-Islamic, non-Chinese, Third World, would espouse anti-American policies to take from the prosperous West and give to this Third World. It is, hopefully now, also understandable why some Americans and

Europeans in power choose to ostensibly support the U.N. in pursuit of its prosperity dooming policies.

If the U.S. has not been able to solve its own Third World, inner city problems with the massive amounts of dollars spent over sixty years of ostensibly assiduously pursuing a solution, it is a certainty the culturally induced problems of Africa cannot be solved with any amount of money in any amount of time.

It is also a certainty those individuals smart enough to have attained their high U.S. Government and U.N. positions must be aware of this reality, but understand their *"show must go on,"* at least for their benefit.

The only roadblock to the U.N. achieving many of its One World Government goals is U.S. veto power in the U.N. Security Council. But this is a very thin line that could easily be crossed should a U.S. President and his (or her) administration be of a mind to join U.N. bureaucrats, Third World dictators, and European Socialists in pursuit of their collectively desired worldwide totalitarian Utopia.

This should have been a major concern in the 2016 U.S. election.

Therefore, the American electorate must insist those in the U.S. Government pursuing pro-U.N.pro-One World Government, *New World Order* agendas at the expense of the sovereignty and prosperity of America be deprived of their power. The next election would be a good time to begin the removal process.

Trilateralism

"Jimmy Carter is but a puppet president, he is the programmed product of the Trilateral Commission which created him, and we must recognize that Jimmy Carter is little more than Charlie McCarthy to David Rockefeller's Edgar Bergen."
- Utah Independent, 1977

So, it has been with all U.S. Presidents since, with the exceptions of Ronald Reagan and Donald Trump, and that Brzezinski's name should be substituted for that of Rockefeller.

But in 1977 Rockefeller was still active, his money was behind it, and he had too high a public profile not to be mentioned by those in the know.

However, since the organization was always intended to be a secret stealthy conspiracy to be kept well beyond the eyes and knowledge of the American public it was never intended to be known, let alone have a public face. Thus, Brzezinski was not the public face of the organization in 1977, nor since.

But the non-membership, non-puppet status of Reagan and Trump, explains the media treatment of both beginning thirty-eight years ago, as of 2018, with *New World Order* media whore Tom Brokaw's anti-Reagan comments at that time of note.

Carter perceived himself having a position of great power within the *New World Order*, as did charter member Bush I, as he proudly proclaimed it from the beginning of his presidency, which explains one reason Reagan did not desire him as his Vice President... and his almost being assassinated confirmed him correct.

But that Bush was Vice President shows the power of *"the Establishment"* Trilateralists in the Republican Party, AND why the veneer, party label should not fool Americans into thinking... as they do... there are two parties when in reality there is only one big *"Establishment"* assiduously pursuing the demise of their freedom and prosperity for at least four decades as of 2018.

It was hoped by some after the two "Republican" Bush experiences Americans would be fool proofed, but we now know what we thought could not get worse, did: Obama.

***

It does not require much to be a *New World Order* puppet U.S. President except obedience, as has been demonstrated by Carter, Bush the First, Clinton, Bush II, Obama, and in 2016 candidate Hillary Clinton who have all demonstrated this in domestic and foreign policy positions and actions.

However, these Presidents do need to be careful about public pronouncements, like Bush II on *"global warming,"* defining America's enemies, and Middle East policy, or he (or she) may have to publicly *"eat crow."*

But the fact the media did not take Bush II to task on his inconsistencies, *"flip flops"* and demonstrated intellectual deficiencies is indicative of his *New World Order* credentials inherited like so many others also not qualified to be anything but a good little second or third generation, or in his case fourth generation puppet, political hacks.

Bill Clinton was of demonstrably smarter raw material than Carter, the Bushes, or Obama, but even he, who was what could reasonably be called a *"give-a-shit"* in terms of assiduously pursuing the accomplishment of *New World Order* goals (or anything else but the *"ladies"*) compared to these other four relative zealots, could not escape public chastisement from *"the Establishment"* that put him in the White House.

Early in his Presidency when Hillary was illegally pursuing revamping U.S. healthcare to bring it in line with Trilateral *"Establishment"* plans for American healthcare when Bill made the mistake of publicly stating some component of it might be negotiable, this was too much for his Puppeteer "bosses."

Thus, lifelong *"Establishment"* member Senator Jay Rockefeller publicly stated, *"The President better consult with his wife."*

This not only confirmed Hillary had better *"Establishment"* ties than Bill, the member, but possibly he was President because it was perceived by the powers *"behind the throne"* that America was not ready for a female president. Nor was it ready for a bachelor President like Bill would have been. So, a compromise; Bill was *"fixed up"* with a wife who would not care what he did? The next eight years seem to substantiate this.

Also, the fact *"the Establishment"* member Speaker of the House at that time, Tom Foley, stood up in the House lauding Hillary for her healthcare initiative provides confirmation of who was behind her in this, her first attempt to harm Americans on behalf of the America destroying *"Establishment"* by implementing what Obama did almost a generation later after Americans had been substantially dumbed down

Too bad for America more of the electorate in 2016 were not aware of what Hillary truly is. "Too bad" because had more been aware of her real background and plans to complete Obama's unfinished business of removing America's sovereignty, and making it a borderless, totally open, non-sovereign state, she might have been recognized for what she would have been: the final nail in the coffin lid of a free and prosperous America.

Substantiation of the length of time she was working toward this goal, and her Trilateral credentials, was disclosed to the very few who even knew about the Commission and some of its top members early in Bill's Presidency when she publicly stated she had *"known Vernon Jordan longer than I have known my husband."*

Since Vernon Jordan is a long time Trilateral member since its beginning, and probably the most powerful Black American in Washington this is interesting because she reportedly did not meet Bill until she was in Yale law school, which means she knew Jordan even prior to this time. This raises the question of how and when she became an acolyte of communist advocate for everything she desires for America: Saul Alinsky.

This background of Hillary and Jordan, and that her name has been conspicuously missing from Commission membership lists, even though other prominent political females such as Diane Feinstein are included, should be of concern to Americans. As should Bill's experience with Hillary, as reported by White House FBI and Secret Service personnel. These facts provide an indication of, beyond what some men will endure for their careers, just what Americans might have had to endure under a Hillary Presidency.

But we can assume it doubtful America would have fared any better than Bill or her supposedly best friend Vince Foster did.

Also, given Bush II expansions and implementation of *New World Order* programs, and his diminution of citizen's rights through these, the prospect of what further damage a Hillary Presidency might have done to America is damned frightening!

***

Senator Jay Rockefeller felt comfortable taking the President of the United States to task publicly because of his long term *"Establishment"* family credentials. These stem from the fact David Rockefeller, Chairman of Chase Manhattan bank was the principal founder of the Commission in 1973, and the Rockefeller name has been synonymous with money and power in the U.S. since the last quarter of the Nineteenth Century.

Thus, this name should lend more than cachet' to anyone looking for, or doubting, substance in this One World Government organization. The name has billions of dollars and dozens of Rockefellers behind it, including major oil and financial interests and ex-governors of New York and Arkansas. This should explain the Rockefeller involvement, but in case it does not, consider: Politics are about M-O-N-E-Y, nothing else!

In the movie *Vanilla Sky*, the Tom Cruise character said his father told him the answer to *"ninety-nine out of one hundred questions"* is *"money."* Where the Rockefellers are concerned, all one hundred answers are *"money,"* unless the answer to the last question is oil. Thus, the genesis of the *New World Order* destruction of once great America was money, money for the few at the expense of the many.

There was recognition of the potential for expanded profits in the Third World due to the great disparity between those countries' labor costs and costs in the industrialized First World. There was also recognition that business needed to have more power in government if the profit potential was to be fully exploited. The prior experience of American global business interests with the U.S. Government indicated a need for money and business to dictate domestic and foreign policy.

The First World, industrialized world is Japan, North America, and Western Europe thanks to American global industrial expansion post WWII. Their geographic dispersion is east to West, lateral, as opposed to North to South. Thus, the world was divided, laterally, into three longitudinal areas, ergo, "Tri" and "lateral."

The idea was that each of these three industrialized areas would have responsibility for those portions of the world to be "helped" through job creating profit exploitation based upon geographic proximity: Western Europe with Eastern and Southern Europe, and Africa; the U.S. and Canada with Mexico, Central and South America, and, Japan with Southeast Asia.

This concept is not without historical precedence.

In 1494, Spain and Portugal entered into the Treaty of Tordesillas, wherein they divided the entire world into halves. The idea was that each would exploit its half for profit without getting in the way of the other.

Just like the *New World Order* brains of today, Spain and Portugal presumptuously ignored the other countries of the world in their plans. Since, as Mr. Machiavelli recommended, *"One should read history..."* to be able to avoid defeat, it might be profitable for these current *New World Order* geniuses to consider how well their concept turned out five hundred years ago, with special consideration to Russia and China.

In the year of the Spanish/Portuguese treaty, France invaded Italy. Less than ninety years later, in 1580, Spain annexed Portugal. In 1587, the English destroyed the Spanish fleet. Then, over the ensuing centuries, the French and English appear to have been the successful exploiters.

The First World at the beginning of the 21st Century reflects the success of the English and French, while the Third World reflects the influence and values of Spain and Portugal.

It is this Third World, sort of the dregs of Spain and Portugal, the *New World Order* "geniuses" are endeavoring to exploit at the beginning of the 21st century. But while they are re-enacting the Spanish and Portuguese parts of five hundred years ago, the Chinese are exploiting the greater potential of Asia, Russia is gaining more influence around the world, and Islam is attacking the First World of the geniuses who are financing them.

Anyone care to guess how this is going to turn out?

Since it is human nature not to learn from mistakes of the past, or of others, and this is an even more pronounced characteristic among those who consider themselves "brilliant," it is a safe money bet these geniuses are not going to be dissuaded from their chosen path toward the destruction of Western prosperity, *à la* Spain and Portugal, in the pursuit of personal profit, since in the forty-five years prior to 2018 they were not.

Money, global business and profits, are all the Trilateral members are about. But to accomplish their goals requires the political element, and that is where the One World Government, *New World Order* is detrimental to the average American, Japanese, Canadian, and European.

The Trilateralists under Brzezinski guidance best explain the nature of the detriment, in their own words, in published statements.

The Commission has stated, in writing; *"...secrecy and deception...are inescapable attributes of...government,"* and *"crisis"* has been caused by an *"excess of democracy."*

Note the underlined because it states the view of America from the perspective of *"the Establishment"* whose members addressed above, the Bushes, Clintons and Obama have been destroying it under the guidance of co-conspirator Brzezinski their entire careers.

But it gets worse, *"The public and leaders of most countries continue to live in a universe which no longer exists--a world of separate nations--and have...difficulties thinking in... global perspectives...and interdependence...,"* i.e. when Brzezinski and his co-conspirators wrote this many years prior to 2018 they thought they had already won: *"separate nations... no longer exist."*

These statements provide credibility for critics' comments, as published in October 1977 by Paul Scott. These were the Trilateral purpose is: *"to influence or take over all the key policy-making positions in government,"* and *"permanent coordination of the entire free world and eventually the establishment of a loosely knitted socialist world government"* into which the U.S. would be merged, greatly modifying, if not destroying the sovereignty of the country and the Constitutional rights of Americans.

PLEASE read this again and understand that Carter, the Bushes, Clintons, Obama and many others... Democrats and Republicans alike... have been working for over forty years toward this destruction of America, and creation of their *New World Order* One World Government to the detriment of all Americans, ninety-nine percent of whom have never even heard of *"the Establishment"* Trilateral Commission mother organization and cannot define the word "plutocracy" they are victims of.

Thus, they do not know why so many Republicans and *"the Establishment"* controlled media in 2016 were doing everything possible to prevent Trump from becoming President and endeavoring to get proven criminal Hillary... according to the F.B.I. Director's July 5, 2016 statement... into the office of President of the United States.

That their view of an *"excess of democracy"* is detrimental to American's freedom should be evident in the fact all but one of the Presidents of the United States in the forty years prior to 2016, were proponents of this concept. And the father of Bush II, Bush I, was a *bona fide* member of the East Coast Brahmin "Mafia" set who have always shared the *"excess"* view. Also, that Bush II worked for his father's interests when his father was President, and he followed the

New World Order playbook every day he was President should send chills down the spines of all freedom loving Americans.

The ultimate results of the cumulative, Carter, Bush I, Clinton, Bush II, Obama and his successor, if not for non-"*Establishment*" member Trump if, unlike JFK, he stays in office long enough to thwart this, would have been further decline in the prosperity and freedom of Americans, with the *de facto*, if not actual, inclusion of America in a Socialist, *New World Order* One World Government, which Hillary would have ensured.

But we are still not out of the woods on this due to the fickleness and short-term orientation of the American electorate, and the possibility of what they might do in 2018.

However, if a majority of Americans were made aware of what is in the paragraphs above, their country and much of the rest of the world could be spared this fate. But no one with the power or platform to inform about this is doing it, especially not FOX NEWS' Hannity, Carlson or Ingraham. They are AWOL on this.

They waste three prime time hours a night, five days a week going on and on about "*the Left, Democrats, Liberals*" and whatever else they can find to avoid telling their viewers the truth of what is being done to us and who is doing it.

If they would address "*the Establishment*," explaining the plutocracy that constitutes it, what their plans and objectives are, give examples of what they have done and name those responsible, "outing" some of those operating adversely to the best interests of America while masquerading as "*Conservative Republicans*" they would do a lot of good.

For examples: Senators McCain, Flake and other veneer Republicans like Romney, Kasich, the Bushes and even registered Republican Bob Mueller are solidly "*Establishment*" members who should be "outed" as such for the benefit of Americans.

But if they do not begin to do this they are just as big a problem for Americans as CNN because what they are doing is continuing to participate in "*the Establishment Divide and Conquer*" program that has almost already defeated us, and will in the not too distant future if the people are not informed what they have is "***one very big problem and what that problem is***" so they will have some idea of how they "***can solve it.***"

Surely with the two to three decades of experience in the Government and reporting on it each of them claims to have <u>there is absolutely no way they could not be fully aware of what is written herein above and below.</u>

Therefore, their failure to use their platforms to inform the American public about this impending destruction they must know has been developing for forty years is beyond irresponsible. In fact, it is not too big a reach to cast their lack of informing their viewers of what they know in the contemporary terms of what they talk about every night.

What their failure to disclose the facts of *"the Establishment"* organization, who is behind it, what their stated goals and objectives are, and who in the Government have been or are members to their audience amounts to is withholding evidence and thus obstructing the justice their viewers and all Americans deserve.

But they are not the only "FOXs" who are not doing their jobs for the American public. FOX NEWS seems like a retirement home for the Bush II Administration.

We don't know how many of them are there, but on camera frequently are ex Bush Press Secretaries Ari Fleisher and Dana Perino, and Bush Family long termer Karl Rove.

The Bush family connection with the U.S. Government dates to at least WWI, over a hundred years before 2018, and its connection with *"the Establishment"* in one form or another, dates to WWII with G.H.W. Bush in the U.S. military OSS, which morphed into the C.I.A. that was his employer for many years, some disclosed, some not.

He was what is referred to in the Mafia as a *"made man"* for his loyalty and deeds in that organization, and he was a charter member of the Trilateral Commission. Therefore, it is a very safe bet none of these people would have held their positions in the Bush Administration or closeness with the Bush family unless they supported what the Bushes do, which is every anti-American *New World Order* One World Government policy of *"the Establishment"* the official Commission membership of G.H.W. Bush connotes.

But for purpose of specificity consider the following three items:

1.) *"Conservatives are just another special interest group."*

- Karl Rove, Bush Administration, 2002

Rove would not have dismissed *"Conservatives"* in such a condescending way if either he or the Bushes were actually the *"Conservatives"* he did not consider them to be.

2.) *"If you believe that you believe the grassy knoll theory"*

- Ari Fleisher, Bush II Press Secretary in response to a reporter.

This statement in defense of the indefensible Warren Commission conclusion JFK was shot in the back of the head when there was a small hole in his forehead while the back of his head was blown off onto the trunk of his Presidential limousine represents *"the Establishment"* position which many there at the time of the assassination and others in the know for many reasons disagree with.

In fact, for years after there were billboards across the Southern U.S. calling for Justice Warren's impeachment for this travesty.

3.) Perino has a sometime guest on her FOX show from the Weekly Standard who is presented as a *"Conservative,"* which she must know is not the truth because William Kristol, the founder and publisher of that *New World Order* rag sheet, was also one of the signatories along with Dick Cheney and Jeb Bush to their on-line publication in August 2000 calling for a U.S. invasion of Iraq thirteen months before "9/11," as well as a *"Pearl harbor-like event on American soil"*... which is a direct quote from their writing.

AND in 2016 Kristol was so vehemently anti-Trump (along with the entire Bush family) he was the one who actively, publicly tried to find a Republican to run against Trump to prevent his being elected President.

Perino must know all of this, pretty much destroying her credibility as an ostensibly somewhat positive Trump FOX commentator.

Hopefully readers of this will use whatever means available to inform these FOX commentators of what they should be doing or call them out for their lack of honesty if they continue as they do every night: deliberately not informing their viewers of the truths of who is doing what to them and their country.

***

The past G-7, G-8 with the inclusion of Russia, represented a lack of unilateral American economic freedom, as evidenced by Bush II's economic aid announcements of years ago, which the expanded G-20 version only exacerbated in recent years.

This collective, or organization, is just one small part of *"the Establishment"* attack on American sovereignty, and one small step of many over the years gradually relieving us of our freedoms by putting much of our future in the hands of non-American, unelected bureaucrats like we see occasionally on TV in the EU either unable to reach decisions or doing what they do to relieve European nations of their sovereignty.

But the biggest attack on America's ability to trade unhindered for the benefit of Americans is *"the Establishment"* supported World Trade Organization, or WTO, that is yet another One World Government organization of unelected, and secretive bureaucrats empowered to resolve trade disputes between nations. Like the U.N., this is a pro-Third World creation to enhance it at the expense of, or damage to, America.

How is this? You may ask. Well, for example; in trade disputes between the U.S. and China the WTO favors China because this growing behemoth of a country with a population over four times that of the U.S., comparable gross domestic product, GDP, more than triple the annual percentage GDP growth, a military rapidly growing to rival that of the U.S., and where General Motors produces and sells more vehicles each year than it does in the U.S. is considered a Developing Nation, or Third World country.

Therefore, to satisfy the *New World Order* One World Government objective of "leveling the economic playing field" to enhance the Third World at the expense of us in North America and Europe the WTO favors China over the U.S.

Trump's actions in many ways, including those on the Paris Climate Accord and The Trans Pacific Partnership indicate his awareness of this, and his efforts are to protect us from destruction the Bushes, Clintons and Obama deliberately conspired (Thus, really a conspiracy.) with these foreigners to do to blend America into their *New World Order.*

Bush and Obama position that all decisions, even regarding prosecution of the War on Terror should be made on a *"multilateral basis,"* are indicative Bush II made *"one giant step"* on the road to elimination of American political freedom that hopefully Trump can restore, regardless of *"the Establishment"* Republican opposition.

Continuity of Government is key to continued success of the cabal of global business, financial and political *New World Order* interests. Thus, as previously explained, *"the Establishment"* Trilateralists have a policy of determining the Presidential candidate in both veneer Republican and Democrat parties.

To ensure this they maintain a stable of candidates waiting in the wings. Republican examples have been ex-governors James Thompson, Tom Ridge, Mitt Romney, and Ohio's Kasich and Jeb Bush who were, thankfully eliminated in 2016.

Their continuity success was demonstrated by primo, long term *"Establishment"* NWO whore Bush II, as he continued, and even expanded, Clinton policies regarding Israel, immigration, amnesty for illegal aliens, etc. that were all acts against American citizens.

He even continued their *"Divide and Conquer"* program, as evidenced by his irresponsible, further incitement of racial division on the issue of home ownership without consideration of the percentage of home ownership among all working Americans rather than along racial lines.

Given his demonstrated intellect he may never have even considered that, but we cannot cut him that slack because of his other puppet acts previously disclosed.

But speaking of the puppeteers; since they have no confidence in democratically derived decisions, really desire there not be any, *"the Establishment's"* written statement, ***"the effective operation of a*** *democratic political system usually requires some measure of apathy and noninvolvement on the part of some individuals and groups,"* comports well with their indoctrination, rather than education, to produce a population that is *"Placidly Governable."*

Here, again, they have been incredibly successful. The *"apathy"* of American voters, particularly so-called *"Conservatives,"* is proof.

A continuation of their success will have long term, disastrous consequences for the freedom of Americans. They will cause foreign policy to continue to be guided by their incorrect Utopian vision of keeping the business marketplace peaceful through avoidance of confrontation at all costs, thereby weakening America and its allies, such as Israel, as it seemed Obama did deliberately. This is another reason they desire to oust Trump.

They and their media constantly rage against his speaking and acting like any successful businessman would in dealing with competitors who are not conducting business as it would be done in a truly *"free market."*

Their failure to deal with the Machiavellian reality that *"without victory there can be no peace,"* and *"war...can only be postponed to the advantage of others"* will result in strengthening enemies, and potential enemies outside of what they *"control,"* like those in the Middle East and elsewhere in contravention of this prescient Machiavelli warning.

They will continue to deplete America's wealth through generous aid to Third World and other failing economies and through depletion of U.S. means of production by shipping it offshore to enhance the wealth of their few at the expense of most Americans.

They think they are the brilliant few, but as one of their so-called *"brilliant elite,"* Henry Kissinger, said, *"I have a first-rate mind, but weak people talents,"* therein defining the problem they are creating because it is people and their human nature that define the fortunes of humans.

Thus, *"brilliant, first rate"* minds such as Mr. Kissinger's and many of his *New World Order* co-conspirators should be relegated to designing aircraft parts, or the field of technology, because they are devoid of that single ingredient necessary when endeavoring to change the course of human events: COMMON SENSE.

Lacking this, they are incapable of recognizing and including the important element of human nature in their policy formulations, as President Trump is able to do.

They cannot understand, as Machiavelli observed: *"Great things have been accomplished only by those who have been held miserly, and the others have met disaster. Miserliness is one of those vices which sustains. There is nothing so self-defeating as generosity; in the act of practicing it, you lose the ability to do so and you become either poor and despised, or hated."*

Please inform all America destroying, communist *"Establishment"* members endeavoring to increase America's vast, growing, dependent populations to increase their power base of this Machiavellian wisdom. They are demonstrably too unread to determine this on their own. But maybe if conveyed in Texas vernacular they might connect the dots: *"What you are doing is gonna come back and bite you in the ass!"*

This truth is already visible in America. Millions who for three generations have never had to work to feed, educate or shelter themselves are protesting their *"oppression."*

Thus, history and empirical evidence are on the side of Mr. Machiavelli's and Texas' wisdom. But the successes of *"the Establishment"* New World Order effete *"elite"* in terms of their own pocket books will continue to reinforce them... unless President Trump is successful in rendering them impotently incapable of continuing the destruction

If not, their personal successes will prevent them considering the broader picture of the cost of their policies and actions to everyone else. But they don't care. They aren't concerned. They are, in fact, empirical evidence of the element they are incapable of including in their policies, plans and actions: BAD HUMAN NATURE.

They collectively are the contemporary embodiment of this millennia old wise observation:

"To expect bad men not to do wrong is madness." -
- Marcus Aurelius, Meditation

But to avoid being called sexist by Hillary Clinton and her *"feminist"* followers or improperly failing to include her based on her personal "embodiment" of many things **"*bad*"** and **"wrong"** we absolutely must add **"*and women"*** in this quote.

They are accomplishing their personal goals and continuing to pursue their strategy without involvement of the electorate by keeping voters *"in the dark"* through their dishonest media or as President Trump correctly refers to it: *Fake!"*

They are accomplishing what they desire even though most Americans would be opposed if they were aware. And, they are endeavoring to ensure they can continue *ad infinitum* insofar as Americans are concerned even though the continuation of their policies will eventually "tank" America and them with it.

Even their congregational dupes in the U.S. Congress mindlessly spout their propaganda to the American public, like during a television "debate" on the FOX NEWS channel between avowed communist/socialist Independent Sanders and Republican Drier of California way back in July 2002.

When Sanders pointed out the American middle class is "*being hurt by the millions*" of jobs moved out of the U.S. to Mexico and China, Drier's obviously uninformed response was, "*that's what 'free trade' is about,*" and "*ninety percent of the world's consumers reside outside the United States.*"

Remember: this was "*socialist*" Sanders, the 2016 Democrat contender for the Presidency against Hillary Clinton who stated Trump's position on this issue, which explains why the Democrat branch of "*the Establishment,*" including most, if not all, FBI and Justice Department "management" connived to ensure Clinton would be the nominee to continue their *New World Order* America destroying agenda.

Of further note is these comments by Drier were right out of the *New World Order* playbook Bush II played by and is thus another example of how their agenda destructive to America is viewed the same by members of both veneer parties, which are also endeavoring to ensure their future through control of what children learn in the Government indoctrination system.

Their strategy of "*Placid Governability*" of the American people is being accomplished by imbuing students with their ideas of avoiding confrontation at all costs, especially when it is the Government in need of confrontation.

The Bush II Administration's irresponsible lies to the American people, as well as Hillary Clinton and Obama's, about Islam and who the real enemy is are another example of this concept of converting the total American population into an Orwellian herd of "*Placidly Governable*" non-questioning sheep.

Thus, they are either woefully unaware, or desire to keep the American people unaware, the only truly viable means of conflict resolution is not avoidance, but confrontation, as President Trump proved many times his first year in office.

But either way, if permitted to do so, the effete "*Establishment*" like never did anything Barrack Obama, will continue to buy America into suicide through policies of attempting to "buy off" enemies and potential threats, by Mexicans, Egyptians, Islamic terrorists or Iran to which Obama paid $400 million cash to ransom American captives in 2016 plus another $1 billion, plus to avoid any further confrontation about the bad deal they made with Iran, which was left by these so-called "*elites*" for Trump to clean up.

They will only confront in cases where the political fortunes of their One World Government strategies, or OIL, are at risk. And they will only deviate in any way, including parting with the United Nations, if their own personal interests are at risk.

They have demonstrated an amazing One World Government policy consistency with the U.N. until the Bush Administration split with it over the International Criminal Court.

This was the correct decision regarding this international "kangaroo court," but being realistic, and not cynical, it was probably the right decision for the wrong reasons.

The Bush reason was protection of American soldiers; particularly those involved in U.N. peace keeping missions. This was, however, not the real reason because other international tribunals, including those in Japan and Nuremberg, and more recently The Hague, did not show a propensity to pursue *"soldiers."*

The targets have been much higher up the political food chain. Besides, American soldiers serving in a U.N. "peacekeeping" mission would be under the command of someone functioning as a U.N. commander.

Thus, the real reasons for Bush "bailing out" on the U.N. in this instance were probably much higher up the political, One World Government, not military, food chain.

The Clinton bombings of Serbian civilians, his missiles into a Sudanese pharmaceutical plant, Vietnam War actions like Kissinger's bombings in Cambodia (doubtful there is a statute of limitations on killing civilians), the destruction of the Iraqi army in the Gulf War, and other actions in Afghanistan and Iraq, including the internationally criminal bombing by Bush of a restaurant in Bagdad before he began his war there, killing six dozen innocent men, women and children, and potential future actions the U.S. Government should decide to undertake unilaterally, such as Obama's in North Africa and Eastern Europe without European consent, which could make the American decision makers and commanders vulnerable, are more likely better choices as reasons for this Bush decision. It was strictly a PYOA decision.

However, this I.C.C. decision was one of those rare instances wherein the interests of the Trilateral, *New World Order "Establishment"* happened to coincide with the interests of American taxpayers. But history suggests these instances will be "few and far between," and demonstrates their agenda is completely at odds with the future of a democratic and sovereign America.

Thus, continuation of this *New World Order* "management" of the fortunes of America is like a loaded gun to the head of the country. Therefore, Trump must be successful!

A proven legitimate argument against their continued destructive "management" is their demonstrated political and business incompetence.

Although they have been winning internally, within the U.S., to the disadvantage of Americans, much like bad managers in businesses incapable of thinking outside their culture's inbred nature, they have been losing for America and themselves on the very global stage they desire to dominate.

Their culturally inbred debates about proper courses or policies to follow that can frequently be witnessed on television "news" talk shows are, as human nature would dictate, also constrained by their egos. It is just not possible for people who consider themselves the *"elite,"* in possession of *"first rate"* minds to prevent their egos from ruling out, at least to some extent, any consideration of their obviously dismal failures.

Examples of these failures outside the United States that confirm the validity of Machiavelli's 500-year old observations on human nature, as well as the typical incompetence of "academics" like Brzezinski due to lack of common sense are:

1.) Middle Eastern policies that, after billions of dollars of U.S. aid and oil money, ignoring Bush crimes there, have yielded hatred and terrorism directed toward America.

2.) African aid and exploitation policies that, after over four decades, have yielded an Africa in worse condition, needing more assistance than before.

3.) Also, don't forget the "brilliant" Brzezinski failed plan for Japanese domination of Asia. This one was literally stupid to begin with because Japan is the one county in Asia that has no natural resources, and its population is only one tenth of China's. Thus, this brilliance cut one of the three legs from under his planned Trilateral domination of the world through his *New World Order "Establishment"* before it was even born.

4.) This last one is the most damaging failure of all. The People's Republic of China has used American dollars garnered through years of massive trade imbalances resulting from *New World Order "free trade"* policies of moving U.S. capital, jobs and production to China to displace America's ally Japan as the dominant Asian economic and political force, thereby weakening U.S. influence and prestige, as well as that of Japan, throughout Asia.

So, thanks to these ridiculous Brzezinski influenced, anti-American prosperity, U.S. Government *"Establishment" New World Order* policies, China has been enriched beyond what it could have expected in a hundred years without U.S. capital investment and one way *"free trade"* policies.

Therefore, due entirely to the "brilliant" minds in and behind the

U.S. Government policies and actions, China has been sufficiently economically enhanced to become the only real threat to U.S. world economic and military dominance.

And even this capacity of China was further enhanced by more "brilliant" U.S. Government *"Establishment"* actions.

Apparently without even considering China and Russia were such enemies half the military might and cost of each was deployed on the Sino/Soviet border, the U.S. *NWO* "brains" decided it a good idea to "take down" the USSR because of its imposition of communism on the part of Europe the Brits and America gave to them at the end of WWII in contradiction to General Patton's advice not to do so at that time.

As a result, these "brains" stupidly drove energy lacking, but relatively economically rich China and energy rich Russia into the waiting arms of one another, further enriching both and creating a new very economically and energy rich alliance that in 2018 is the only real threat to U.S. military/economic supremacy.

Not in the history of human experience... except maybe fifteenth century Portugal and Spain... has there ever been a government so blunderingly incompetent and arrogantly dismissive of the rest of the world... or suicidal.

Since they have destroyed the Japan "leg" of their Trilaterial "stool" from which it seemed in 2018 is still their intent to control the entire world, thus turning their plans into another type of "stool," are they going to rename themselves "Duolateralists" and continue their quixotic quest for world domination at further expense to America, without considering their entire vision is turning into "stool," rather than expanding?

Well, since they are a secret, conspiratorial organization ninety-nine percent of Americans have never heard of... thanks in part to our friends at FOX NEWS... there is no concern about the name of their America destroying organization.

Considering *"the Establishment"* full court press via dishonest media, crooked Government agencies like the "Justice" Department and F.B.I., and every *New World Order* whore in the Government endeavored to prevent Donald Trump becoming President, and their postelection efforts to remove him, it appears they aren't going to give up until they turn America into a proverbial "~~Shit~~ *Stool Hole Country"* like those Trump allegedly addressed from which they import their dependent cannon fodder fuel for the *"Divide and Conquer"* part of their destroy America for profit program.

The empirical evidence of human nature argues, and conduct demonstrates they will stick with their name and game regardless of what happens to one of their legs, continuing on their chosen course to the detriment of all citizens of North America, Japan, Western Europe and the entire world, as has been the case in their doing nada but fucking up the entire world since the end of WWII. Therefore, to date Brzezinski can RIP.

That there is a growing confluence of anti-Western sentiment, economic interdependence and assertiveness on the part of Islamic countries, Brazil, Russia, the People's Republic of China and others accounting for about six billion of the seven and one-half billion world population that is primarily the result of their actions and worldwide known plans... except in America... will nary cause a twinge in their arrogant, hubris laden heads.

"The dangerous clashes of the future are likely to arise from the interaction of Western arrogance, Islamic intolerance, and Sinic assertiveness."
- Sammuel P. Huntington, 1996,
The Clash of Civilizations and the Remaking of World Order

Although the arrogant ones in charge are not evidencing any concern about what their stated positions and actions are eliciting from outside their world and are continuing their course of the last four decades, average Americans should have great concern about how we got to our sorry, current state of world affairs. How did the destroyers in *"the Establishment"* gain control of their country and wreak so much damage on it without their knowing?

To answer these questions, we must look at the history of when, why and what happened, or was done, and by whom.

CHAPTER FIVE
PROLOGUE TO DESTRUCTION

"Plutocracy" is defined as "government by the wealthy" -
"a group of wealthy people who control or influence a
government."

Since the beginning of civilization, possibly before, there has always been a small group in charge of every tribe, village, town, country, religion, culture, or any establishment or organization humans have created.

Human nature, and that of all herd, pack, flock, pride…all non-solitary animals require leadership to be successful. In the animal kingdom this leadership is for survival.

In primitive man it was for the same reason, and leaders were chosen for the same reason as the animals: wisdom, knowledge, intelligence, strength, etc. for protection, knowledge of food and water, for survival.

But when the basic needs, the hierarchy of needs, for survival are satisfied things change. The leaders are not always chosen by others in either the human or animal kingdoms. The leaders frequently choose themselves and one way or another eliminate the current leader to take his or her place.

In humans, a very long time ago, the currency to obtain leadership positions, in addition to elimination of competition, became just that: currency in one form or another.

Power became rooted in wealth, physical things like gold, silver, land, shelter, etc., the ability to "buy" the labor or loyalty of others or to tell them what to do, as well as how, when and where to do it.

Physical wealth became the currency to influence or control whatever or whoever one with the currency desired. Wealth became THE means of power, and the wealthy became powerful enough to exercise it over many others, including other groups, organizations and governments, which has been the human condition for at least five thousand years in what we call civilizations.

This was the condition of the Egyptians, Persians, Greeks, Romans and Europeans before us. But the word to describe these groups of wealthy powerful people, Plutocracy (Greek; *ploutos,* wealth and *kratos,* power), was first used in1652, likely in England.

U.S. Founders could accurately be described a Plutocracy because they were a collective of wealthy, powerful men who were businessmen, traders, shippers, financiers and others involved in the businesses that built the country by creating jobs and commerce, including trading with other countries.

Also, although not a requirement for a Plutocracy, in bringing together the colonies into a sovereign independent United States they did a good thing for the people because united they were stronger and able to make decisions for their benefit.

But in 2018 and for a century and a quarter prior the U.S. could not accurately be described a Plutocracy because it was no longer a collective of just the wealthy or anyone else who exercised power and influence over the country, or in concert, for any reason, but especially not for the good of the entirety of the population.

Somewhere along the way, first evidenced just before the turn of the Twentieth Century, it became obvious there was not just one cohesive group, Plutocracy or not, in control of the U.S. supposedly working for the benefit of all the people. The assassination of President McKinley accurately demonstrated this, which has been further demonstrated more than once since.

At that time President Roosevelt accurately summed up what those who had grabbed control of the U.S. ship of state were interested in was expanding their personal power beyond the borders of the U.S. Even Zbigniew Brzezinski confirmed this when he described the 1898 Spanish/American war as America's *"first overseas war of conquest."*

Please note *"conquest"* connotes by force of arms and is more of a personal act than one for the good of others, especially in a country wherein its "arms" are, according to the law, specifically only for protection of the people and their country, ergo the title of the person supposedly in control of the arms has been for some time: Secretary of Defense.

But having gotten away with this little treasonous act and the sacrificing of three hundred American citizens to do it, since then they have been off and running, running for the empowerment and enrichment of themselves and their cronies at the expense of taxpaying Americans while serving only those they think can assist them. "They," being whoever is in control of the Government at any time, and "those" being two groups:

One; people who have never created, been in, or earned a cent from business in the private sector exercising the power of government solely for the benefit of themselves and their controlling Government puppeteers who have also never created, been in or compensated for producing or creating anything.

Good examples of each would be the FBI and "Justice" Department employees and others of their ilk in elective positions who in 2016 through 2018 did everything within their power, including breaking multiple laws, to take down Trump and endeavor to get Hillary elected.

Two; sufficiently large segments of the population they have divided that can be bought via welfare and other benefits to support whatever nefarious endeavors "they" decide to engage in at the expense of other Americans who are producing and contributing, and others in big business, special interest groups and the media that can be rewarded in any of several ways for their support.

Unfortunately, money and power corrupt and create or encourage bad people who do bad things to others. Zbigniew Brzezinski is the best contemporary example of this:

"The nation-state as a fundamental unit of man's organized life has ceased to be the principal creative force; International banks and multinational corporations are acting and planning in terms that are far in advance of the political concepts of the nation-state"
- Zbigniew Brzezinski, *Between Two Ages*, 1971

What this says in plain English is Brzezinski's objective was eliminating sovereign countries like the U.S. from the face of the earth and having the big international banks and global corporations that have no regard for the law, due process, Congress or the will of American citizens replace these aspects of every American's life.

This should be frightening to every American because this is from the co-founder of the Trilateral Commission whose stated goal is to create a *"New International Economic Order,"* i.e., *New World Order,* that was represented by eleven members in key positions in the Obama Administration, appointed in his first ten days in office after Brzezinski was the one who groomed him for the Presidency, just as he did Jimmy Carter.

That these positions had control over U.S. financial, economic, national security and foreign policies explains Obama's negative impact on the economy, border control and trade, which demonstrates he did not have an agenda that favored working, taxpaying Americans, and thus the massive loss of jobs and decline in their economic status.

All this also explains Obama's total disregard for Congress, ruling by executive order, usually in opposition to the economic welfare of Americans, as well as the conduct of those in his "Justice" Department ensuring Trilateral darling Hillary not be subjected to due process so she could continue his *NWO* America destroying agenda while also ignoring and breaking laws to try to prevent Donald Trump becoming President.

Could anyone cognizant of the foregoing quote and paragraphs about what *NWO*, anti-American Obama, those he appointed and reported to, including Brzezinski, doubt they do not represent "bad people" doing "bad things" to Americans?

***

More Bad People Doing More Bad Things to Americans

In 1913 the Federal Reserve banking system was legislated ostensibly with the intent to stabilize the U.S. economy through decisions and controls regulating U.S. money supply and interest rates. In short, the "thinking" was a self-serving group of over educated in the overly complex field of economics, a field of study that totally ignores the real-world market place wherein other humans are conducting business, could control or determine the future outcome of millions of individual transactions in the macro economy.

Interestingly the impetus for this was another of those secret, conspiratorial meetings. This time six of the richest and/or most influential men either in control of or dependent on profits from the banking system met on a private island off the coast of Georgia.

But let's not forget shortly thereafter the same kind of control of a large economy was commenced in Russia, and the "wise" financially savvy men supporting this in the U.S. spent the next seven decades making negative comments about the folly of *"Central Control"* of an economy. Surprise! They were correct.

Possibly these were related to those in the U.S. space program who continually attacked Russian efforts in this arena that are now sending U.S. astronauts to the International Space Station on Russian rockets?

- Since 1913 the U.S. dollar that did not lose any of its purchasing power in the hundred years prior to implementation of the Fed lost over ninety-five percent of its purchasing power as of 2018, helping impoverish working, dollars earning Americans.

- The Fed did not stop the Great Depression, but through its actions likely caused it. It also did nothing to prevent the early 1980s recession or the 2008 financial panic that its actions in concert with the Bush Administration war in Iraq and "banking" greed likely caused, crashing much of the financial system worldwide.

- Since 2008, after creating trillions of dollars out of thin air to fund "on demand" needs of the Federal Government "debt" that was passed through the big banks that actually own the Fed and receive six percent interest, by law, on their percentage ownership of it, as well as interest from the Government, i.e. taxpayers, on every one of the "out of thin air" dollars created, Obama increased Government debt 100% to ten trillion dollars.

Surprise, again; during this time the *Too Big To Fail,* banks, the biggest of which is J.P. Morgan Chase, grew even larger and richer.

Therefore, so everyone can understand whether the Fed accomplished what it was intended to, consider rather than what was stated; two of the men at the meeting over a hundred years ago were financial "*titans*" of the time, J.P. Morgan and Paul Warburg who were even more richly rewarded after the Fed was created.

As we depart the Fed and TBTF banks, PLEASE let's not forget these are the institutions and people who run them in whose hands Zbigniew Brzezinski and his *New World Order* co-conspirators have spent four decades endeavoring to place one hundred percent control of U.S. finances and ours, while not being subject to due process under laws, Congressional oversight or Constitution.

In considering this, please also do not forget the fact that not one single bank or its management was subjected to U.S. due process as a result of their proven criminality and serious adverse effect on the finances and lives of millions of Americans, as well as the impact on the U.S. economy when puppet Bush II's Secretary of the Treasury bailed some of them out of certain bankruptcy with billions of U.S. taxpayer's dollars.

The foregoing occurrences under, and actions by, both Republican Bush II and Democrat Obama consistent with Brzezinski's guidance and goals should prove, even to the most skeptical, there really is only one *New World Order* party/organization in control of these Presidents and the U.S. Government. It should also prove it is not just "*Democrats, Liberal and the Left*" that are assiduously endeavoring to remove Trump.

***

We have earlier probably sufficiently addressed Franklin Delano Roosevelt's nefarious, illegal actions of withholding information and unnecessarily sacrificing Americans to get the U.S. into WWII against the desires of most of the people, thus satisfying his promise to his beleaguered third cousin Winston Churchill to do this. We also stated his other cousin's actions forty years prior seemed to be the model for this, as well as for others post WWII. But we haven't discussed the economic factors involved.

The Great Depression was world-wide but began in the US after the US stock market crash in Oct 1929, only fifteen years after implementation of the Federal Reserve that was ostensibly created to prevent occurrences of this nature. Also, of note is the fact big banker Andrew Mellon was Secretary of the Treasury under Hoover at its beginning.

So those in control of the big banks and the Fed were incompetent or enriched themselves, as they did after the 2008 financial crisis. But either way, the Fed was useless or complicit both times because it has done very little, if anything, to enhance the U.S. economy or the lives of average Americans during the 100 years, plus of its existence.

This time the Depression lasted for ten years until the beginning of WWII. During this time world GDP dropped 15%, and U.S. unemployment rose to 25%, industrial production declined 46%, and foreign trade dropped 70%.

Initial cause of the Depression was monetary contraction of 35% due to bank failures, resulting in 33% deflation, or decline in the valuation of components in the economy.

According to economist Milton Freidman the Fed exacerbated the Depression by not lowering interest rates, not increasing the monetary base, not injecting liquidity into the banking system and just passively doing nothing.

Thus, those in control of the Fed who should have known better, and taken appropriate action, just sat passively and watched what would have been a normal recession, had they taken aggressive action, turn into the Great Depression. Why didn't they?

***

The Great Depression was the enabler of Hitler who must have been smarter because he rose to power due to his prompt action ramping up military industrial production in Germany that resulted in his being the economic savior of the German people.

Could British and U.S. intelligence really have been totally unaware of massive, industrial resurgence in prewar Germany? Following Occam's theory; the simplest answer requiring the least assumptions, is usually the correct one: certainly not.

Thus, can we accept the level of supposedly unintentional high-level incompetence could really be accidental over, and over again, and again for a hundred years?

Could highly educated economists, bankers and also highly educated, experienced "management" of the FBI continue to fail to act in the face of constantly monitored economic factors or constant reports about potential terrorist acts by those they were warned about as many as twenty-three times? Same answer as above.

So, it looks like we the American people have continuously "been had" for over a century by a Government never intended to be our friend, but has continued to increase in size, ever adding more worthless appendages and components that have done nothing but rob us of our hard-earned dollars and wasted them to no avail.

Thus, the Fed, seemingly, was never, nor ever intended, to be what those who would massively benefit from it then or today present to the rest of America. Surprise!

But FDR who inherited the Depression did try public works,

farm subsidies and other obviously ineffective efforts to end the Depression. However, according to British economist John Maynard Keynes whose solution to every recession was always spend, spend, FDR never spent enough to end the Depression until the beginning of WWII, which also seems the model for ending all recessions in post WWII America.

There you go! The reason for the U.S. war-based economy since 1945. The precursor of other similar actions by Presidents: 1.) Truman when U.S. unemployment reached 7.9% in 1949, and the unlikely event of relatively economically successful North Korea invading not so South Korea when South Koreans were fleeing to the North, 2.) Kennedy/Johnson when unemployment averaged 7.5% the four years prior to 1962 the military buildup that ended in Johnson starting the Vietnam War, 3.) Bush I when 1990 unemployment was over 7% again and he attacked Iraq, and 4.) Bush II when, after Clinton's good economic times unemployment was headed back up over 6% again he invaded Iraq.

All these actions indicate a high probability of war and thus sacrifice of Americans to solve economic problems that persist frequently even though the Federal Reserve continually adjusts interest rates and money supply based on their obviously unsuccessful academic non-real world, central planning models, or just bad forecasting.

All this aside however, the 2018 position of economic "whizzes" was the government should maintain equilibrium between money supply and demand to prevent economic crises. There you go again: government to solve everything. We see where this has gotten us on multiple occasions, so due to widespread and confidently predictable government ineptitude, this is not likely.

However, following Occam's rule this could be the solution, only if more directly and plainly stated to avoid typical government probability and deliberate obfuscation of the term "equilibrium" which means balance, and removing consideration of all special interests and other primarily government generated impediments to any common-sense solution to any problem:

Forecast future economic growth, based on objective analysis and extrapolation of recent past growth, then gradually increase the monetary base on this basis only, and raise or lower interest rates, which are nothing but the price of money, like any other product, solely on the economy's... not the Government's... demand for it. This should eliminate the speciously based argument for the Federal Reserve and its politically based projections.

But there is no way "*the Establishment*" populated by Brzezinski acolytes would go along with this that would seriously hinder at least one component of their business plan for the destruction of America and roll it into their envisioned *New World Order*.

Anyone who might have the audacity and be in position to pursue this and reinstatement of a solidly backed currency, rather than the *fiat* money supply that has accommodated the horrendous Government expansion of the fifty years prior to 2018 would not likely be any safer than the last President to pursue this course.

The Day America [that was] Died

"President John Kennedy has been shot in Dallas."
- Texas radio announcer

This is what Americans heard on the radio newscasts just before 1:30 PM Central Time on November 22, 1963. Then spent most of the rest of the day listening to the coverage of what was unfolding that was unbelievable… and still was in 2018.

The story was a guy named Lee Harvey Oswald, with a bolt action rifle, shot Kennedy through the head at about 12:30 PM as his limousine was going downhill around the curve on Elm Street in Dealey Plaza toward the railroad underpass that would take him westward out of downtown Dallas… and he did it from the 5th story window of a building in Dealey Plaza at the top of the hill.

Many people around Dallas familiar with the area remember thinking; *"That Oswald guy must be one hell of a shot, hitting something the size of a human head at that range is damned good, but doing it when it is moving away, downhill and around a curve at over twenty miles per hour? Well…….."*

After he supposedly killed Kennedy, Oswald managed to get to the Texas Theater on Jefferson Boulevard in Oak Cliff several miles to the west across the Trinity River where he was captured a few hours after Kennedy was shot.

Upon hearing this, and for years since, many familiar with the area could not fathom why he would have gone there because to get there he would have had to cross the area where Kennedy was shot and all that was going on there, unless he went east, then south and back to the west to take the Zangs Boulevard bridge that was the only other route to Oak Cliff from that part of Dallas. This did not make any sense if he was endeavoring to get away.

If Oswald shot Kennedy and was trying to get away it would have made much more sense to keep going either east or north to get away and avoid capture. To double back, he would not have been terribly bright, or something else was going on with this.

There was a lot more going on with this.

The previous June 4th Kennedy signed Executive Order 11110 authorizing the Treasury to again begin issuing silver certificates backed by the nation's silver reserves, essentially curtailing Federal Reserve control of the money supply, thereby potentially limiting the expansion of the Government and its activities like unnecessary wars to the availability of silver in the reserves or what the economy could actually afford.

This one act could have sealed the President's fate, but he had also recently taken action to begin getting the few troops there out of Vietnam and stop the building nonsense of invading that country. But to many, especially all the young American males being drafted into the military, it was obvious anything but that was happening. The troop build-up was accelerating.

All most could do in November 1963 and for a time thereafter, was wonder why, or who killed Kennedy. However, in intervening years that question has been answered for anyone intelligent enough not to choose to believe the lies of the Warren Commission of which Gerald Ford was a member and accept reality.

Anyone sufficiently intelligent to connect the dots can go on line, Google Kennedy Assassination, click the site "Secret Service ordered to stand down," watch the video and question why the head of the Secret Service detail assigned to protect the President ordered his Agents on the steps at the back of the President's Limousine to abandon it a few minutes prior to his being killed.

If you do this, watch the agent who would have been between Kennedy and Oswald on the right rear of the limo ordered off the car shrugging his shoulders and holding his arms out asking why? in total incredulity.

This video, more than anything else, demonstrates who killed John Kennedy and covered it up, especially given the Zapruder home movie that shows the shot that killed Kennedy came from his right front, the direction of the "*grassy knoll,*" not from behind, as has been confirmed by over six dozen forensic investigators in recent years, and as a U.S. Marines Officer trained as a sniper during Vietnam stated upon visiting the site of the shooting years later said, *"I can't tell you who shot Kennedy, but I can tell you who certainly did not!"*.

Multiple writings and research behind them indicate the warmongering powers within and behind the U.S. Government did both the assassination and the cover up.

According to the book "*JFK And the Unspeakable*" by James Douglas, in addition to likely stopping the Vietnam War, Kennedy was at odds with the C.I.A. over Cuba and the Joint Chiefs of Staff over their plans for false flag events and their desire to attack the

Soviet Union while they thought the U.S. had the advantage.

Of course, as the removal of the agent from the back of the Presidential limousine to eliminate the possibility of questions about how Oswald could have made the shot around him shows, the Secret Service was also involved.

This was a vast conspiracy, contrary to what the naïve "*It can't happen here*" American public choose to believe.

Had he remained alive as President, JFK would likely have stopped the invasion of Vietnam and the following twelve years of useless war costing fifty-eight thousand American lives, tens of thousands of seriously wounded and hundreds of thousands of Vietnamese and other lives, as well as the death of the America that was... the America of promise and prosperity that has also since been further brutalized by more unnecessary war and unbridled expansion of the Government permitted by inflation of the monetary base through Federal Reserve issued *fiat* currency not backed by silver or anything else.

That day Kennedy was killed, November 22, 1963, was the day the real America died. That day was the zenith of the American dream, and the death of it and the concept of America that existed since 1776. But it was also the day those who have willfully been destroying America for decades for personal gain began to seize a firm grip on the tiller of the United States ship of state prevailed over the dream, the concept and the people of America. That was the day of the biggest government coup of the Twentieth Century.

Anyone who chooses not to believe this will inherit his just rewards. But anyone who desires to be informed about the reality of what America has become in the years since JFK's death, and under control of the evil shepherding it into the waste bin of history amid the company of those failed states that took similar courses the United States is on, need read only two books, in addition to "*JFK And the Unspeakable*": Jesse Ventura's book, "*63 Documents the Government Doesn't Want You to Read*" and "*Family of Secrets*" by Russ Baker about the Bush family that details much about this family, including where George H.W. Bush was in the A.M. of November 22, 1963.

The fact people within the Government and military of the United States produced official documents, including plans and details of operation for assassinating leaders of countries in the same way Kennedy was killed, killing people whose only "crime" is to disagree with those in control of the Government, planning to kill American citizens by flying a commercial airliner into a building in this country and blaming it on a foreign country to enable them to start a war against that country, and many other criminal acts, should be sufficient evidence to cause any law-abiding citizen to desire to distance himself and his country from these people by whatever means within his or her power.

This written evidence of the moral and ethical decay wrought on their country from the top down by its Government *"Establishment"* is more than sufficient for the removal of these people via impeachment, through votes, imprisonment for the guilty, and seeking the ultimate penalty for those still alive who were key participants in the assassination of President John F. Kennedy.

The evil disclosed in these books that continued through 2018 and likely beyond is like an operating manual not only for the assassination of Kennedy but of the America that was for over 200 years Reagan's *"shining city on a hill,"* an assassination of the beacon for the entire world... the killing of a bright future for all.

The day President of the United States John F. Kennedy was assassinated was the day the real America died.

***

In confirmation of the above, shortly after taking office, Lyndon Johnson supported Federal Reserve currency, money "out of thin air" that carries an interest cost payable by the people but is not redeemable for gold or silver from Government reserves, i.e., free money that permitted tremendous unaffordable Government expansion without cost except to the people thru interest payments and denigration of their purchasing power, and impoverishment through inflation. Then he eventually reversed JFK's Executive Order and began removal of Silver Certificates from circulation.

He also expedited the buildup for the Vietnam invasion, then he and others in his Administration created the Gulf of Tonkin false flag event, treasonously lied to the American people and United Nations about it and began that conflict in earnest.

Also, during this time, he was criminally beginning the War he did something at least as destructive to America, or possibly long term more so. He created his *Great Society* that is among the country's most expensive debacles because it increased poverty and strife among America's most economically vulnerable population, black Americans.

Just one aspect of this so-called *"liberal Democrat"* idiocy, some think deliberately to increase numbers of the Government dependent electorate, discouraged black families through more welfare to single black women with children than to married ones.

The result has been most black males being raised in single parent "families," without added income or guidance of a father, causing them to grow up in poverty, more susceptible to tribal gang life and its concomitant crime.

This has torn apart and created an underserved, especially educationally, permanently poverty stricken, underclass of millions of angry, actually *"divided and conquered"* and frequently racist people to the disadvantage of the entire country.

By the time he left office in January 1969, following in FDR's footsteps, he was responsible for tremendous unnecessary war costs in lives and money, massive Government expansion through his *"Great Society"* welfare programs, and spending more than all previous Presidents combined, beginning a seemingly unstoppable spending spree of destruction that continued for fifty-three years as of 2018, with no end in sight.

***

In 1970 Zbigniew Brzezinski called for a ***"coordinated policy among developed nations necessary in order to counter global instability"*** caused by ***"increasing economic inequality."***

This comment alone should prove to the intelligent mind; he was intellectually little more than any of his typical left leaning "egghead" Harvard "academic" United Nations One World Government sycophants devoted to only two objectives: 1.) creation of a One World Government with control over all nations and all people without regard for any of the empirical evidence of the causes of the human condition available to show the differences between the thoughts, actions and desires of people of different cultures and religions, and the results thereof, and 2.) through that government endeavor to impose their cultural beliefs and way of life that would satisfy their goal of a homogenized Utopian Socialist world they would control, i.e., a much larger example of the failed United Soviet States of Russia, the USSR.

This should be very frightening, and frustrating, to all of us with reasonably well functioning minds and a modicum of world experiences that this man, as the architect of this quixotic adventure, was able to create such a wide following among those in control of the U.S. Government and "education" system for so many years he has been the major force in the destruction of the greatest country and best experience in human history.

But it does bring-to-mind what the Chairman of the regional branch of the Republican Party soliciting him to run for Congress in 1982 said to this Author, *"How do you think you will feel trying to work with your intellectual inferiors every day?"* Then compounded this with his answer to the question of why he would say this, *"I have known a lot of Congressmen."*

Seems he experienced *"a lot of Congressmen"* either untouched by reality and lacking common sense or blinded by the possibility of the *New World Order "Establishment"* offering them previously unimagined power and wealth... or victims of both.

If the former, they may have been uneducated of the fact rampant population growth among some cultures inculcated either by their religion to increase the wealth and power of the Plutocracy of that religion or their culture, or just their ignorance cause them to be less wealthy than others unburdened by religious or cultural enticement or simply sufficiently intelligent to ascertain those with the greatest increases in population are collectively much poorer, or less wealthy than those that practice sensible procreation relative to their ability to sufficiently provide for their next generation.

They may also be unaware of the fact neither can be overcome because this is a religious or culturally imbued burden that cannot be eliminated due to inertia unlikely to be overcome by more than six percent of the population.

However, if they are either lack knowledge of these facts or not concerned with them as Harvard Ph.D. Brzezinski was not, as well as possessing his same narrow-minded focus on more power and wealth they would not likely be interested this simple world reality:
The major cause of poverty is the percentage increase in humans exceeding the percentage increase in production of goods and services, resulting in less wealth to be divided among greater numbers of humans.

The obvious fact of this reality in Africa, most of Latin America, Mexico, and some Asian sub-continent and Eastern European countries or elsewhere is not going to be overcome by any number of *New World Order* One World Government or Brzezinski acolytes like Obama, Hillary or any number of members of *"the Establishment"* because they are also aware of these Winston Churchill cited realities, and not interested in overcoming them, but relying on the ignorance of the uneducated to their advantage:

"The main vice of capitalism is the uneven distribution of prosperity. The main vice of socialism is the even distribution of misery."
"You don't make the poor richer by making the rich poorer"
- Winston Churchill

And they will continue their deliberate America destroying journey because of their drive for personal wealth and power best demonstrated by both Clintons and so many others of their ilk, or because they are but ignorant followers who really are so intellectually challenged they satisfy this bit of Churchill's wisdom:
"If you're not a liberal at twenty you have no heart.
If you're not a conservative at forty you have no brain."

Given the fact of the ages of the two generations that have been indoctrinated by our Government's *"education"* system and even all the older ones populating *"the Establishment"* Government and its media, plus the uninformed, self-styled *"millennials"* who with regard to most facts of history, geography, cultures, economics, business, trade, and almost everything else they cannot see on their phones or ~~think~~ believe might personally affect them, those of us who possess "intelligent minds" are going to find living in the America of 2018 and beyond very challenging.

Beyond that, <u>unless Trump is more successful than we can imagine; immediately redirects U.S. *"education"* back to what it was pre 1976, immediately removes all Obama holdovers continuing to permit tens of thousands from south of us to overrun our border monthly, "outs" those really behind our destruction other than *"leftists, liberals, Democrats, fake news,"* and many in Government who have committed crimes like Hillary, members of her entourage and the Democrat Party, the top people in the Obama "Justice" Department and FBI are prosecuted and found guilty of their crimes average Americans will never know, and he will have failed to *"**Make America Great Again.**"*</u>

Then it will not just be "challenging" to live in the U.S. We will be done as a successful democratic country. *"The Establishment"* will have won, and "America" will be no more in a fairly short time. Brzezinski will have won posthumously!

But ninety-nine percent of Americans will not have a clue what happened to them or their country because neither Brzezinski, his co-conspirators nor any of their evil America destroying *Globalist New World Order* One World Government agenda have been disclosed by the media or anyone in the Government even though the lies about everyone who should be opposed to them and their evil America destroying schemes are broadcast twenty-four seven by Mika and her father's other media co-conspirators.

Even the multimillion dollar a year talking heads on FOX News seem to be willing to leave their viewership in the dark about what is being done to them and their country. They are demonstrably willing to continue to pick up their millions while absolutely <u>lying by omission</u> to the millions of people who trust them.

Given the stakes, the future of America, this is almost as "criminal" as the lying by Mika and her co-conspirators on MSNBC and other media. The difference is it is not intended, but it is difficult to understand why they never "out" what they must know.

Mika *et al* are broadcasting in support of what they believe or desire while lying about Trump and others for the same reason. But those on FOX and elsewhere who know precisely what and who are the problems are keeping their mouths shut, permitting the status quo of America's destruction to progress relatively unimpeded even though they have the platform from which to inform and arouse Americans to cure what ails them.

Are they nada but just some of the *"pawns"* Brzezinski summed up the effete "e*lite"* consider all to be?

Must be! They and other so-called *"Conservative,"* but obviously phony nothing media have had forty-five years to inform Americans about what they have known was being done to their country. However, they have not. So, let's do it now.

***

July 1973, Brzezinski and Rockefeller formalized their Trilateral organization and began implementing the American part of their *New World Order* socialist totalitarian plans with a "Business Plan for America" that was the necessary First Step because it was the keystone of the *"Globalist/Internationalist"* house of cards they planned.

"House of cards"? Yes, because it ignores common sense and like the Spanish and Portuguese five hundred years before, they ignored other powerful countries except to target them as enemies to be dealt with later. We saw how that turned out, but onward.

***

The Brzezinski Business Plan for America

Objective: to gain control of the U.S. Government and direct it toward the U.S. becoming a member of their envisioned *"New World Order"* with all countries under a One World Government like originally envisioned in creation of the United Nations, but with the realization that would require full support and cooperation from the top rungs of the U.S. economic ladder.

Therefore, to ensure these influential people would be on board with the concept of internationalizing or globalizing the world economy it must further enrich big business, the financial and political classes because their money and power were the basic requirements for success. But "unfortunately" the major source of the money had to be the pockets of taxpaying American citizens.

- *De facto* **Single Political Party: c**ontrol of the Government required controlling the Presidency, which meant controlling the two parties, or ideally having only one party. But given the U.S. system and human nature this would have to be *sub rosa,* i.e. under the surface, secret and confidential, not known to the U.S. electorate that must think they have a choice.

- *Sub Rosa* **Party Presidential Candidates:** of each veneer party must be a member of or committed to loyalty to the only single party actually in control. This would not be a problem because win or lose the election the candidates would be compensated via handsome financial compensation and/or positions for their loyalty and service by member or supporting business organizations or their veneer party organizations.

- **Enriching Business:** to obtain full support of big business required having them increase profits and value without waiting for slowly increasing gains from business as usual. They would need another means of accomplishing this widening of the spread between cost and revenue by producing at lower costs. Producing in lower cost countries like China and Mexico and being enabled to import those goods into the U.S. with no or minimal import duties would solve that problem.

- **Rewards:** corporate management would receive higher compensation, as would the financial class due to resultant increased profits and market capitalization, and the political class would also benefit because the growth of cash flowing to the business lobby would be increased tremendously enabling increased largesse available to it.

- **The Problem:** the American working, taxpaying Middle Class would lose jobs and suffer a wealth decline due to capital investment and production being moved offshore to enhance corporate profits, which would eventually, but sooner rather than later, cause unrest among these masses. Even though corporations could offer some products at lower prices, possibly slowing inflation, Middle Class historic economic gains and increasing wealth would be dramatically slowed, even reversed.

- **Solution Part I Control:** "Education" and Knowledge by imposing a loss of history to accomplish the required loss of knowledge of the American culture and economy that preceded the Brzezinski *"New World Order."*

Thus, as proven in Hitler Germany, Mao China, even pre-reformation Catholic Europe that was the model for these two, it was necessary to control the minds of the people beginning with early education, then controlling the media was an absolute must.

- **Solution Part II Change:** the nature of the population into one more accepting of more government control like those of Third World countries. In other, politically incorrect, words a largely Government dependent, less well educated, less productive, complacent, passively governable population was needed. Solution: Mexico and other Third World Countries.

However, this would further adversely impact lives and finances of the principally Eurocentric majority population that would not be terribly receptive of the financial and lifestyle changes they would suffer, even after they were reduced to a minority, as planned.

- Solution Part III More Control: a <u>two-pronged solution;</u> take <u>control of the healthcare,</u> <u>and disarm</u> the historically productive, controlling population, both slowly, but surely, as their electoral and physical power is reduced via mass immigration of the desired largely Government dependent third world immigrants.

Following chapters *SIX* through *ELEVEN* present details on implementation of these Brzezinski/Rockefeller immoral plans *"the Establishment"* has ardently pursued since 1973 to secure control of the U.S. Government and accomplish their objectives of 1.) moving U.S. production off shore to increase corporate profits, 2.) changing education to indoctrination to control knowledge, 3.) creating a majority Government dependent electorate, 4.) implementing healthcare controls to control the people, and 5.) removing the ability of people to defend themselves... all to enhance their wealth and power to enable them to guide the country into their desired *New World Order Socialist* One World Government, all of which most, if informed, would recognize is reality given the opposition to Trump and his *"Make America Great Again"* plans.

CHAPTER SIX
" THE ESTABLISHMENT"

CREATING AN ORGANIZATION INTENDED TO PLACE CONTROL OF AMERICA IN THE HANDS OF AN INSTITUTIONALIZED TOTALITATARIAN CORPORATE/GOVERNMENT PLUTOCRACY

The Webster Dictionary definition of "*the Establishment*" is those *"regarded as holding the chief power and influence"* - *"the ruling inner circle of any nation, institution, etc."*

There is, and has been for a long time, a great conspiracy against the American people by these people adversely affecting their lives and prosperity. Generations of the greedy, effete "elite" using America and its people for personal gain at their expense have been actively involved in their nefarious deeds since the beginning of the 20th Century. But the events of 1973; the primarily West Coast "Outsider" Nixon Administration quitting the gold standard, proposing tariffs against imports into the U.S. because the country faced its first trade deficit in over eighty years, and suggesting legislation to lift import tax exemptions for products of U.S. global businesses produced offshore because it was perceived their trade practices were already costing American jobs were much too unilateralist for the big business and old East Coast Brahmin establishment money. This spurred the already planned Rockefeller/Brzezinski "New World Order" One World Government, pro-multilateral takeover of the U.S. Government in the interest of large global businesses to begin in earnest.   - The Author

Therefore, since 1973 America no longer has had a government "*of the people, by the people, for the people,*" which it actually had not for over a hundred years prior.

But it did have until this time a government that functioned at least partially for the benefit of a majority of working, producing, taxpaying Americans, a government of at least some people who possessed the goals and objectives of the founders, who did their best to endeavor to make America the best place on earth for the people who lived and worked here because they were dependent on them for their Government's income.

However, since 1973 that has changed. The Government was taken over by, and has since been, one hundred percent controlled for the benefit of members of *"the Establishment"* who are destroying the America of yore, Ronald Reagan's *"shining city"* that was a beacon for freedom and prosperity. And they are willfully doing this for greed; for money and power, which has more recently been even further facilitated.

As recently as 2010 the U.S. Supreme Court under its Justice appointed by the second Bush President again ruled against the people in favor of *"the Establishment,"* of which the first Bush was a charter member, in its *Citizens United* ruling that proved it is just as politicized as the FBI Director and Attorney General proved they were in deciding not to charge Hillary for her Email criminal actions, and as it did in its ruling on Obamacare.

In this decision it essentially ensured *"the Establishment"* will become even more firmly entrenched in its control of the U.S. Government by eliminating limits on campaign spending by corporations and labor unions and limiting the possibility of preventing corruption in campaign financing, as has been disclosed Hillary's campaign likely engaged in during 2016; this potentially created a system of unlimited bribery.

Now big money from these entities and the very rich will substantially offset the votes of average Americans and thwart the democratic process because big money will satisfy the extant greed of lobbyists, politicians, heads of the Government agencies, and the rest of *"the Establishment"* as they apparently endeavored to do in Hillary's campaign.

***

It was July 1973... just four months shy of ten years after President Kennedy's death... when the most widely unknown important event having the most adverse long-term effect on Americans, their economic well-being, security, freedoms, and future occurred.

David Rockefeller, Chairman of Chase Manhattan Bank, the youngest of six children of oil baron and world's richest man John D. Rockefeller's son, John D. Rockefeller Jr., and Harvard PhD Zbigniew Brzezinski founded the formal organization that has become the preeminent organization of the America destroying *"Establishment."*

To understand the nature and character of this organization and the effect its members are having on Americans and their country let's revisit the following, some of which were addressed in Chapter One, because these comments provide the insight into the structure for what has so adversely affected us for over four decades:
- Rockefeller stated in response to a characterization of him *as internationalist, conspiring with others around the world to build a more integrated global political and economic structure—one*

world, **"If that's the charge, I stand guilty, and I am proud of it."**
- He is also credited with the statement **"Americans have too much democracy."**
- Polish born Democrat Zbigniew Brzezinski attended Harvard to work on a doctorate he received in 1953, and later collaborated on a book on the concept of Totalitarianism, which seems to have been his guidance for structuring his organization, as well as his "Business Plan for America" to fund and support the implementation of his plans.
- He also supported Lyndon Johnson's Presidential campaign, his "Great Society," his criminal Vietnam War, and selected Jimmy Carter as a member of the organization, then personally groomed him for three years before he announced his candidacy for President in 1976. He also did the same for Obama, but for four years over three decades later.
- Carter proclaimed himself an *"eager student"* of Brzezinski who became his foreign policy advisor, and his National Security Advisor.
- In 1979 Brzezinski led the United States in a new arms buildup. *In* an interview he admitted the U.S. supported and armed radical Islamists to undermine Russia. (It has been reported these terrorists morphed into al Qaeda.)
- He also admitted U.S. covert action got Russia to start the Afghan war in 1979.
- Asked if he had regrets about this, he responded, *"Regret what? That secret operation was an excellent idea. It had the effect of drawing the Russians into the Afghan trap and you want me to regret it? The day that the Soviets officially crossed the border, I wrote to President Carter: We now have the opportunity of giving to the USSR its Vietnam War."*
- When asked if he regretted "having given arms and advice to future terrorists" he responded, *"What is most important to the history of the world? The Taliban or the collapse of the Soviet empire? Some stirred-up Muslims or the liberation of Central Europe and the end of the Cold War?"*
- When he was told, "Islamic fundamentalism represents a world menace today." Brzezinski responded, *"Nonsense! It is said that the West had a global policy in regard to Islam. That is stupid. There isn't a global Islam...."* [Le Nouvel Observateur (Paris), 1/15/1998]
- In 2008 Democratic Presidential front-runner and supposed anti-war candidate Barrack Obama obtained the endorsement of and foreign policy advice of his creator and mentor, Zbigniew Brzezinski, after four years of his grooming him, obviously ignoring

his endorsement of the creation and support of militant Islamic forces in Afghanistan that were directed by accused "9/11" mastermind Osama bin Laden.

- Obama has since stated, *"I've learned an immense amount from Dr. Brzezinski who is one of our country's most outstanding scholars who has done a lot for our country."*

- In 2016 Hillary Clinton went on the campaign trail with Barrack Obama signifying she agreed with and would have represented a continuation of "*the* (Brzezinski stated) *Establishment*" policies of wars for purposes other than protection of America, as well as the position " *There isn't a global Islam*" Obama followed like a good little puppet, regardless of the continuing death toll of Americans and others throughout the world.

***

Given this, is there any doubt Hillary who also refused to acknowledge Islamic terrorism, was a member and sometime chair of the "*leftist*" New World Foundation from 1982 to 1988, would have been anything other than another representative, like so many other members of "*the Establishment*," Democrat and Republican alike, who have been responsible for most of the bad policies and actions Americans have suffered the results of since 1973?

Examples of what members of this unsavory "*Establishment*" have wrought are : 1.) elimination of conscription to create a military non-representative of the population so it will not protest unnecessary wars as it did the Vietnam War, 2.) the foundation for moving U.S. capital investment, production and jobs offshore to enhance corporate profits for the benefit of the corporations and their political benefactor favorites, 3.) forcing management, i.e., control, of trillions of dollars of retirement money into a few hands on Wall Street, enhancing banks, corporations and politicians at the expense of retirees, 4.) the massive U.S. arms buildup, 5.) more wars like the 2014 U.S. *coup d' état* in the Ukraine and in Libya removing Gadhafi, 6.) starting a new Cold War with Russia, per advice from Brzezinski's 1997 book, it is necessary to remove Russia as an obstacle to his cabal's desired *New World Order* One World Government, and 7.) ensuring Americans are unaware of this by keeping it a secret through control of the media.

***

But as bad as all of the above is, consider the following some attribute to communist Saul Alinsky who wrote <u>Rules for Radicals</u> that was inspirational for "*Counter-Culture*" college organizers, as well as Caesar Chavez, Jesse Jackson, Hillary Clinton and Obama.

Although some say he wrote them and others say he did not, these exact statements cannot be found in this book. But he wrote a lot, they are not far off his espoused communist leanings, and someone wrote them in sympathy with his communist philosophy... possibly Hillary, since she was close to him, or even Brzezinski since they describe his Harvard professor mentor and co-author Carl J. Friedrich's statements which outline much of his *New World Order* agenda for America.

These instructions on how to create a totalitarian socialist state, no matter who wrote them, represent an outline of what has been done to America over the forty-five years prior to 2018 by Brzezinski, his comrades and his protégés in the Presidency, State Department and elsewhere:

1) Healthcare. Control healthcare and control the people.

2) Poverty. Increase the Poverty level as high as possible. Poor people are easier to control and will not fight back if they are provided everything for them to live.

3) Debt. Increase the debt to an unsustainable level. That way you are able to increase taxes, and this will produce more poverty.

4) Gun Control. Remove the ability to defend themselves from the government. That way you are able to create a police state.

5) Welfare. Take control of every aspect of their lives (Food, Housing, and Income).

6) Education. Take control of what people read and listen to, and children learn in school.

7) Religion. Remove the belief in God from the government and schools.

8) Class Warfare - Divide people into the wealthy and poor. This will cause more discontent and it will be easier to take (Tax) the wealthy with the support of the poor.

These points represent a simplification of much of the Communist Manifesto used by Russian communists to convert and subdue the Russian people who Stalin described as *"Useful Idiots."*

Alinsky, born of Jewish Russian U.S. immigrants died in 1972, the year before official creation of the organization whose members have been in control of America over forty years as of 2018, *"the Establishment."* But for the benefit of those who might doubt this is happening in the U.S. today, or that Alinsky influenced those in control... and one who could have potentially been in control of America in the future, let's look at the influence of his teachings that coincide with the communist/socialist/totalitarian plans of Brzezinski and his co-conspirators.

But first; note: Hillary did her college thesis on Alinsky's writings with his personal assistance, and when Bill became President this thesis was removed from public access.

Why? We can only guess since Hillary has been described as a "*leftist*" legal scholar whose first law internship was with an Oakland, CA law firm that supported "radical causes," including the Black Panthers, and whose two partners were communists.

Obama also writes about him in his book, likely in addition to sympathy with his "*Counter* [American] *Culture*" ideas, because he was also the founder of "community organizing," which he began in Chicago where Obama engaged in the same under his guidelines that also influenced his 2008 Presidential campaign.

Many argue about "*conspiracy theory*"... mostly those in, or in support of "*the Establishment*"... to endeavor to disavow or disprove what those with minds unobstructed by indoctrination or an inability to connect the dots can easily "see."

For there to be an actual "*conspiracy*" only two people must conspire, i.e., combine for evil purposes, to plot, or devise.

There is no evidence Hillary and Obama conspired to do what was in both their minds fifteen years apart. But implementing the same "health insurance" program near the beginning of their tenures in the white House should cause recognition of the high priority both gave this action for which the idea to do the same thing at the same relative time came from somewhere.

Given the two people both Hillary and Obama had a connection with, or for whose ideas both have stated admiration are Brzezinski and Alinsky, that both were influenced by these two in their actions to hasten creation of a "*socialist state*" in America fifteen years apart has a high degree of probability.

1) Healthcare. Go back to shortly after the Clintons were in the White House. Hillary secretly developed a "healthcare" plan "to control the people" via cards that had to be presented to receive healthcare. These cards were geographically limited. There was also much more in the plan that caused it to be rejected at that time.

Now, flip forward a decade and a half, after further dumbing down of, and lying to, the people, as well as Congress, the installation of a Bush "*Establishment*" Supreme Court Justice who was willing to ignore the Constitution and bend the law, and *voilà;* the Affordable Care Act... that was not "affordable."

Surely anyone who was an adult in 1993 could recognize the similarity of the two plans and connect the dots between these two and their mutual mentors.

2) Poverty. 2008 to 2016; fewer jobs, millions more unemployed, lower pay and household income, more citizens on food stamps, interest rates so low people could not get any income on their savings, need we say more?

3) Debt. Obama almost doubled Government debt, increasing it ten trillion dollars to an amount in excess of the *faux* national Gross

Domestic Product, an amount unequaled by all Presidents during the 220 plus years prior to him.

4) Gun Control. Democrats, especially Hillary and Obama, have consistently campaigned against citizens owning guns, i.e., against the Second Amendment.

5) Welfare. This has been greatly expanded under all Democrats since Lyndon Johnson's *"Great Society"* in 1965 that also satisfied numbers 2) and 3) by tremendously increasing debt.

6) Education. This has been deliberately, greatly denigrated in the decades since Jimmy Carter formed the Department of Education. It has been changed from educating to indoctrinating by "teaching" what to think and eliminating history, the language and geography so the people will lose their culture, and not be able to recognize what their Government is doing to them. Check out the *"common core"* of public education.

7) Religion. Everyone is aware it has been under attack by Democrats for years.

8) Class Warfare. This has been a major program of *"the Establishment"* through its *"divide and conquer"* program for at least forty years as of 2018.

All this destruction is the result of actions by Johnson, Carter, Clinton the Bushes and Obama following the ideas of *"the Establishment"* represented by Brzezinski, and others like Alinsky advocating implementation of socialist/communist programs destructive to America and its people.

Now, three questions: a) does anyone doubt the America they have known and loved has been deliberately destroyed by members of *"the Establishment,"* Jimmy Carter, the Clintons, Bushes, Barrack Obama, Brzezinski, Rockefeller and scores of other members, b) how was this destruction accomplished, and c) how could anyone other than one of Stalin's *"Useful Idiots"* vote to install anyone else as President who is desirous of continuing and even expanding this destruction of converting a freedom providing and prosperous America to what will eventually become a totalitarian *"Socialist"* police state?

The answer to a) is hopefully *"no"* because *"yes"* equals *"Useful Idiot,"* and it would mean America is done for, and c) provides its own answer. So, let's look at b).

A booklet entitled <u>Members of the Club</u> published several years before this is being written disclosed many companies and individuals who were at one time members of *"the Establishment"* organization created by Rockefeller and Brzezinski in 1973. Here is a partial list of companies it shows either have, or have had, senior members of management represented among the membership:

General Electric Corporation (which owns NBC, CNBC and MSNBC), *US NEWS AND WORLD REPORT,* CNN, *WASHINGTON POST, NEW YORK TIMES,* Time Warner Corporation, Xerox, Archer Daniels Midland, PepsiCo, Molson Companies, Goldman Sachs, RJR Nabisco, TRW, American International (AIG), Levi Strauss Company, Corning, S.C. Johnson, Coca Cola, Exxon Mobil, General Motors, Smith Kline Beecham, Nissan, NEC, Sony Corporation, Toshiba, IBM, Toyota, Ford, Chase Manhattan Bank and Citibank.

Additionally, here are some individuals it states who have been members you might recognize: George H.W. Bush, Alan Greenspan, Lawrence Eagleburger, Walter Mondale, Tom Ridge, Bill Clinton, Charles Rangel, John Danforth, John Chafee, Strobe Talbot, Casper Weinberger, Alan Simpson, Diane Feinstein, Donna Shalala, William Cohen, Charles Robb, George Schultz, Brent Scowcroft, Andrew Young, and Paul Volker.

Given this list includes large media, pharmaceutical, auto, personal products, energy, technology, banks and other companies, as well as Presidents, their senior staff and cabinet members, senators, chairman of the Federal Reserve and other highly influential people, question b) "how was this destruction accomplished" should be answered. But that is not the end of it.

In early fall of 2016 Wolf Blitzer on CNN was citing some of the names who are Republicans saying they would be voting for Hillary Clinton to endeavor to discredit Trump's Presidential bid without pointing out, as he obviously knew, they were doing this because they are members of the same club as the Clintons, Bushes and others whose *New World Order* continuing destruction of America for personal wealth and power could possibly be stopped by Trump.

The next day, September 20th, it was announced Trump was about even with Hillary for electoral votes. Also, while showing a photo of the enfeebled ex-President, long time member of *"the Establishment"* Trilateral club, C.I.A. and several America destroying activities it was announced George H. W. Bush would be voting for Hillary. What, a *"conservative"* Republican?

The fact of all these prominent Republicans voting for Hillary rather than Trump was an effort to further lessen Trump's chances because all these characters were aware they and their controlled media had been successful in depriving Americans of knowledge of the Trilateral Commission one party organization they were all members of and beholding to, rather than their Democrat and Republican veneer party affiliations.

***

For half a century, U.S. Government policies have been guided by *"the Establishment"* because of the highly placed officials, including all U.S. Presidents since Carter, except Ronald Reagan, who have either been members, or appointed by members.

The U.S. job destroying, *"free trade"* treaties like NAFTA, the American culture destroying immigration policies, billions of dollars to Mexico and Africa, and appeasement of Arab regimes regarding the Arab/Israeli conflict are all a result of *"the Establishment," New World Order* influences within the U.S. Government.

Like most of these actions and agreements, the Trans Pacific Partnership, being promoted by Obama, and Hillary "waffled" on, continuing potential damage to America, its people and economy until Trump became President. Ditto the Paris Climate Accord.

Both were like other "trade" agreements *"the Establishment"* entered to enhance global corporation's finances, and those of other countries to the detriment of America.

Both were just more *New World Order "globalization"* trade deals that, like the WTO, World Trade Organization, agreements and NAFTA, were designed to disadvantage Americans by setting rules to further enhance the coffers of multinational corporations, *"trampling democracy, national sovereignty and the public good."*

As Donald Trump accurately states, *"It is a rigged system!"* that has adversely affected Americans as Ross Perot pointed out over two decades ago: *"In the 1960s, our standard of living doubled every generation and a half. At our present low growth rate, it will take twelve generations for our standard of living to double."*

Almost everything has gotten worse since the *1960s*.

As of 2018 in the intervening years since JFK's death the United States has been at war unnecessarily, on a preemptive basis for twenty-five years, almost fifty percent of the time, in countries that posed no threat to the security of the United States.

The U.S. military has been greatly expanded into occupations in more than one hundred and twenty countries. The "defense" industry has experienced phenomenal growth, as has the wealth of those involved in it.

The Government has greatly expanded control over the population, especially since Bush II began deemphasizing the title of Chief Executive Officer of the United States... a position that desperately needed to be competently filled... favoring Commander-in-Chief of the United States Military... clearly demonstrating the misplaced priorities of *"the Establishment"* Barrack Obama studiously followed... nay, greatly expanded, as would Hillary had she been elected the next President.

One of those priorities is taking as much money as possible from every productive citizen to continue to fund the out of control Government that is a failed financial basket case, generating only half the revenues it needs from the economy, especially the Commander-in-Chief's preemptive military being utilized in pursuit of world hegemony, as proven by the collection arm of the Government, the I.R.S., especially since Obama and his *"Affordable Care Act,"* aka Obama care lightened the pockets of each average American family annually by thousands and small businesses to the point of extinction caused recently by *"the Establishment"* membership incompetence of Barrack Obama.

***

America could not have withstood another four or eight years of an *"Establishment"* President. That would likely have been the absolute end of America as we know it.

No matter what anyone thinks about Donald Trump, <u>he was the only non-"Establishment" choice</u>, even if he were not the competent international businessman at the right time in America's history.

He does NOT represent *"the Establishment"* represented by Hillary and Obama, and even Republicans like all the Bushes, Mitt Romney, and others who refused to support him, and even campaigned against him, like William Kristol who "showed his stripes" by endeavoring to get a third-party candidate to run against him for the purpose of ensuring Hillary would be elected.

All these *"Establishment"* member, phony, veneer "Republicans" showed where their loyalty lies through these actions. They and the rest of their "Republican" ilk would have much preferred the *status quo* destruction course for America represented by Hillary because they have been beneficiaries of it for forty-five years.

The United States of America, Reagan's beacon of freedom and prosperity, has been dragged down and into the gutter among the worst states the world has ever known by these people... the states so many Americans died to bring about a cessation of their evil.

Evil that has been replicated in the United States of America for over four decades as of 2018 by Zbigniew Brzezinski, his acolytes Jimmy Carter and Barrack Obama, both Bushes, both Clintons and multitudes of NWO whores in politics, the media and corporate America who have placed their desire for personal power and wealth above their country, its people and their future!

Everyone must recognize President Trump is theirs and America's last hope for its resurrection, and their freedom and prosperity as it was before Zbigniew Brzezinski with Rockefeller money and influence literally got control of the tiller of the U.S. ship of state and began guiding it onto the rocks of destruction of his *"New World Order."*

Therefore, it is mandatory President Trump and his team of saviors have eight years to do all in their power to *"Make* [and keep] *America Great Again"* because if any more *NWO* whores like Carter, the Bushes, Clintons or Obama become President you can be certain they will quickly redirect American onto its previous course to destruction.

There is too much money at stake, and they have a solid foundation of support of their kind in Germany, France, the U.K., Canada, Mexico, the E.U. in Belgium and others wherein the "leadership" have benefited greatly from Brzezinski's *"New International Economic Order,"* as well as the World Trade Organization, Paris Climate Accord, NAFTA and other anti-American organizations.

Also, let's not forget the American media where *NWO* members and operatives like Diane Feinstein, David Gergen and many others are constantly given a platform to lie and attack Trump on behalf of the *NWO* without their real affiliation or membership being revealed. Then there is even FOX that never reveals the reality of what has been adversely affecting all of us for decades that could be stopped if the people were informed.

So, it is entirely up to us Americans to protect ourselves and save our country. The only way we can do this is to be informed and seriously vet anyone seeking any position of power and authority before voting for them.

CHAPTER SEVEN
TRADE

DELIBERATELY INCREASING CORPORATE PROFITS AT THE EXPENSE OF AMERICA'S MIDDLE CLASS IN A WAY THE FUTURE OF ITS ECONOMY WOULD BE ADVERSELY AFFECTED

When Brzezinski and Rockefeller founded their *New World Order* organization in July 1973 that would soon thereafter become the breeding ground for the population of *"the Establishment"* we had in 2018 and for over forty years prior they knew what they were doing. They had their **"Business Plan for America"** previously presented in Chapter Five of which at least three parts had been in effect since Lyndon Johnson.

***

Rockefeller was fifty-eight, attended Harvard and the London School of Economics with John Kennedy, was already the head of one of the biggest banks in the world, Chase Manhattan Bank, in 2018 J.P. Morgan Chase, that did business with other big banks worldwide, big oil and others, and was heavily involved in international trade which enabled him to count among his friends, leaders of big businesses around the world.

He was also an "insider" with the CIA, and already expressed his support for a *"one world,"* in a way that connotes one world government or political establishment, that could be interpreted as his not placing the good or wellbeing of the U.S. foremost. Incidentally, he also visited China in 1973.

Brzezinski was forty-five, a descendent of Polish nobility from part of that country that is now the Ukraine. He also attended Harvard where, as stated before, he received his Doctorate. But previously spent his pre-pubescent youth in Hitler Germany, Russia and Canada where he grew up before coming to the U.S.

As previously addressed; he was responsible for Carter being President and all the damage to America's education system by changing it to indoctrination, and disruption of the country's internal harmony through immigration Carter wrought. But prior to that he was an advisor to both Presidents Kennedy and Johnson... where a decade before the damage he did to America through Carter, Johnson's tremendously destructive *"Great Society"* had his fingerprints all over it.

Rockefeller classified himself a Republican, although seemingly a very moderate one. Brzezinski was a Democrat. No question.

These credentials provided both with sufficient credibility to claim their new organization was "*bipartisan*," which it definitively was and continues to be, as demonstrated by the bilateral... or some might say bilabial given what it has done to language in America... makeup of its actual one party, *faux* "two party" sham we have in American politics since implementation of their plans.

Their **"Business Plan for America"** took this into account because it was necessary for them to appeal to both veneers of their "*Establishment*" organization to be able to accumulate the money and power they desired and needed for their plan to be successful. They knew money was the key to the power their plan was all about...as it always is.

After formalizing "*the Establishment*" organization, a broad based "trade" plan both had to know was bad for the American economy was set into motion to get as much more money as possible into corporate coffers. And they knew where the money was, and how to generate it.

***

In 1973... before Brzezinski and Rockefeller... the U.S. was still the largest, richest and most powerful business and industrial economy in the world. It was still a net exporter of oil. Also, China's internal conflict that began with Mao's Communist Revolution in the early 1920s ended with Mao's success in 1947, a quarter century prior to 1973.

In the next quarter century ended, conveniently, just before Rockefeller and Brzezinski's "business" venture began, China had begun to put its billion, plus population back to work, and was producing and exporting on a massive, wealth creating scale consistent with the country's prior history of almost two millennia.

This was the key to their plan. And as is oft said, "*Timing is everything.*"

The decades long prohibition on trading with communist China, a defined enemy of "*the Establishment,*" was lifted by the U.S. in April 1971, two years prior, but the U.S. ostensibly still did not have diplomatic relations with the country, which posed a limitation on what big business corporations were willing to do there.

The British colony of Hong Kong was different. It was a longtime bustling hub of business activity, much of it with the U.S.

On its Victoria Island there was much wealth on display. In the Kowloon part of the colony that was on the Chinese mainland there were massive port facilities.

What was the real source of all this activity and wealth?

Short answer: China. Long answer: a combination of British organization, unfettered capitalism, the long ostensible aversion of

U.S. "*Establishment*" hypocrites to anything communist, and China. But without China the other three would have been meaningless.

To demonstrate this there were many examples of suppliers of such items as furniture, housewares, electronics and other items widely used in the U.S. located on the island in high rise, predominately office buildings in a highly congested, densely populated area where space was very expensive.

There were also many in Kowloon where one would expect to find manufacturing facilities, but some of them desired to be in the commercial area on the island, rather than the industrial area, and they could afford it

These usually had a small office and one other room in one of the multistory office buildings. The office was not huge or fancy. It was just adequate and comfortable for conducting the business of selling to one or two people at a time. In the other room would usually be no more than four Chinese working, producing one or two of the items the supplier was selling.

How could businesses like this with such small production afford the space?

Answer: the fact is; hardly anything was made or manufactured in Hong Kong except the red and blue Union Jack "*Made in Hong Kong*" labels and tags the guys in the small "production" rooms were producing when customers were not visiting, and thousands of other workers were engaged in placing on all the merchandise headed for the U.S. as they unloaded it from trucks that brought it from communist China before putting it into the shipping containers in Kowloon that were headed to the United States.

Hong Kong's business was never manufacturing. It has always been a financial and distribution center. Its wealth and manmade physical awesomeness were entirely attributable to it being the major distribution point for products manufactured by a billion Chinese workers.

Everything in stores, and everywhere else in the U.S. sporting "*Made in Hong Kong,*" red, white and blue British Union Jack labels and U.S required "*Made In*" stickers and printing on packages was made in mainland China by Chinese communist workers.

This was well known by most of the hypocrites in the U.S. Government "Establishment," especially David Rockefeller who visited China, and probably Hong Kong in 1973… if he was required to go through there to get to the mainland as ordinary Americans and business people were required to.

They were aware of the enormous labeling operation named "Hong Kong," and that they had no ability to do anything about it through U.S. businesses because they were buying from vendors in

Hong Kong representing their merchandise was made there.

But stopping this was not what *"the Establishment"* U.S. Government, corporations and financial institutions, Rockefeller or Brzezinski, were interested in doing.

They were seriously pursuing legitimizing, maximizing and participating in the enormous profits of Chinese manufacturing for years before this time, but they recently turned on the afterburners in this effort, and were in the process of accomplishing it.

In April 1971, two years prior, the U.S. ceased its blockade of China and ban on China trade after U.S. National Security Advisor, *"Establishment"* operator and years long Brzezinski Harvard associate, Henry Kissinger, paid China a visit. Then in October Taiwan was expelled from the United Nations and replaced by China. After the U.S. ping pong team was there in November, China was given a seat on the U.N. Security Council.

The "paving of the way" for the biggest negative impact on its economy by any government in world history was laid. Billions, eventually trillions, of dollars and millions of jobs of U.S. production were going to be moved to China to fatten profits of U.S. corporations to enhance their market capitalizations, thus lining the pockets of their executives and filling the coffers of lobbyists to affect U.S. politicians' decisions, unnecessarily, at the expense of American workers, the manufacturing based American Middle Class, U.S. productive capability, and ultimately its economy and wealth was *fait accompli,* as was *"the Establishment"* New World Order destruction of America.

The next task for Rockefeller and Brzezinski was to get U.S. Corporations to start the ball rolling in a big way to begin manufacturing in China where they were not burdened with U.S. Governmental regulations, unions, costs of construction of facilities, or, of course, U.S. high wages so they would have more cash flow and enhanced market capitalizations. But this did not take long.

The U.S. Liaison Office was opened in Peking in 1973. Then in August 1974 charter member of Brzezinski and Rockefeller's new organization, and longtime C.I.A. "made man," George H.W. Bush, was appointed Chief of the Office. The rest is, as is said, *"History."* And that *"History"* ain't pretty!

Since that time U.S. wages have stagnated, productive capacity utilization declined, as has the investment in plant and equipment, etc., etc. to the extent some have estimated fifty percent of the dollar value of shipments from China to the U.S. are attributable to American companies producing their products in China.

Corporate coffers have bulged as Rockefeller and Brzezinski planned, corporate executive compensation wherein CEOs were making eight or ten times their employees in the 1970s, are now paid hundreds of times the salaries of their employees, U.S. Government salaries are fifty to one hundred percent higher than those of employees in the real, productive economy, Congressional salaries are more than three times what they were in the 1970s, and… at the expense of American workers… American corporations are producing more and making more money from their interests in China than in the U.S.

Example; in 2016 General Motors produced more autos in China than in the U.S., and the Chinese are getting richer because they do not have their money taken away from them by their government to enable it to engage in foreign interventions, and other *New World Order,* unnecessary actions like those of the Bush Presidents, especially Bush II.

So, the Rockefeller/Brzezinski **"Business Plan for America"** was wildly successful for them and theirs. They got the money flowing where they desired, and what Ross Perot forecast in 1992 was a rosy scenario compared to the economic destruction they wrought.

The standard of living for average Americans has continued to decline, not improve, since 1974 as follows:

- 80% of wealth generated has gone to the top 2% of the population.
- 65% to the top 1%.
- Increase in real wages for salaried workers has only been 20% to 28%
- while real national Gross Domestic Product increased 110%, or over two times.
- After tax income of top 1% has increased 8x more than those in the next lower 60%
- and 10x more than those in the lower percentiles.
- Overwhelming amount of the wealth created for the last the two generations went to the top of the income pyramid
- while real net worth of 90% of Americans declined 25% between 2000 and 2012.
- And Americans have substantially less democracy than before *New World Order,* America destroying, One World Government, sovereign nationless world seeking, Harvard "academic" lacking common sense… like his also America destroying Harvard associate Kissinger, egghead Zbigniew Brzezinski began his campaign of destruction of the world's greatest nation.

None of this happened in other countries during this time, which is a clear indication it was entirely the result of Brzezinski initiated policies and associated actions of Carter, the Bushes, Clinton,

<u>Obama and other willfully America destroying *NWO* co-conspirators acting against the interests of their country and its people, such as:</u>

- Economic drain of immigration begun on a big scale by Carter, and his adverse effect on education that did irreparable damage to knowledge and abilities of the work force.
- Bill Clinton reforms of the 1990s permitting the big, TBTF banks "free rein" to trample American consumers, lax enforcement of rules and the massively destructive NAFTA.
- The unnecessary, massive debacles and trillions of dollars cost of the Bush wars.
- Obama attacks on oil and gas production, coal, energy pipelines and implementation of stiff, unnecessary regulations on others, land confiscations, and much more, including his giving blanket immunity for their criminality to big banks and financial institutions for money laundering for drug cartels, their fraud that caused the 2008 worldwide financial and economic meltdown, as well as to those that committed fraud in forging foreclosure documents on millions of innocent home owners that cost them dearly. All clearly demonstrating Barrack Obama was the financially and culturally most destructive President in America's history.

***

This legacy might be sufficient to cause many conscientious, thinking Americans to think of the adage *"they should be taken out back and shot,"* but not seriously consider this that is just one of those responses to terrible acts. Nor would it be a solution because of the massive numbers willing to take their places if they can replicate their personal financial gains.

However, failing that solution, all working, contributing Americans should strongly desire not to have any members of *"the Establishment"* that wrought all this destruction remain in charge of the U.S. Government or be elected to influence any part of it.

But there has been much more, especially from the Democrat veneer of the *faux* "two party" system. Some of it before the Rockefeller/Brzezinski organization was formalized.

This was likely largely a result of their constant drive, as demonstrated in 2018 by the arrogant Nancy Pelosi, to increase income tax revenues to "feed" their dependent base, rather than thinking about or even understanding the best way to accomplish these objectives is to enhance industry to increase Government tax revenue because that is just not the socialist way. Somehow, they manage to perpetually ignore, no matter whatever happens; the empirically proven destructive results of socialism versus the success of capitalism.

Meanwhile, as previously explained, it was these same Democrats who were responsible for the new emerging, dominant Japanese steel industry.

Even during the Democrat, Vietnam War in the 1960s under the Johnson Administration some U.S. "defense" production was moved to South Korea. That "some" was sufficient to provide a kick start to the Korean economy that resulted in it growing five hundred percent in just a few years, and creating massively competitive companies like huge POSCO Steel, which in addition to the Japanese is a reason Trump has endeavored to rebuild the U.S. steel industry.

Also, the $250 million the Johnson administration paid the South Korean Government to provide troops for the Vietnam War endeavor could have assisted.

Another example: in the 1960s and into the seventies the mostly Democrat controlled U.S. Government was also successful in destroying two more American industries.

As previously explained, they literally drove U.S. ocean surface shipping out of business by imposing government determined freight charges on all U.S. flag carriers carrying shipments to all U.S. ports, and they imposed union wages on U.S. flag vessels greater than those paid on foreign flag vessels.

These rules prohibited U.S. companies successfully competing in the worldwide market by those who style themselves champions of *"free trade."*

Thus, many years prior to 2018, U.S. shipping companies were gone along with thousands of jobs and billions of dollars of contribution to the U.S. economy.

Along with the U.S. shipping industry went the U.S commercial shipbuilding industry, and who knows how many jobs, as well as more billions of dollars of contribution lost to the economy?

South Korea further benefited from these U.S. Government actions by becoming one of the few major producers of large oceangoing freight and commodity transport vessels... no doubt aided greatly by their successful steel industry.

For four decades, thanks to the Brzezinski American versions of Stalin's *"Useful Idiots,"* many of the manufactured goods shipped to the U.S. from China, Japan, Korea, and elsewhere are shipped on vessels made in Korea of Korean, Chinese or Japanese steel, flying flags other than American and owned by foreign based companies.

Don't believe this? Go to any major American port and look at the names and flags on the ships and the containers they are carrying. Then try to envisage how many hundreds and hundreds of thousands of lost American jobs and trillions of dollars contribution to the U.S, economy all this represents.

It is impossible to begin to imagine how Americans could do this to their country and their countrymen. But facts are; they have. AND foreign born... which could explain his part in this... Zbigniew Brzezinski was personally responsible for greatly enhancing this destruction of America's economy for the forty years prior to 2018.

The important, obvious fact of this is: *"the Establishment"* whores in the U.S. Government are not friends of American citizens. They are, "first and foremost" as shown by their actions, One World Government, internationalist/Globalists of the ilk of David Rockefeller who, like he and Brzezinski, were willing to sacrifice the prosperity, lives and future of America on Bush I's stated *"New World Order"* altar of personal greed.

***

Here are some other egregious examples:

First, as previously briefly addressed, Bill Clinton oversaw the NAFTA moving to Mexico of manufacturing of vehicles, appliances and more that were doing fine in the U.S., providing profits for American corporations and continuing to enrich and enlarge a large part of the still growing, at the time of his "election," great American Middle Class.

Why would he do that... being the smart guy he is... when he knew it would adversely affect the entire U.S. economy, driving a big stake into the heart of the economic well-being of the manufacturing based American Middle Class, driver of a large part of the economy he was supposed to represent, as Ross Perot told everyone, including Bill, during the election campaign this is what would happen?

Well, we can only guess. But appearances indicate it was M-O-N-E-Y, pure and simple, because when he entered the White House financial disclosures indicated he and Hillary had a net worth of $250,000 to $400.000, even after Hillary's controversial conversion of $1,000 into $100,000 in ten months "trading" cattle futures.

In 2018 he and Hillary were reportedly worth over $50 million, if not much more if the strange Clinton Global Initiative that has received many tens of millions of dollars of contributions from many foreign regimes... for what unknown purpose... is included.

This by a couple holding no wealth producing positions other than engagements speaking to the heads contributing foreign regimes and members of the U.S. plutocracy for which they were paid hundreds of thousands of dollars for each speech.

Next, probably to the dismay of diehard, but self-imposed, ignorant Republicans, is little George W. Bush who would not have been President if not for his father who has a decades long history of serving no one, but "*the Establishment*" in each of the Offices he was given for that purpose.

It is not possible for anyone not to know the damage he did to America as President with the absolutely, unnecessary, strategic blunder, Iraq fiasco that has cost trillions of dollars to date and was a major transfer of wealth to "defense" industry members of "*the Establishment.*"

This also qualifies as one of the bad trade deals for Americans because of the bulk of these funds being spent outside the U.S., rewarding others - not Americans.

Also, no one could be so intellectually lacking as to not understand what he did, and why he did it for the sole benefit of "*the Establishment*" member agricultural company Archer Daniels Midland unless they are unaware of this action.

So, let's also ask why he is responsible for legislating converting corn, a worldwide basic food source, to energy, driving up its price, and adversely affecting hundreds of millions of people, when Brazilian sugar cane ethanol was at least fifty cents a gallon less expensive and would not have adversely affected anyone?

Further, let's ask why he oversaw creation of a new pharmaceutical Part D Medicare in which he specifically excluded pharmaceutical prices from being negotiated on behalf of millions of elderly Americans paying for them, thus enhancing pharmaceutical companies' ability to greatly increase profits by taking more money from the pockets of these older Americans in need of those drugs whose interests he was supposed to be representing, as well as also further, greatly enhancing profits of insurance companies?

Should anyone doubt he did this they should look at the billions of dollars pharmaceutical companies spend on TV advertising for prescription drugs since, including those made by foreign companies, and the multi-million dollar a year position and benefits package the Louisiana congressman who pushed this through Congress for Bush received in his new position as head of the pharmaceutical Congressional lobbying group he resigned from Congress to take immediately after passage of this legislation.

Also, some might wonder if they were aware of it: why did the head of the Harvard University Endowment who was a friend of George H.W. Bush authorize, in the late 1980s, the largest ever, before that time, single investment by the endowment in the failing oil company where George W. Bush was on the board?

Possibly because shortly thereafter, before he became Governor of Texas, shrub George received millions of dollars for his stock.

M-O-N-E-Y! *"The Establishment"* greed, corruption and destruction will go on and on until there is nothing left unless it is stopped by a non-*"Establishment"* President like Trump and his Administration.

As the esteemed Harvard Business School Professor, now Emeritus, stated to his class in spring of 1969, and Donald Trump has demonstrated he among few understands;

> *"The economy that does not produce the things it consumes and uses will not survive."*

But of the "few" who do understand this we can count *"the Establishment"* whores who initiated shipping U.S. capital and manufacturing of American global corporations to China, Mexico and elsewhere to increase profit margins, and at the same time eliminated or substantially minimized U.S. import duties on these foreign manufactured U.S. company products.

Thus, it is an established fact: neither China nor anyone else is responsible for *"stealing"* American production or jobs and destroying the American Middle Class.

This can be laid squarely at the feet of puppet, willfully complicit American Presidents Clinton, Bush I and II, Obama, Congress and their constituents in Corporate America, and on Wall Street who following the Brzezinski Business Plan for America deliberately did this to Americans and have been lying to us about it for decades.

No one other than these people is responsible for the economic destruction they have wreaked on America!

So, God help Trump clean out this America destroying swamp!

CHAPTER EIGHT
EDUCATION

TAKING CONTROL OF WHAT PEOPLE READ AND LISTEN TO AND WHAT CHILDREN LEARN IN SCHOOL TO CONTROL KNOWLEDGE

"A nation that forgets its past has no future"
- Winston Churchill

Before 1973, thinking was not a threat to the Government. It was still encouraged in education system classrooms. But 1973 was the year the evil that has been creeping toward total control of America since the time of Kennedy's assassination was formalized, and unfortunately for America, knew "education" was the key to the long-term success of their desired *"placidly governable,"* indoctrinated population.

The founder of that "evil," along with David Rockefeller of *"too much democracy,"* was again; Zbigniew Brzezinski who wrote in his 1970 book about the desirability of *"the gradual appearance of a more controlled society... dominated by an elite unrestrained by traditional values"* that could exploit *"the latest techniques to manipulate emotions and control reason"* of individuals who are *"citizens"* of America and presumably everywhere else given his stated desires for a one world government.

Now everyone reading this should understand this evil man was advocating Americans have more Government control in their lives, and that *"control"* to which we should be subservient to is a small effete *"elite"* group of his making or liking that would be *"unrestrained"* by traditional American religious and moral values, and would have the legal right to *"manipulate"* our *"emotions,"* AND imbue us with whatever values they desire to cause us accept whatever they do or tell us is *"reason"*able.

It is impossible to differentiate this man's ideas and desires from those of the most-evil men in the 20th Century among whose names he should also be listed. They are an exact restatement of what Hitler and Stalin created in Germany and Russia and Mao in China.

They are the ideas of the totalitarian communists and fascists rightly vilified by numerous American "leaders" and the U.S. media that, if it were not also in 2018 an exact replication of Hitler and Stalin's media, would be supporting President Trump, rather than endeavoring to get him out of office because he is the only one trying to salvage what is left of America after the protégés of this man, Carter, the Clintons, Bushes and Obama, spent the last forty years assiduously endeavoring to turn America into exactly what he stated above... a program for the destruction of America Hillary Clinton believed in and if elected President would have assiduously pursued to our very end.

If the four preceding paragraphs are insufficient to cause great concern the following should awaken some fear, actually "scare the living hell" out of you.

Polish Zbigniew Brzezinski and German Henry Kissinger both of whom spent their formative years and received their first years of formal education during the pre-WWII years in those countries were at Harvard University in their twenties in the 1950s pursuing their doctorates and doing work for the U.S. Government - Brzezinski in totalitarianism and Kissinger in mind and *"emotions"* control.

Since then these two men, co-conspirators in every way, were the two most active and influential non-elected officials in the entire U.S. Government with the full support of some of the wealthiest people in the country, and the, stated from their own mouths, adulation of the two Presidents responsible for the most damage to the ideals, education, economy, foreign relations, freedom, international relations, and future of every living American as well as those not yet born.

Both Brzezinski puppets Carter and Obama made statements of adulation of him, and the Clintons who attended Trilateral and Bilderberg meetings with him and Kissinger for years implemented and expanded his trade economic destruction while proven, communist Hillary followed his guidance in everything she did.

But referring to Brzezinski's desire to *"manipulate emotions"* we cannot avoid considering the possibilities of the results of his Harvard relationship with Kissinger while he was deeply involved with the Government in mind control there.

Seems to inquiring minds the two cannot be disassociated, especially given time spent and proximity of them to one another at what has been for years... since the development of Napalm there in WWII, as well as its graduates and Professors involvement in that and Vietnam, like McNamara and many other unsavory ones highly placed in the U.S. Government, their destructive influence on education and so much more, as well as the words and actions of its Presidents and the Presidents "educated" there over the decades... the epicenter of the destruction of America.

Now consider for a moment the stated desires of Alinsky and Brzezinski, the totalitarian need to disarm any potential opposition, the oblique commentary in this regard of many in *"the Establishment,"* including Hillary Clinton, leaving no doubt there is a long running and building desire/plan to relieve Americans of their Second Amendment right to bear arms.

Then consider the above while questioning the growing spate of school shootings that "kicked off" during the first Clinton term, and with each such event the clamor to relieve us of the ability to protect ourselves from a totalitarian takeover of our country. Exactly for what purpose and what kind of "mind control" was Henry Kissinger involved in with or for the Government sixty years ago?

We should also consider the "outsider" Trump hating FBI failures to stop school shootings for which it had prior notification more than once just like its conduct and connections with Nine Eleven, the Pulse Night Club and Garland, Texas shootings. Is there a pattern here? We might know if the "Justice" Department ceased withholding evidence.

But if anyone chooses not to see a pattern here, possibly he or she might be able to ferret out some sort of pattern in F.B.I. actions to prevent Trump attaining the Presidency with the additional knowledge this Agency had a mole in the Trump campaign, but highly likely not in the Clinton campaign, and at least five of its top employees were actively anti-Trump.

When so many facts and knowledge lead to one place and one agency with the obvious results on the minds of the people, intelligent minds should want to know what for, why, or for what purpose by whom, and who are the beneficiaries of all this?

Also, did a first or second year Harvard dropout who supposedly conceived and developed Face Book with a couple of other students, engage in endeavoring to *"manipulate emotions"* for U.S. Government research, not unlike Kissinger fifty years prior, for any reasons other than nefarious ones associated with Brzezinski's objectives? Did he also engage as well in censoring conservative thoughts or commentary opposed to what Brzezinski, Kissinger and their acolytes have been doing to America for almost a half century for any other than the same reasons? O.K. why?

"The task of the leader is to get his people from where they are to where they have not been." - Henry Kissinger

Is this quote an oblique reference to him and others, as "leaders," getting the American people from their freedom loving of democracy and what America is to acceptance of the totalitarianism under their control he, Brzezinski and the rest of the America destroyers desire to take us? Think not? How about this?

"Power is the ultimate aphrodisiac." - Henry Kissinger

O.K. No further questions.

But do not forget Brzezinski is the principal architect of the Orwellian Totalitarian state desired by *"the Establishment"* rapidly developing since the beginning of the Twenty First Century, a willful unmitigated proactive proponent of the destruction of personal freedom, individualism and free will of humans who are to be completely subjugated to the will of despots who control everything in America and the rest of the world... and also willing to reward him for his assistance in the destruction of advances of mankind since the Magna Carta in the year 1215.

***

It was not an accident Brzezinski was chosen National Security Advisor to President Carter, this "evil's" first puppet President and ostensible creator of the Department of "Education," elected entirely through the understanding by Brzezinski of the importance of religion in all cultures, including the Christian culture, especially in the United States.

After using religion on the unsuspecting electorate to get into office, Carter acted quickly under the direction of his puppet master, Brzezinski who was responsible for his being President, to eliminate what they perceived the biggest threat to their ability to take and keep control of the country's economic and military power.

The planned "educational" destruction of knowledge, free thought and the ability to reason promulgated by Brzezinski through his advocated *"controlled society"* was immediately instigated under the direction of this "evil" as "National Security Advisor," thereby providing to us the knowledge of what *"the Establishment"* members in the U.S. Government and media really mean when they refer to *"national security"* It is their security they refer to, not that of the nation or people of America.

The act of Carter putting "education" of American youth under Federal Government control, removing the local influence of those most interested in ensuring they be as well educated as possible to succeed in life, placed their minds under control of those whose only concern is that Americans are not a threat to *"the Establishment,"* but to the extent possible, an extension of it, was the death knell for upward mobility and the future of a free and prosperous America.

Since that time those in control of the Federal Government have been in absolute control of the "education"/indoctrination of American youth.

Given the importance of this topic, if not **THE most important topic of this book,** it is appropriate to explore and expand on this subject that provided the foundation of America's 20th Century success and is at the root of the difference in the life of someone born in 1940, versus the lives of those born post 1960.

The following on this subject was published, in part, in 2003 in *Connecting the Dots of American Politics.*

"Placid governability"

"In America 2018 education is a misnomer. Indoctrination is closer to the truth, just as it was in Mao's People's Republic of China.

"American children, stuck in Government schools, and even in the universities, are being indoctrinated, much more than they are being educated.

"The *'Placid governability'* concept of the first President Bush's *"New World Order"* is preferable to true democracy for Americans, and David Rockefeller's *"excess of democracy"* comment connoting the *New World Order* disdain for democracy required the rectification of the *"excess"* if the *New World Order* "brains" were to achieve their greedy objectives.

"What better way to do this than to emulate someone who was wildly successful in changing the direction of an entire country of one billion plus people, and who developed a method of controlling those masses by gaining control of the minds of all of the young people in the country who would eventually be the majority?

"To emulate Mao's success required gaining control of the means of indoctrination, the public-school system, and converting it into the U.S. Government system. But to gain control of such a large system required personnel in the form of many already inculcated with the ideas desired to infuse the young minds of America with. This meant universities producing those who would be "teachers" of young American minds would be the place to start.

"The 1993 edition of *Members of the Club* listed eight influential, universities with deans, professors, presidents, honorary fellows, or chancellors as members.

"Some of the prominent persons it showed associated with these universities, who might be recognizable were, in addition to Zbigniew Brzezinski; John Deutch, Harold Brown, George Schultz and Paul Volcker.

"With these highly placed people, who have also held senior Government positions, in such esteemed institutions of higher learning, "*the Establishment*" had more than its foot in the door of America's "education" system.

"Also, the White House, having been occupied by members for all but eight of the last forty years [excepting Reagan], and the President being the one who appoints the Secretary of Education has likely resulted in influence of note on the "education" system.

"The members who have been in both houses of Congress, including ex-Speaker Thomas, had a hand in furthering destruction of the "education" program and have had control of Government "education" money that is never distributed without "strings."

"Members of "*liberal*" influential "think" tanks, like Brookings Institution, have conveyed their message throughout Government, the media, and have had a strong influence in academia.

"Lastly, but not the least influential person who has been a member and would have helped cast a very long shadow over those indoctrinating the young minds of America was Albert Shanker, President of the American Federation of Teachers in the 1990s.

"Has "*the Establishment,*" through all of this influence, been successful in replicating Mao's China success in America?

"An important Insight magazine article documents how U.S. public schools continue to develop as a tool for the left-wing to condition American school children to accept dependence and servitude...Yes, the cultural Marxists have a plan for America...poorer families have no choice but to accept whatever is handed out by the failed public school system...a huge new generation of docile, ignorant adults will emerge-much to the detriment of liberty in the United States. Even on U.S. university campuses, many administrations now require students to herd themselves into designated 'free-speech' zones before they are allowed to talk without restrictions on content."
-The American Sentinel, April 2002

In 2018 we have already seen the results of this education denigration, but "According to Ann Coulter, writing in HUMAN EVENTS, June 18, 2001, *'It is simply taken for granted that it's desirable for children to revere 'authority figures' at government schools...Children must be taught to love Big Brother, welcoming him to take over our schools, our bank accounts, our property...'*

"How could this have happened in America, 'land of the free and the brave,' the country that has been a bastion of capitalism and democracy; that has provided a beacon for those desiring to experience the liberty and democracy it has offered for over two hundred years?

"Schools Training Cultural Soldiers, Not Teachers"

"Imagine Dan Rather is your son's history teacher, Barbra Streisand teaches your daughter's English class, and Jane Fonda serves as the school's guidance counselor. Yes, it really is that bad.
- Robert Ortiz, Ed. M., Harvard University 2001.

"Mr. Ortiz, 2001 graduate of Harvard Graduate School of Education can provide, as well as anyone, real knowledge of how successful those desiring to destroy America's Capitalistic Western democracy through the Government indoctrination system have become. Writing in *HUMAN EVENTS*, in June 2001, he continued:

"As conservatives endeavor to reform public education they will face stiff opposition from the very people with whom they entrust their policies -- and their children. Perched well to the left of American society, the nation's graduate schools of education have produced an educational establishment that considers itself to be on the front lines of the culture wars. Conservatives cannot afford to ignore the radical ideology and activist intentions of teacher education programs...Education schools not only lean radically leftward, but also equip their graduates to promote the liberal creed in American schools and classrooms... The academic course at HGSE resembles a casual luncheon with Ralph Neas and Martin Sheen. As Election Day neared last November, numerous classmates and even teaching fellows implored me to 'Pray that Gore wins!'...In my spring semester courses, students and faculty denounced conservatives easily and often as either stupid or dangerous or both...resplendent in its righteousness, HGSE (Harvard Graduate School of Education) precludes thoughtful debate by summarily excluding conservative views. Students regularly brand opponents of bilingual education as racists...the absence of conflicting viewpoints...encourages students and staff to believe that liberalism represents the only reasonable vision of a just society...defines itself through opposition to concepts of Euro-centrism, competition, patriarchy, and heterosexism. Courses rest on foundational assumptions that racism is rampant and gender is socially constructed, and prospective teachers debate the best way to teach adolescents these fundamental truths...Students and staff generally cite the under-representation and misunderstanding of minority experiences as the fundamental problem of American education...From this philosophy emerges a radical egalitarianism that values personal experience and cultural affirmation over skill acquisition and content knowledge...Dialects like Ebonics are not wrong; they illustrate the oppressiveness of a 'hidden curriculum.'...standardized evaluation, and reward systems are all rejected out of hand because they are believed to reinforce society's racist, sexist, and capitalist structures...the centerpiece of HGSE's annual student research conference was a panel discussion that seriously asked, 'Cuban Education: Our Role Model?"

"Mr. Ortiz experienced a speech at the HGSE, on the role of arts in education, by Bill Ivy, the Clinton-appointed chairman of the National Endowment for the Arts, in which Mr. Ivy said, the <u>arts *"are more important than reading and math* ....</u> *I believe in the message, and I will use any weapon in the arsenal."*

"This comment from the head of the Government agency responsible for fostering the arts in America, appointed by President Clinton, member of *"the Establishment,"* is right out of the communist handbook.

"There is in fact no such thing as art for art's sake"
- Mao Tse-Tung

"With the chairman of the National Endowment for the Arts spouting Maoist philosophy for education of American children and the Harvard Graduate School of Education promoting the Cuban Communist "education" system that is also right out of Communist Mao's handbook, anyone attempting to determine the future of America should not have to look any deeper into the Government system for indoctrinating the children of America to understand the true nature of America's "schools."

"Every concerned American should very seriously consider Mr. Ortiz' final cautions regarding American classrooms and teacher training; teachers *"...so casually link conservatism to such undeniable evils as racism and the Holocaust."* And, *"Education schools are not teaching teachers to teach; they are training cultural soldiers. With an estimated 2-3 million teaching* [jobs created in the first decade of the 21st Century] *conservatives must either take teacher education seriously or, for the foreseeable future, concede our classrooms to activist liberalism."*

"There is no doubt *"activist liberalism"* is a euphemism for anti-capitalism, anti-Western and American culture, pro-Socialist indoctrination *"The Establishment"* is bringing American education down in flames along with everything else, and every concerned American should be yelling, *"FIRE!"*

"Ignoring schools turning out *"cultural soldiers,"* one has to look no further than U.S. Presidents since 1974 to see the effectiveness of *New World Order* Socialist training programs.

"Leftist" Clinton *"loathed"* the military. Bush II had a proletarian manner of speech to belie to the American masses his real, North East, so-called *"elite"* background. Both are products of Yale at a time programs advancing the *New World Order* were just getting off the ground there.

"These two Presidents unmistakably advanced this same political agenda on both domestic and international fronts. Most Americans are either confused or lulled into complacency by Bush being a veneer Republican. But, make no mistake about it; he accomplished much of the agenda Clinton could not because he was a Democrat."

As did Barack Obama because he, as well as the first Bush, the second one and Clinton all danced to the pulling of their strings by the same anti-American... the "America" in which many of us grew up... puppet masters who control and enrich them and themselves at the expense of the American people, and would have continued to do so if not for the election of "outsider" President Trump who is adamantly opposed to the One World Government *New World Order* that is approaching the beginning of its fifth decade of screwing up America and the entire world.

***

On that note, it is important to point out the fact of no perceptible difference in the method utilized, and in effect, between *"leftists," "liberals," "Communists," "Fascists," "Marxists,"* and *"the Establishment" faux* "two party" political machine in control of America through its two branches of veneer "Democrats" and "Republicans."

So, no one should get "hung up" on the references to "Marxism" and *"Liberalism"* in the foregoing. It is only important to understand all the above are only slightly variant political concepts utilized to empower those in government at the expense of the masses, including the two superficial veneer American political parties that are nothing more than contrivances to cause members of the electorate to think they have a choice where there really is none.

Little do they know as followers of each, they are merely being stupefied into believing there is a difference while both parties do nothing but serve *"the Establishment"* destructive powers behind and in the U.S. Government, represented by the faces of Hillary and Bill Clinton, the Bushes, Obama and so many more, including CNN and network TV "talking heads" trotted out daily to lie to them.

They have no idea they are fallen victim to one of the oldest power grab concepts in history: ***"Divide and Conquer."***

All the political concepts stated above, even if not originally intended as such, due to the insatiable desire for power of the nature of those who seek government as their refuge, eventually evolve as totalitarian political concepts whose adherents abhor free thinking and free speech. Thus, indoctrination into their "thinking" is their foundation for control, as we have been witnessing on college campuses since Donald Trump came on the scene.

The ultimate objective and consequences of all these forms of political thought is elimination of free thought and speech and implementation of totalitarianism that is not unique to "Marxism," *"liberalism,"* "Fascism" or any other political concepts, including what Brzezinski was doing to America for over forty years.

It is the *"Placid governability"* concept employed by each that is important.

Brzezinski knew indoctrination via "education" is the foundation upon which all totalitarian governments are built because it is the thinking person who is a threat.

Thus, indoctrinating people, imbuing them with desired doctrines, lies, and contrived "facts," rather than encouraging them to analyze and think things out for themselves serves to eliminate a lot of thinking among the masses that would be detrimental to the goals and objectives of the *"the Establishment"* Government.

The result of diminution of thinking results in *"Placid governability"* we previously demonstrated was employed by Hitler via Joseph Goebbels' *"If you tell a lie big enough and keep repeating it, people will eventually come to believe it... for such time as the state can shield the political, economic and/or military consequences of the lie."*

How can the state *"shield the political, economic and/or military consequences of the lie"*? This quote, also from Goebbels, should answer that: *"Think of the press as a great keyboard on which the government can play."*

Just insert the word "media" for *"press"* and think about the government being at play with your mind the next time you are watching CNN, MSNBC, or the network "news" on ABC, NBC or CBS. Then think about the fact that, as Propaganda Minister, Goebbels had complete control of all forms of media during Hitler's rein in Germany, and he was provided a large budget to ensure only what the state desired the people to know was disseminated through films, magazines, books, radio broadcast... the available forms of media at the time. In 2018 FOX NEWS was the only big exception to this in America.

So, given this and the following consider what *"the truth"* of all things about Trump is up against.

"A lie gets halfway around the world before the truth has a chance to get its pants on." - Winston Churchill
***

In America 2018, the FCC, Federal Communications Commission, a Government agency has the power to revoke licenses of broadcast companies or stations, and thus function much like a Propaganda Minister, which they do. Thus, FOX could be in danger.

Couple that with the fact Hitler's rise to power was greatly facilitated by the difficult economic times of the Great Depression and Goebbels' comments these hard times facilitated getting the media people of his day to become party to *"shield[ing] the political, economic and/or military consequences of the lie"* from the German people.

Think about Bill Maher's extremely ignorant June 2018 wish for a recession to bring down Trump, and Barrack Obama's lies about the economy, unemployment, inflation, the reasons for attacking Libya and removing Muammar Gaddafi, and more that will eventually be disclosed as the lies they, that continue hammered into the heads of Americans seven days a week by the willful "news" liars of "*the Establishment,*" but "changed their tune" to attacking Donald Trump with lies as soon as he won the election.

Thus, they deliberately continue lying as co-conspirators endeavoring to destroy the economy, freedom and rights of Americans and any hope of a bright future, as though they have been indoctrinated into believing in their America destroying crap, which given the ages of most of them is impossible. They are simply "*the Establishment*" whore mouth pieces, just as the F.B.I. is its enforcement arm as demonstrated by its ant-Trump actions.

But there is much more than the media and the FBI for all Americans to worry about. It goes much higher than just criminal actions of the top management of the FBI.

In June of 2018 the Deputy Attorney General of the U.S., the third highest law enforcement Officer in the U.S. Government, threatened Congressional staff members with an investigation of them, their phones, Emails and correspondence in response to their requesting from him documents they are entitled to in their positions of Constitutionally authorized oversight of his department.

It appears, based on the facts available about the conduct of him and others in the "Justice" Department, he did this in a continuing effort to conceal information that could show deliberate actions in "Justice" and the FBI to endeavor to prevent Trump from being elected, and others possibly showing their endeavoring to assist Hillary to be elected.

This should be frightening to all Americans because this conduct is on a parallel with that of President Obama using the Internal Revenue Service to attack his political opponents, as well as his formal, post Presidential OFA operation continuing to endeavor to remove President Trump from Office.

All these actions by top Government Officials in support of the anti-American "*Establishment*" that put Obama in Office and a dozen members at the top of his Administration within the first week he was in the Presidency should prove beyond a doubt the existence of a huge anti-Trump and thus anti-American democracy conspiracy that is definitely not just a "*theory*" but a fact!

This fact proves all these high-ranking Government Officials, including the ex-President are opposed to the form of Government

Americans have enjoyed since the beginning of the country.

This in-our-face criminal conduct without even a flicker of fear or remorse proves they are fully on board the Brzezinski train taking America to their obviously desired *New World Order* destination because their conduct would not be tolerated in any other than a totalitarian form of government.

Their blatant conduct since 2016 is no different than that of members of Stalinist KGB or Fascist Gestapo. They have used their positions as the head of our Government and those empowered to enforce the laws of the country to endeavor to prevent one opposed to them and their desired form of government becoming President, and they have continued since to use their powers to endeavor to incarcerate others opposed to them.

Thus, there is no way any honest person can argue there is one iota of difference between the current conduct of these people and those of these past, failed totalitarians.

However, these are just a few examples of what only the worst kind of people, the most-evil ones like Zbigniew Brzezinski and those who by their own words are his ardent followers, like Presidents Carter and Obama... could be part of a government doing what it has to America and its people or be extensions of that Government by being the media keys on the *"great keyboard on which the government can play"* its lies of destruction.

It is thus the opportunity for upward mobility was deliberately removed from the playbook for average Americans born after 1973 by Brzezinski and his acolytes who by Webster's definition, *"to seek or pursue ardently that which is immoral,"* are whores for him and *"the Establishment"* of which he was the creator and implementer of its anti-American, "immoral" evil for forty-four years.

***

"How fortunate for governments that the people they administer don't think." - Adolph Hitler

The American public-school system deliberately inhibits upward mobility because *"poor families have no choice but to accept whatever is handed out by the failed system"* that has eliminated imbuing youths with knowledge and the ability to be free thinkers in favor of indoctrination to enhance Government power, rather than empowering the individual.

Thus, a majority of American youth reach adulthood having their intellectual legs cut from under them before they have a chance. Then they and their ever increasing *"huge new generation[s] of docile, under-educated adults"* form sort of a "glass ceiling" for everyone, limiting upward mobility from the top down through self-serving imposition of reverence for *"authority figures,"* which serves to impede free thinking as in Mao's China.

There, Mao Tse-Tung who was in total control of China's population for almost three decades at the time of his death in the mid-1970s and had written *"...we must constantly carry on lively and effective political education among the masses..."* i.e., indoctrination, was revered, as happened in many cultures throughout history, and his political concept of communism was as revered by the youth of China as he was, **much like the American youth protesting in the streets and supporting avowed Communist, not socialist, Bernie Sanders in 2018.**

They indicate with exception of the single "Authority Figure," America is not far behind 1970s China on its road to Brzezinski desired communist totalitarianism, not socialism.

Non-thinking Americans better awaken and act now... in 2018 or whenever this is read... before they fulfill Hitler's comment about *"how fortunate"* their conduct is for *"the Establishment"* indoctrinating their children and destroying their future.

The "education" legislation and related conduct by Carter and Obama under Brzezinski's guidance put any American President desiring it in much the same position *vis-à-vis* average Americans as Mao relative to average Chinese. That includes Alinsky's and Brzezinski's acolytes like Hillary and Obama or anyone who unwittingly supports her veneer party comrade co-conspirators. All of them are demonstrably communists.

Also, the Brzezinski totalitarian inspired members of each house of Congress continuously legislate rules and regulations to enhance big business at the expense of taxpayers and small business, **further impeding upward mobility among the less privileged,** and moving America closer to corporate Fascism; an unhealthy relationship between government and big business, as we have already witnessed in the health insurance industry, big banks and pharmaceutical companies.

The failed American "education"/indoctrination system in impeding upward mobility has played its part in the destruction of the American Middle Class and causing America to be more divided along socioeconomic and cultural lines. And let's not forget that effete *"elite"* Harvard University has been at the forefront of the destruction of U.S. education for well over three decades, as demonstrated in Mr. Ortiz' words above.

Those with the financial means spend a lot to keep their children out of the hands of the public-school system. Their children, especially those of the so-called *"elite,"* are educated in private institutions that prepare them for private universities, giving them an intellectual leg up on life, rather than cutting their intellectual legs from under them.

The difference in education of the majority and those from the higher rungs of the socioeconomic ladder is comparable to the difference in the military indoctrination of draftee or volunteer enlisted men and that of the Officer Corps, which is vastly different.

But who would know. Few enlisted ever know the difference between their lot in life and that of an Officer. The abyss between the two lives is wide and deep, and few are equipped to cross it.

Ditto: the abyss between lives of products of the American Government indoctrination system and those with private school and private university educations, as the protesting, communist indoctrinated Bernie Sanders supporting youth in America under the control of "*the Establishment*" following the guidance of Hillary, Obama and their veneer party also will never know.

"Take control of what people read and listen to and children learn in school, has been the task of the "*the Establishment*" controlled American indoctrination system as planned by Brzezinski to the detriment of America since soon after Jimmy Carter entered the Oval Office in 1977, **AND PRESIDENT TRUMP NEEDS TO WAKE UP AND CHANGE THIS ASAP!**

***

The big question of 2018 is; why did President Trump during his over one year in office do nothing to take American education out of the hands of the indoctrinators and put it back where it was before Brzezinski and Carter redirected it forty years ago?

Does he not understand education, real learning of how to think, not indoctrination in what to think, is the very foundation of what made America great before Brzezinski changed it, and he can never really "*Make America Great Again*" for the long term until he gets real education back into the schools of America?

He immediately took on the media lying and indoctrination machine, exposing it for what it is, but has done nothing about the other half of Brzezinski's Goebbels-like mass indoctrination of America. Why not?

He cannot accomplish what he says he is going to do until he treats the "educators" as he has treated the media. In fact, he does not have the power to change the media, but he does have the power to do what is needed in education where what is being purveyed to the youth of America is a pack of lies bigger than what the media is selling... and with longer term and more destructive results.

He must realize he cannot be successful in his big endeavor for America long term unless he fixes education because it is currently a slowly disintegrating house of cards rather than the

solid foundation any successful business, country or structure of any kind, whether physical, conceptual or Donald Trump must have for long term success!

We who have no platform for input can only hope he gets on this most important task ASAP. So, if anyone who reads this does have a platform, please tell the President he is failing in this important part of his self-designed task to *"Make America Great Again*!

What can be seen on television that is happening in the streets and on the campuses of America should be more than sufficient for him to shake free of whatever inertia is holding him back and begin assiduously pursuing this, as he has illegal immigration. If not, his effect on America and his legacy will not be what it could have been, or he would like it to be!

Freedom and democracy require an educated population with knowledge of the facts of their history and culture, not an indoctrinated one, as is being produced now, imbued with lies about the culture and history of America.

CHAPTER NINE
"DIVIDE AND CONQUER"

"Culture is not a substitute for life, but the key to it."
- William Mallock, *The New Republic*

CREATING "DIVERSITY" VIA IMMIGRATION TO CHANGE THE NATURE & CULTURE OF THE POPULATION TO ONE MORE DEPENDENT AND ACCEPTING OF MORE GOVERNMENT CONTROL

That *"diversity"* is a weakness, not a strength, has been proven over and over, and again and again, in contemporary times. Northern Ireland, Belgium, Spain, Yugoslavia, Czechoslovakia, the Middle East... and unfortunately post Obama America... have all proven the divisiveness of language and religion, the two most definitive elements of all cultures, especially when one is productive, and the others tend to be dependent.

"Diversity" has proven disruptive to the peace and harmony of any place in which there are large, critical mass size culturally different segments of population... as has been proven more and more often in America since 2008.

However, even with this knowledge *"the Establishment"* under Mr. Brzezinski's guidance has pursued the **Objective** of **"The Brzezinski Business Plan for America"** to gain control of the U.S. Government by changing the nature of the population through Third World Immigration since implementation of Jimmy Carter's 1980 Refugee/Immigration act began providing "freebies" in the form of money, welfare, healthcare and more to the poorest and least educated peasant class of Mexico.

Their *"Diversity is our strength"* program was a pivotal part of that endeavor, continuously indoctrinating young minds with this big lie in the schools and older Americans through the media.

They were aware of the adage *"divide and conquer,"* and have been assiduously pursuing division of America for this purpose... to *"conquer"* in the literal sense of the word; to overcome, to defeat the people of America... for over forty years as of 2018.

A divided America, one wherein there is cultural, racial, language and religious strife serves, by plan, to strengthen *"the Establishment"* control of the Federal Government. A government that is, clearly, no longer a *"government of the people, by the people, for the people."* It is a government of, by and for those in power and those they serve.

The purposeful cultural, racial, religious and language division of America for strengthening the Government over the people conceptualized by, according to his writings, Brzezinski, was put into operation under his *"eager student"* President Carter who was either complicit or terribly out of touch with reality, and naïve.

Thus, it was during the Carter Administration restrictions on welfare, food stamps and other benefits to illegal aliens were lifted, resulting in an immediate increase in the flow of illegal aliens from Mexico, people who are racially, culturally, religiously, linguistically different from the majority of Americans; people who, prevalent in large numbers, would *"divide"* the country.

This effort has proven successful in accomplishing this in subsequent years.

Carter signing the Refugee Act in March 1980 opened the floodgates of illegal immigration from Mexico providing for ***"placement for economic self-sufficiency, cash assistance"*** and covering the estimated cost at that time of $4,000 for each immigrant's ***"distribution to the states,"*** to spread them among the population for ***"diversity"*** purposes, a program even expanded aggressively by *NWO* America destroying Obama.

Carter also had an "open arms" policy toward Cuban immigrants who were immediately granted refugee status. But that was apparently insufficiently aggressive for either Carter or Obama in the plan to further expand a divisive population segment.

Between April and October of 1980 Carter cooperated with Cuban dictator Fidel Castro in shipping one hundred twenty-five thousand Cubans, many of questionable background, to the U.S. and granting them "refugee" resident status.

He employed the U.S. Coast Guard, Navy, Marines and Army in that five and one-half month effort to get all those Cubans into and settled in the U.S.

To see one, "little" result of that effort, all one must do is go to the West Lake, Lafayette Park area of Los Angeles where many of these "refugees" were settled.

This area of beautiful parks, once utilized by people of Los Angeles, upscale shopping and affluent residential areas has been turned into the most crime ridden, Rampart Division area serviced by the Los Angeles Police Department. Parks have chain link fences around them. They are closed at night. The shopping is gone. The whole area is a crime infested, gang war ridden, combat zone, as has happened in many American cities... large and small... since.

***

But many years before this the U.S. Government under Democrat, Lyndon Johnson, also under guidance of Brzezinski 1964 to 1966, implemented immigration that combined with later immigration created *"diversity"* problems they were not sufficiently astute to foretell... but probably not for "brilliant" Brzezinski. He knew.

It was more Government stupidity gone wild at the expense of taxpayers and less future harmony in the country that was going to be done without regard to the consequences, even if anyone in the Government was sufficiently bright to realize, which is doubtful, it was part of the *"diversity"* for Government power plan also with Brzezinski finger prints all over it.

It was just months... officially less than a full year... into the Vietnam War, which shows it was going badly almost from the beginning, as most involved or receiving reports from family or friends on the ground there were aware.

Thousands of indigenous people were being brought to the U.S. purportedly for their safety because they were known allies of the U.S. military that invaded and was wreaking destruction for no discernable reason. They were being resettled all over the U.S. No one except those doing this knew the criteria for this, but whatever it was, relatively small cities were on the list.

Some of those being resettled in the U.S. were Laotian Hmong from along the Vietnam border who were not viewed favorably by the indigenous Vietnamese even before arrival of the U.S. military.

These and the Vietnamese were village people who lived in huts with dirt floors and had never seen indoor plumbing or cooking over anything but a fire. (We should note this expensive and destructive stupidity has not ceased. Four decades later it was Somalis that were being given this "free ride.")

The Housing and Urban Development agency, HUD, was given responsibility to resettle these people in one small predominately homogenous city, and probably others like it.

It is not known what they did elsewhere, but in this city of about fifty thousand the agency went into the poorer white parts of town, condemned houses as not fit for habitation, tore some down, remodeled others and created new immigrant neighborhoods.

After the houses were remodeled, they were "sold" to the immigrants for one dollar. They also built new houses at taxpayer expense on some of the lots where houses were torn down and "sold" those to the immigrants for a dollar also. But that was not the worst abuse of the taxpayers by the Government in this program

Because these people did not know how to live in houses with bathrooms and kitchens, while their free housing was being readied for them, the Government set up schools on how to utilize and take care of their new bathrooms and kitchens, and paid them $125, over $1,000 in 2018 dollars, per week to go to "school" to learn this.

Essentially, they were being paid by the taxpayers to learn how to cook and go to the bathroom in their new taxpayer provided homes.

After the Vietnamese were taken care of HUD, for self-preservation, as government agencies are inclined, began to also take care of the relatively small numbers of Mexican immigrants before Carter's Refugee Act, also at taxpayer expense when the programs were expanded to the growing Latino community.

That required spending as much as fifteen thousand dollars per house for upgrades and repairs they could not afford out of their welfare checks they were receiving while they were, according to reports of some familiar with the program, watching TV as others were being paid by taxpayers to repair and upgrade their homes.

Remember: this was a predominately homogenous small city of fifty thousand. Guess what happens to a town that size after a few years growth of two diverse ethnic populations like Vietnamese and Latinos competing for the largesse and drug selling territories.

We don't have to guess. We have seen it growing for over four decades. Since the 1970s, this ethnic *"diversity"* has resulted in increased violence, gang warfare, and huge economic and social costs. Asian, Latino and black gangs are engaged in armed conflict on the streets of America thanks to the stupidity of empirically disproven, *"diversity is a strength,"* U.S. Government policies.

By 1998, the subject city had a population of over 150 thousand that was 29% white, 20% black, 43% Latino and 8% Asian.

An interview with a funeral home owner who was still operating the funeral home his family owned in the 1950s when he was in high school told that over half the funerals he was conducting in the 1990s were for Vietnamese and Mexican males under the age of thirty killed by gunfire. Yep; *"diversity is strength."*

The worst abuse of the taxpayer citizens by *"the Establishment"* resulting from idiotic Government strengthening *"diversity"* programs continuing to be imposed on towns and cities that continued in 2018 was the deliberate destruction of the previous relative peace and harmony of homogenous populations, social and educational decline, and tremendous concomitant economic costs, as well as loss of life.

"Liberal progressive" members of *"the Establishment"* like Hillary and Obama, and all the holdovers from these two whore's time in Government are still hell bent on continuing with more Latin immigration, plus Islamic immigrants of questionable intent.

This is another of those *"Establishment"* Government created problems of which anyone smart enough to make his or her way into Congress could not possibly be unaware. Thus, this destruction of small towns and cities all over America through civil strife and the economic cost of it must be deliberate.

It is the classic *"divide and conquer,"* weaken the population and create a greater need for more government. There is no other explanation for this imposed *"diversity"* in small towns and cities all over America. But it must stop if "America" is to survive, if it is not already too late.

Yet, amazingly, based on their statements, only one of the two 2016 Presidential candidates desired to put a stop to this idiocy. The other, preying on the ignorance of her primary constituency, guaranteed expansion of this immigration most detrimental to her base because of the prospect of an expanded socialist electorate in this segment of the population, which was shortsighted on the part of the candidate, as well as her constituency.

She cannot be forgiven for irresponsibly promoting this continued destruction. So maybe even her base constituents should be grateful for President Donald Trump. If not, no amount of increase in socialism could even begin to save them.

ILLEGAL IMMIGRATION
"United States shall protect each of them [states] *against invasion."* - **Article IV Section 4.** *United States Constitution*

Because Mexican military and federal police actions on the U.S./Mexican border against U.S. citizens, the U.S. Congress has the authority to place U.S. military on the border to treat Mexican nationals crossing the border as enemies of the United States.

Further, in addition to this power provided in the Constitution, questions about Mexican illegal immigrants "rights" are moot. They can, and should be, arrested and detained, or sent back, which they could be anyway, if the laws, rather than political correctness, were enforced, since, by definition, they are breaking the law by illegally entering the U.S.

Although the illegal immigrants probably do not think of their entering the U.S. as invading with a vision of conquest, or making a Latin inroad against Western culture, it is clearly their intent to intrude upon, infringe, and even plunder the U.S. healthcare, welfare, education and social security systems.

The Mexican military and federal police, on the other hand, have definitively, consciously and deliberately made armed incursions into the U.S. wherein it was their intent, through use of armed force, to impose themselves and their illegal activities upon America and American citizens. Thus, they violated the rights, and endangered the lives of U.S. border patrol agents on the U.S. side of the border.

Thus, they invaded! No question about this.

Entering with a view to conquest and make a Latin inroad against American culture may not be in the minds of illegal immigrants, even though many demonstrate that after here, but it is implicit in the words of Mexican Officials who refer to illegal immigration of their nationals into the U.S. as *"natural migration."*

They refuse to recognize the sovereignty of the United States and rather than endeavor to prevent illegal immigration by their citizens, have a policy of encouraging it. This policy was echoed by the ranking Mexican Government representative in Los Angeles. He stated Californians should just accept Mexicans are there to stay.

***

The political elite in Mexico have a reason for wanting their less fortunate citizens to leave their country.

Of the over one hundred million citizens of Mexico forty percent live in poverty. The economic system and culture in Mexico, even with the industrialization resulting from NAFTA created jobs cannot adequately provide for these forty plus millions.

The per capita Gross Domestic Product of Mexico is one seventh that of the U.S. with a third of the population even though the country is rich in gold, other metals and oil reserves. It also has very large auto and appliance manufacturing industries, thanks to NAFTA, and it exports to Asia and Europe because of its long coast lines and deep-water ports on both Atlantic and Pacific Oceans.

Therefore, the reason for Mexican poverty is its culture that does not promote education and intelligent procreation relative to its productivity that is deliberately being imported into the U.S. by *"the Establishment"* in cooperation with the Mexican Government that was greatly increased under Obama.

Also, the Latin Church, the dominant cultural institution in Mexico, thus the dominant force in the country, has a policy that is not in the best interest of Mexican people. The Pope suggested during a visit he would prefer to see more rather than fewer members of his church there, proving either he does not give a damn about the people, but only the money they give to his church, or he is unaware the cause of so much poverty there is a result of the annual percentage increase in humans being significantly greater than their increase in production of goods and services.

Smart money would be on the former rather than the latter mindset of the church.

Given the splendor of the Vatican, the lifestyle of the church hierarchy and the culture of poverty and ignorance of populations of countries in which Catholicism is the dominant religion it is obvious the primary cause of their poverty is the religion.

Contrary to the politically correct message of the U.S. Government indoctrination system and Washington politicians, Mexico is not a democracy. Its form of government is an oligarchy wherein very few citizens have any political power.

It is not a government of, for, or by, the people. It's a government of the few, by the few, for the few, in which it is exceedingly difficult for average citizens to move up the socioeconomic ladder, as it is becoming in *"the Establishment"* controlled America.

The oligarchy... in neither country... have any interest in instituting reforms that would change the country into a more democratic one, and even if they did, it is doubtful the change would take hold quickly enough to provide the needed benefits because of the nature of the people, the extent of the role of the church in their lives, and the sheer magnitude of forty million uneducated, poor people, unqualified to contribute to the country's advancing economic prosperity other than through manual labor.

The more religious, indigenous segment of the population is the poorest, the least educated, and potentially the most volatile. This means the country has forty million potential rebels, some with communist proclivities on the U.S. southern border, not unlike Cuba pre1960 with its also strongly U.S. supported President. But there is not a body of water between the U.S. and Mexico.

Rather than deal with this segment of the population, the oligarchs prefer to get rid of the problem by exporting it to the U.S. where it becomes an American problem that will send much of the money made in the U.S. back home to help its families remaining in Mexico: a win-win situation for the Mexican oligarchs, but a losing proposition for Americans.

In the real world, if that concept exists in Washington D.C., the U.S. Government would act to protect interests of the country and its taxpayers, as it is Constitutionally charged to do. But when the Brzezinski cabal got its hands on the tiller of the U.S. ship of state the Constitution was relegated to the hold with the rest of the undesirable baggage.

If not, it would have stopped illegal immigration and put the Mexican Government on notice its policies, actions of some of its government personnel, and the effect of these actions on citizens of the U.S. qualify Mexico as an invading enemy of the United States.

This is serious. *"The Establishment"* should not permit Mexico to solve its problem by moving them to the U.S. But they are smarter than past Presidents and Government of the U.S. They understand the real world and are not subject to political correctness.

Although recently Mexico had only a thirty-five-hundred-dollar per capita Gross Domestic Product, only one seventh of the U.S., the average per capita GDP of the Central American countries immediately South of Mexico is only one quarter of that.

To those people, Mexico looks pretty good. Thus, they desire to engage in its government approved northward *"natural migration."* However, this is where the Mexican oligarchy prefers to depart from the U.S. fiction and have real world, pragmatic policies.

Mexico stops *"natural migration"* of Central Americans at its southern border and detains them unless they are being guaranteed safe passage into the U.S. by Obama Administration holdovers, as desired by *"the Establishment"* for its *"diversity"* plans.

The Mexican Government supports its ridiculous concept of *"migration"* only when it benefits by getting those deemed undesirable out of their country. This makes them hypocrites on the order of the Brzezinski U.S. Government *"Establishment."*

Some Americans may envisage *"migration"* as the migratory flights of birds wandering back and forth, from North to South, on a seasonal basis, rather than the fact the illegal immigrants are moving into the U.S. to take up permanent residence with the historical encouragement of Hillary, Obama holdovers and the rest of *"the Establishment"* to fulfill their *"divide and conquer"* plans to empower themselves over other Americans.

***

There is nothing natural about an illegal invasion of foreign nationals across a border into a sovereign nation. What is happening is patently unnatural, and the Mexican Government demonstrates it knows this through its actions on its Southern border.

<u>Mexican nationals are unnaturally, illegally immigrating into the U.S. solely because of an acquired taste for U.S. Dollars, free schools, welfare, food stamps, the availability of Social Security payments, and free healthcare available to them,</u> but not to taxpaying Americans with assets to lose.

They are seeking these benefits in the U.S. because, due to the forty percent poverty rate in their non-productive, biased, Oligarchy culture, they are not available in Mexico.

Once these immigrants are here and have "tasted" these benefits, and the ease with which they can obtain them, they are not going back to Mexico. And those in the U.S. Government charged with the responsibility to enforce the laws have demonstrated, because of political correctness, they are not going to enforce immigration laws against minority immigrants.

They are more concerned with political correctness than the law, health, safety and welfare of American citizens it is their desire to further sideline from political power through *"diversity."*

American citizens would be arrested, fined and imprisoned for doing what millions of illegal immigrants are doing every day. They are stealing from the U.S. Government, and by extension from U.S. taxpayers, by illegally obtaining welfare benefits with the use of fraudulent documents and failing to pay income taxes when working for cash.

They are also stealing from American taxpayers by being here illegally, and obtaining the benefits of schools, jobs and healthcare that are rightfully benefits of only those legal residents of the country who pay for them through their taxes.

Also, there are tens of thousands of Mexicans living along the U.S. border stealing these benefits without immigrating into the U.S. They obtain welfare benefits through use of fraudulent documents, obtain a U.S. post office box address, have checks mailed to the box, and come across the border to pick up their checks, or to obtain free healthcare.

***

Arizona is referred to as the health maintenance organization, HMO, for Mexico. The U.S. Government is aware of this but does nothing. Thus, the U.S. Government is condoning the theft of taxpayer funds by foreign nationals at the same time its position is certain benefits for American citizens are not affordable.

Mexican nationals come to the U.S. to have babies for free. Some estimates are those citizens living in areas where there are large numbers of illegal immigrants are paying for as many as seven babies when they go to the hospital to have one. But these people are not a drain on the American taxpayer only because they have their babies in U.S. hospitals.

A baby born in the U.S. is an American citizen. Since U.S. immigration policy favors families of U.S. citizens, the new U.S. citizen, "anchor baby," has the right to have his or her family with him as welfare receiving, non-contributory residents of the U.S.

Of course, it would not make sense to say the citizen baby could not have its mother or father with it, but this is not where it ends. The new citizen's entire family will probably be permitted to immigrate via "chain migration." Even the grandparents who have never paid a penny into Social Security may come to the U.S., retire, and draw Social Security. (Let an American citizen who has not qualified attempt to obtain Social Security.)

Mexican Government officials have openly articulated a policy of complete disregard for U.S. laws and sovereignty. They are actively promoting the Mexican invasion for their economy and more peace and harmony at home due to benefits previously stated.

Most of *"the Establishment"* Washington politicians from both sides of the aisle are going along with this politically correct displacing of America's Western culture, and eventual destruction of great swaths of American prosperity, by doing nothing to stop illegal immigration, and by lying to the American public about *faux* *"advantages"* of it.

It is obvious the foolish and deceitful *"liberal, progressives"* of *"the Establishment"* are doing this to broaden their power base, but is it possible the veneer Republicans are so intellectually challenged they actually believe they can convert Mexicans into Republicans, or is there something more sinister in their position?

It should be obvious to anyone who can read, or has a television; there is no positive, no advantage, to Mexican or other Latin immigration, legal, or illegal.

The differences between American and Latin cultures, the immigrants' resistance to assimilation or adopting the English language, should be sufficient warning that millions of Latin Nationals bringing their culture and language to the U.S. cannot, in any way, be positive for the future of any American.

But with total disregard of empirical evidence of the adverse effect of illegal Mexican immigration *"the Establishment's"* *"liberal progressives,"* through their mouthpiece media accomplices like the *NEW YORK TIMES,* and so-called *"liberal"* think tanks continue to promote the *faux* advantages of illegal immigration.

They say immigrants do jobs Americans are unwilling to, and advocate *"illegal, otherwise law-abiding immigrants"* should not be arrested by state, or local law enforcement agencies. Thus, they are providing "sanctuary" cities and states.

This is what everyone should expect from the non-"thinking" so-called *"liberals"* who consider themselves the *"elite."*

This amounts to selectively enforcing or not enforcing laws based on the ethnicity of the individual lawbreaker. They are, now, demonstrating the form of government they would like to see in America would subjectively determine which laws are to be enforced, and against whom. The logical progression in this type of "thinking" would lead to selectively enforcing, or not enforcing, laws based upon against whom a crime is perpetrated. (Look for this next.) What is it they do not understand about "illegal"?

How about this? Inform local law enforcement agencies they are not to arrest *"ordinary ... otherwise law-abiding ..."* citizens who trespass, break and enter, commit fraud against American citizens, companies, or the Government by illegally obtaining welfare or other benefits, cheat on their taxes, etc., etc.

C'mon! The laws must either be enforced against all who break them, without regard to ethnicity, origin, religion, or citizenship, or they must be taken off the books. <u>A democracy requires impartiality in the administration of justice.</u>

But "*liberal, progressive*" members of "*the Establishment*" like Hillary, Obama *et al* and their media mouthpieces understand what they are doing. They are endeavoring to destroy American democracy, and replace it with their Utopian, Socialist vision.

They are the ones Alan Keyes referred to in the 2000 Presidential debates with the "*house burning down*" before he was barred from the debates because he made the significantly less intelligent, and less articulate but chosen one, Bush II look so bad.

Remember, they "think" they are in charge, and the type of government they desire in America that would be consistent with their Socialist views, and those of every oligarchy and dictatorship in the world, permits those few who are in charge to determine what the laws are, and against whom they are applied.

This is the reason they promote the immigration of millions who have never experienced the democracy they desire to deprive Americans of with such avidity.

These people are exactly the types John Adams warned America about when he wrote: ***"Our Constitution was made only for a moral and religious people. It is wholly inadequate to the government of any other."***

Therefore, when it is argued "*moral clarity is dead,*" as has been done in media like the *NEW YORK TIMES,* given "*moral*" is about distinguishing between right and wrong and "*clarity*" indicates free of confusion, this suggests there is no longer a clear distinction between right and wrong. The extension of this "logic" is ethics, the standards of moral conduct, have ceased to exist. Ergo by definition, we have a bunch of NWO political whores in charge!

<u>What they are really arguing is the historical standards of Americans who created the country that is a magnet for people from other cultures should not apply to immigrants of different cultures in the U.S.</u> or those of Latin, African or other cultures should not assimilate or be bound by American ethics, standards of conduct, or what is considered right or wrong in America.

It is selective application of laws, morals, ethics and values for which they are arguing. Thus, they are arguing against American values and democratic ideas.

The insanity of this should not need to be addressed. But **<u>what this suggests is in addition to there being no national borders, there should be no cultural "borders" of conduct, laws or anything else. Every place should be a "sanctuary" for everyone to do whatever he or she desires without any parameters.</u>**

This defies logic and common sense. **Without distinction between what is considered right and wrong, or standards of moral and physical conduct there would be no internal strength, unity or harmony. America would be dead!**

But considering the thoughts conveyed in writing by Brzezinski about his desired no nation states, no borders and a One World Government this has to be the world he and his acolytes in the U.S. Government, including the afore named two U.S. Presidents, plus Hillary and others have been endeavoring to guide and legislate America toward.

Although this is insanity, or possibly stupidity resulting from lack of any real-world experience, like the "sanctuary" nuts are demonstrating, this would satisfy their objective of empowering whatever government happens, although **no government could control or survive the resultant anarchy.**

No people, society, or culture can exist, nor can people live together without collectively accepted standards of conduct and shared knowledge of what is considered right and wrong among them. Recognized parameters of conduct developed over time, or proscribed by laws or religion, define culture. This is what provides its strength, thereby blowing the insane stupidity and obvious societal weakness of *"diversity is strength"* out of the water!

***

Also, regarding the nonsense about certain immigrants *"doing jobs other Americans won't.* This is just more *"liberal, progressive Establishment"* hogwash!

If welfare were eliminated for those mentally and physically capable of working and earning a living, they would do those jobs the immigrants are doing when they are young, learn the benefits of working, progress up the income scale, AND the culture of dependency, drugs and crime, those supporting illegal immigration and welfare are directly responsible for, would be dealt a healthy blow to the benefit of all Americans, especially black Americans about whose self-esteem these same *"liberal, progressives"* and "educators" express so much concern.

Mexican immigration is particularly unhealthy for the education, health and safety, incomes, wealth and self-esteem of black Americans… more so than for any others.

All black Americans should reconsider their position of siding with the other major minority against America's Western culture they erroneously define as "white" when they have been a part of the same culture sharing the same language and religion, and no other, for hundreds of years, and the other is vastly different in that it promotes poverty through promotion of larger families without regard for the ability to support them.

They have been "sucked into" this position by the *"the Establishment leftist, liberal progressives"* through their denigrating "pitching" of the benefits of a culture of dependency to those they perceive susceptible because of the legacy of their African culture. And they have done this, not to benefit black Americans, but entirely to broaden their power base.

<u>Black Americans, most of whom can trace their "Americanism" back a minimum of five generations; have much more in common with white Americans than with Latino immigrants, including language and religion, the two most significant cultural elements.</u>

As previously stated, black Americans have always been part of American culture. Only since 1973 have "*the Establishment liberal, progressives*" on their "*divide and conquer*" for power mission of weakening the United States internally, marketed a contrived African culture to black Americans through indoctrination.

They are deliberately exploiting the natural, inherent cultural imperative of black Americans to "belong" to African culture just as they are in cahoots with Mexico in exploiting those of Latin culture for the same purpose.

***

The cultural imperative is visceral. It is not intellectual. But cultural adherence can be mental. When people are not bound by geographic or governmental constraints, and free to choose, as American residents are, they may choose to view the world through the cultural options available. The key word being, "choose."

Therefore, black Americans, being citizens of the U.S., and having all the rights and privileges of citizenship can, as many have, choose to fully participate in their American Western culture, or they can reverse the progress they have made, and adopt a mythical African cultural mindset to the detriment of themselves and the entire country as was the intent of Johnson's *"Great Society"* to *"divide and conquer"* for Government power.

Should black Americans choose to continue to permit themselves to be used by their African-like, despotic Congressional "leadership," and "*the Establishment*" as a part of their power base in their anti-Western culture support of illegal immigration, they will be the ones to suffer the most among all citizens of America.

Therefore, black Americans should ask: can we commit the same illegal infractions as illegal immigrants and expect to have the same people who are calling for a suspension of law enforcement against them, do the same for us?

They should also be cognizant that language and religion are *the* two most divisive cultural characteristics. Then, consider; in the decade between the 1990 and 2000 census, due to illegal immigration, the population of Latinos in America grew to parity with the numbers of blacks, and fifty percent of all those of Latin heritage were foreign born.

Plus, illegal immigration is not subsiding. Unless Trump is successful, likely in very few years, major areas, a large percentage of black Americans call home, could become home to a majority Latino, Spanish speaking, Latin Church population, that tends to be culturally intolerant, and favors a less free, socialist, oligarchy form of government.

Further, in 2018, over fifty percent of the Spanish speaking population got its news solely from Spanish language media.

In 2002, the under-estimated nine million Spanish speaking, illegal immigrants in America were only equal to about twenty five percent of the entire black population and were taking jobs and benefits that would otherwise be available if not for illegal immigration being fostered by those individuals who also purport to be advocates for blacks.

In many states, the Latino population has become so large the states are already being redistricted to provide more Latino backed representation in Congress.

Black Americans should also ask themselves whether they believe their circumstances would be better when living under a culturally cohesive, and less tolerant, Spanish speaking, Latin majority, than they are with a proven generous, compassionate, democratic, Protestant majority with which they share both language and religion.

Then, they should ask those advocates of "African Americanism" what they will be advocating when the Spanish speaking population numbers twice that of black Americans.

***

Latin America immigration is bad for all Americans, culturally and economically, but it is worse, near term, for black Americans. Thus, they, like all Americans, should wake up to the reality of the situation, rather than continue to listen to "*the Establishment progressives*" who will sell them "*down the river*" whenever and wherever the numbers of the Spanish speaking population surpass their numbers. Political power which equals M-O-N-E-Y is the name of the game!

Waiting rather than pragmatically looking at trends or current real-world situations and failing to take actions to stop this immigration will result in a Latin American United States being *fait accompli* during the lifetimes of a large percentage of us.

Any illegal immigrant who makes it across the border into the

U.S. under current Mexican Government supporting mentality of most of "*the Establishment*" and the pro-immigration laws they created in support of their "*Divide and conquer*" program is probably home free. There have been as many as one million of these each year.

But black Americans are not the only ones who should be concerned near term. Veneer Republicans and black Americans are in the same boat. Primarily illegal Mexican immigration of the poorest, least capable to support themselves will be the end of the Republican veneer of the *faux* "two party" system and Western culture in America.

Thus, black Americans, the Western culture that affords them so much opportunity, and honestly conservative, capitalistic Republicans are on the losing end of Mexican immigration. The "*leftist, liberal, progressives*" will be the big winners because they will have a greatly expanded power base with a demonstrated, socialist proclivity.

"*The Establishment liberal, progressives*" in America will finally realize their heyday. Hell! Given they were already almost there before 2018 they will surely have a sufficiently large base of support with socialist proclivities to whom the appellation *"socialist,"* as with Bernie Sanders, does not carry any negative connotation. They might even change their name to reflect their real identity as *New World Order* communists.

But whether they change their name, it is a sure bet they will pander to and support the large Latino population's culture in every way, including language, which they will have to begin to speak or be out of office.

The only winners will be immigrants and the new, enlarged Socialist Party. Everyone else loses, even Americans of Latin heritage whose families have been Americans for generations. As people are prone to do, they will paint these Americans with the same brush as the immigrants, even though many of them do not even speak Spanish.

Profiling may not be politically correct, but it is natural to define others on the basis of their appearance and the observed conduct of the majority of the same appearance.

There is another fact of Mexican immigration of which all Americans should be cognizant. The U.S. is suffering a loss of highly paying manufacturing jobs at the same time it is absorbing large numbers of a growing Third World population from the least capable to contribute economically and thus less desirable segment of the Mexican population.

This fact, despite illogical arguments to the contrary, is America and its population is culturally and economically regressing. At a time when the Western world and even Mexico are advancing, America is moving backward toward Third World status as its population of those of a Third World cultural mindset increases.

Mexico is advancing solely as the result of U.S. jobs moved there under NAFTA, and they represent advancement, not regression. It is NOT those capable of filling those manufacturing jobs that are illegally "moving" into the U.S. It is the least well-educated, least capable to contribute who are *Coming to America.*

***

The Mexican Government wants to get rid of those who restrain Mexico's advancement. And even though this advancement is compliments of America, it is Americans to whom it is more than willing to transfer their burden. Does this sound like friend, or foe?

That illegal immigrants are really aliens, foreign in culture, and different in nature, although not politically correct, should be obvious. That large numbers of them are having an adverse effect on American civilization should also be obvious.

The United States, its civilization, like any country or functioning system is much like a large, living organism. It has, per Webster, *"diverse parts that function as a whole to maintain its life and its activities."*

Invader, as defined by Webster, is one who chooses to *"crowd into, throng, intrude upon, infringe, violate, to enter and spread through with harmful effects, to make an invasion."* The synonym of invade is trespass, *"go beyond the limits of what is right or moral, do wrong, transgress, unlawful entry upon the property or rights of another."* These are words, terms and concepts appropriate for the discussion of illegal immigration and its effects on America.

As previously stated, unlike the Mexican Government and its agents it is probably not the cognitive intent of illegal aliens to invade. They do not think of themselves as invading in the true sense of the word. But the consequences are nonetheless the same. They are knowingly crowding into the U.S. in violation of U.S. laws. Much like any trespasser, they are deliberately, violating and unlawfully infringing the property and rights of Americans.

Permitting illegal aliens to knowingly violate U.S. law, to come into the country and go beyond the limits of what they know is wrong without there being any consequences to them for this willful wrong doing will have severe, long term, negative consequences for Americans that cannot be overlooked. This will result in an expansion of the numbers of the criminal class and increased economic and social cost to the country beyond what has already happened that is extensive.

In California, this is obvious. In 2000 when only fourteen percent of the citizen population was on welfare, twenty-one percent of immigrants were on welfare and fifteen percent of violent criminals in California prisons were these immigrants.

The foreign, different nature of the immigrants cannot help but have an adverse effect on the American system and its people, especially since they persist in speaking a language that is alien to this system, and they are accustomed to different cultural values and a less free form of government.

Also, accommodation of non-English speaking millions is costly and dysfunctional to the otherwise relatively smooth functioning of the American system. This can already be observed in schools and the provision of essential Government services.

According to *THE NEW YORK TIMES, "The number of students with limited English skills, most of them Hispanic, doubled to five million in the decade* before 2000 or *more than four times the rate of the general population...We are now experiencing the largest wave of immigration in the history of the United States,"* and per the U.S. census this immigration is resulting in a decline in the median income in American cities.

The invasion of millions of aliens who know they are violating American laws, know their government encourages this violation, and are intent on imposing their customs and cultural characteristics on America, rather than assimilating to derive the greater benefits of the American system, can do nothing except wreak havoc on it.

This is totally dysfunctional. The invading aliens are a threat to the health and safety of Americans and the integrity of our system.

They are a threat for the reasons cited as well as their alien, Third World culture mentality.

***

Thus, the ultimate consequence of unchecked, illegal invasion of Latin immigrants into the U.S. will permit them to become the largest ethnic group. Then this will result in dissolution of a free, democratic, capitalistic and prosperous America that was developed by Western Protestant culture which is alien and uncomfortable to the invaders.

If Mexico had a culture or a system anything like the American democratic, capitalistic system, Mexicans Nationals would not be leaving their country to come to America for what they perceive a better life. But it does not and cannot. The Mexican system is not capitalistic. The availability of capital is extremely limited primarily because wealthy Mexicans send their money to the U.S.

Without capital availability for business investment and home purchases, Mexico will never be able to provide a satisfactory,

Western-like, standard of living for its population. And the oligarchs have never demonstrated any desire to help advance the welfare of their own citizens. They prefer to place most of their capital in a safer environment than that which they have wrought. They put their money in U.S. investments.

Although most are not cognizant of it, the nature of a country and its culture, or system of government is a direct result of the mindset and characteristics of the people who comprise it.

Therefore, it is mandatory to consider what wrought the Mexican system the illegal aliens are leaving, and that same system they will impose upon any part of America where they reach majority, critical mass status. This will be Mexico in America. No question.

To view this future America, all anyone has to do is visit Los Angeles and go downtown, or to the Wilshire District that were so attractive and prosperous prior to the massive Latin invasion that turned them into Latin, crime-ridden, ghettos.

Then go to Mexico City where it is not safe to drive a nice car, wear a good watch, or take a taxi if you are a "gringo," to see the future of Los Angeles. Both of these experiences would be prophetic trips into the future of a Latin America United States.

"*The Establishment liberal progressives*" either desire to ignore or are incapable of intellectually grasping the empirical evidence of these adverse consequences of Mexican immigration. They think they will not be affected. They will be above it, and in charge, as did Hillary Clinton who so assiduously pursued turning America into Mexico.

This is short sighted on their part. But average Americans, who will be adversely affected in their everyday lives, should not overlook the consequences of what unchecked immigration holds for them, and should act to avert the future it will bring.

To save America, its form of Government, its culture, its civilization, and continue to provide a free, democratic and prosperous future for it, requires an immediate cessation of Mexican and Central American immigration. But this will not happen unless sufficient numbers of American citizens become well enough informed to demand it.

***

Both the Mexican Government and "*the Establishment*" are fully cognizant of the negative impact on America by its Mexican invasion even if the "*liberal, progressives*" life of privilege has sheltered them from these world realities.

The Mexican Government demonstrates knowledge of what unchecked immigration of those from a less economically successful culture can do to the prosperity of a country by stopping

Guatemalans, Hondurans, Salvadorans and Nicaraguans at its Southern border. Too bad "*the Brzezinski Establishment*" in the U.S. wants what Mexico does not.

This policy to prevent adverse effect on the prosperity of their country while, at the same time, enhancing its prosperity by having its least desirable engage in northward *"natural migration"* shows, unlike the U.S. Government, the Mexican Government is working for the benefit of Mexicans who choose to remain in Mexico.

It is not possible "*the Establishment*" in the U.S. cannot see and understand what the Mexican Government is doing. The Mexican Government is working for the benefit of its citizens who can contribute to its future, while those in successive U.S. Government Administrations have also been working for the benefit of Mexico and others that benefit from moving production to Mexico and importing cheap labor from there into the U.S. to the disadvantage of taxpaying Americans who are paying their salaries. Why?

Unfortunately, the answer always has to be M-O-N-E-Y. The U.S. Government is not working to enhance the lot of average working Americans. The last four "*Establishment*" U.S. Presidents clearly demonstrated to those aware of it, they have been working in accord with the Brzezinski Business Plan to enrich big business powerful interests that will benefit from production in Third World countries and Third World labor for production in America to secure their support for his *New World Order* goals.

But those unaware of his plans would not know of the obvious negative consequences of the outflow of production <u>and</u> the unchecked inflow of immigrants President Trump is trying to stop.

O.K! So, U.S. Presidents and the rest of "*the Establishment*" U.S. Government have been working for economic interests other than those of taxpaying Americans. But permitting U.S. sovereignty to be attacked, and do nothing about it? How could these Presidents of the United States get away with ignoring these attacks and calling the leaders of the country perpetrating them a *"friend"*?

Simple: as previously explained: <u>the controlled complicit U.S. media is the gate keeper that determines what information the American public is privy to.</u>

There have been over one hundred known incursions, invasions of the sovereign United States, by Mexican government military and federal police. Many of these occurred while Bush II was in office and since. On two of these occasions, in the fall of 2001, near El Paso, Texas, and in May 2002 in Arizona, U.S. Government Border Patrol officials were fired upon by the Mexican military.

During the incidents in May 2002 reported by a U.S. congressman on Bill O'Reilly's FOX NEWS show Mexican military intruded five miles into Arizona and shot out the windshield and a tire on the Border Patrol agent's vehicle.

Bill O'Reilly questioned why the U.S. media did not report this. This was a good question that O'Reilly could have answered easily. But the more important questions are why would the President of the United States and his Administration permit hostile military incursions into the sovereign territory of the United States, wherein the lives of U.S. Government agents were put at risk without mentioning them, or taking actions to stop this conduct well before the occurrences reached over one hundred in number?

And having reached over one hundred, why was President Bush II not only silent on the subject, but still embraced the leader of the Mexican Government perpetrating these actions against America?

The answer to that is also simple: because George Bush II just like his father who was a charter member was also a whore for the anti-American *New World Order* his father Bush I proudly announced just twelve years prior to this son being put into the Brzezinski *"Establishment"* controlled Government for the benefit of almost everyone in their world except working taxpaying American citizens.

Also, the Goebbels-like U.S. media would not report these incursions because it is also controlled by the same interests as both Bushes, and they did not want the American public to know what Mexicans were doing to America.

Bringing to their attention an actual act of hostile invasion other than the media supported illegal immigration could raise a red flag that might have resulted in an outpouring of negative opinion against Mexicans, and their immigration, which would not be good for the Brzezinski plan and its supporters like the Bushes.

This is just another media action, or inaction, that more than justifies President Trump's appellations of crooked, fake, biased, dishonest or anything else he desires because they are all accurate. It is just that their dishonesty is against the President in 2018 whereas it was protective of all four of the Presidents that preceded him.

But it is a safe bet they would not have been silent about it if it had been the U.S. military venturing into Mexico to stop the illegal drug trade the Mexican incursions are supporting. They and their *"liberal, progressive"* friends would have made anti-U.S. military, pro-Mexican, media hay!

What was the policy of *"the Establishment"* Oval Office occupied by Bush and Obama regarding protecting U.S. borders and citizens when a foreign country police or military invaded U.S. territory and fired on U.S. Government agents?

Since the U.S. was supposedly engaged in its "War on Drugs," and the Mexicans were making their incursions in support of the Mexican drug runners who have strong ties to corrupt Mexican Government, military and police officials who benefit from the sale of illegal drugs in the U.S., should not these invasions have been viewed in the context of the "War" just as the perpetrators of terrorism are viewed in the "War on Terror"?

To fail to put the U.S. military on the Mexican/American border and pursue the Mexican invaders who attack U.S. citizens and property in the United States across the border into Mexico just as the U.S. is pursuing terrorists in the "War on Terror" half way around the world, is intellectually and operationally inconsistent.

It makes a joke of the "War on Drugs," and continues to send the wrong message to the President and citizens of Mexico that U.S. laws and sovereignty do not apply to any Mexicans whose desire it is to break them. Is this not, yet, another example of political correctness run amuck in the previous two Administrations and by many others like the Governor of California in 2018 that President Trump is endeavoring to stop?

***

Let's see: U.S. agents operating in Mexico in the drug "War" are not permitted to carry weapons for their own protection. Some have even been murdered by the Mexicans. Yet Armed Mexican Government agents, on the other side in this "War," can invade the U.S. over one hundred times, fire at U.S. Government property and U.S. citizens with impunity, the media never reports it, and the two previous Presidents of the United States never mentioned it or did anything about it.

But when Trump puts the military on the border and endeavors to protect Americans the Brzezinski *"Establishment"* media and Democrats go after him full bore. Does this not prove to thinking average Americans the media is not their friend, nor were the previous two Presidents? If not, it should because if the people do not rise in support of Trump and his policies against this insanity America is definitively done.

It may be anyway. It might be too late. The last four U.S. Presidents were better friends to Mexican Presidents than to the American people. Could this be because *"the Establishment"* has already been pursuing visions of a greater political clout of the combined borderless North American countries under Brzezinski's *NWO* plan?

Whatever! Their policies, and lack of action, made the "World's Only Superpower" a laughing stock to all Mexicans... especially drug cartels... and most others in the world.

They were also a disaster due to the negative impact of Mexican drugs and immigration on the future of America. So, every thinking American should forcefully get behind Trump on this:

The U.S. Government is supposedly still conducting its "War on Drugs," and the President as the Chief Executive Officer of the Government agencies involved in the "War," as well as Commander in Chief of the U.S. Military, should utilize the full force of all law enforcement and the military in this "War" to stop the terrible damage it is doing to America. The large numbers of American citizens dying as result of drugs being brought over our southern border require and legally justify this.

Even though none of the three most recent U.S. Presidents or other politically connected members of their generation had even a passing acquaintance with the military, save one for a couple of weeks for political career purposes, they should know the title confers not just respect from others, but an obligation to fulfill the roles the titles confer.

Therefore, when officials of foreign government agencies or military such as the Mexican National Police or Mexican Military the drug cartels they support invade U.S. territory and take hostile action, firing on U.S. citizens and property, this should trigger the Commander in Chief and the Chief Executive Officer of the United States, and the U.S. Congress, into action.

The fact the U.S. is engaged in "War" against these very elements perpetrating the attacks should elicit a prompt response from it. For the President, and the Congress, to ignore these attacks, fail to address them, or act to prevent them, represents a failure to fulfill the responsibilities of the position the title connotes.

Also, given the fact several U.S. Presidents previously created *false flag* events, lied to the American people, Congress and even the United Nations to start unnecessary wars then wasted trillions of dollars on these wars does it not make sense that when there was a real attack from a country actually adversely affecting the U.S., resulting in the deaths of tens of thousands of Americans, at least one of these Presidents should have acted strongly against that country rather than against those that did nothing to deserve being attacked?

***

The following should serve to prove what worthless political hacks, rather than protectors of Americans and their country, those Presidents, especially the most recent two, Obama and Bush II were. Also, in addition to these two Clinton, Carter and Bush I were also hacks who did nothing while in Office except serve their *"Establishment"* puppet master Brzezinski to further weaken the United States of America in pursuit of his ultimate *NWO* goals.

Note:

Article I Section 8. of the *Constitution of the United States* states, **"The Congress shall have Power to ... provide for calling forth the Militia to ... repel Invasions."**

Article I Section 8. Also states, the Congress shall have the power **"To make all Laws which shall be necessary and proper for carrying into Execution the foregoing Powers."**

WELL? What the hell held back the previous five Presidents and Congress from doing their duty to protect the American people as they were supposed to, as President Trump began endeavoring to do in 2017... over thirty years after it should have been done?

Answer: the goddamned *New World Order* of which all were either members or nothing but obedient little puppets.

If Bush II had used the military to quell the invasions and drugs from Mexico instead of lying about "9/11" and Iraq, then invading, bombing and killing hundreds of thousands of people in the Middle East, the U.S. and Americans would have five trillion dollars less wealth depleting debt, thousands of us would still be alive, Islamic terror would not have been dramatically ramped up by his wars, the Mexican immigration and drug problems of 2018 would not be with us, and Bush would be a hero rather than the International War criminal reviled by much of the world he legitimately is.

But the failure of Presidents and the U.S. Congress to take actions against Mexican Government invasions, by definition, is indicative of the problems plaguing the Government at ALL levels, in all three branches: Incompetence, greed and a focus on satisfying the Brzezinski *New World Order* "Plans for America."

If these people were in private enterprise, or public companies, they would probably have been fired for incompetence and negligence because it can easily be proven none of them were attempting to fulfill their obligations to their shareholders, the American public, to protect them, their borders, or their civilization from invasion and destruction.

They were playing at their "jobs," reaping the benefits without providing that which they each took an oath to provide. They were spending their time traveling and making speeches because this is much easier than taking care of the business of America, and it is much more profitable from a fundraising point of view.

***

As previously stated and proven by these hack Presidents; the U.S. Government is no longer *"of the people, by the people, for the people."* It is like Mexico's government of the oligarchy for the oligarchy. Maybe this is the reason U.S. Presidents prior to Trump feel such kinship with their Mexican counterparts rather than with the American people (?)

The U.S. Government is a bankrupt, corrupt and incompetent institution in every way, including morally, as recently proven by its Obama Presidency, many members of his Administration, "Justice" Department, FBI, and oh so many also America destroying, "*Establishment*" members of Congress.

Since the Mexican actions should have, long ago, ended any debate about putting the military on the U.S. border with Mexico, but this has not been done, nor has the media bothered to inform the American public about this, what is afoot?

Official agents of the government of Mexico have gotten away with murder of agents of the U.S. Government and with, at the same time, promoting the illegal invasion of millions of their country's citizens into the United States. Is there a connection?

Article I., Section 2. of the U.S. Constitution states: *"Privilege of the writ of Habeas Corpus shall not be suspended, unless when in cases of Rebellion or Invasion the public safety may require it."*

Note that Mexican Government agents and military crossing the U.S. border and shooting at Americans represents *"Invasion,"* and endangering the *"public safety"* of at least some Americans. And note: the Constitution does not place any quantitative qualifier of how many citizens' *"safety"* put at risk *"may require it."*

The intention of *"the writ of Habeas Corpus"* is to prevent, or correct, violations of personal liberty by directing judicial inquiry into the legality of detention. The supporters of illegal immigration have taken the position the illegal aliens cannot be detained because, after they are on U.S. soil, they have the same rights as American citizens, including *Habeas Corpus.*

Therefore, they cannot be detained, which is idiotic, given the *prima facie* evidence they have committed a crime is their very presence on U.S. soil.

The connection between ignoring the *"invasions"* and attacks on Americans by not acting under Article I., Section 8 of the Constitution to call *"forth the Militia to ... repel"* these *"invasions,"* and Article I. Section 2., *"the writ of Habeas Corpus,"* is that action under the former would appropriately define the *"invasions"* for what they are and trigger the latter. The *"Privilege of the writ of Habeas Corpus"* could be *"suspended."*

In other words, should the President and U.S. Government do what they have responsibility to do, protect the U.S., its property and citizen's *"public safety,"* in accord with the Constitution the nonsense argument of illegal alien immigrants having the same "rights" as citizens would be moot! Illegal aliens could be stopped, rounded up, and detained, which they should be, anyway, because

<u>illegal entry into the U.S. is breaking the law.</u>

But this is another case where the *New World Order* U.S. Government demonstrated its bias against American citizens.

Although it has violated the constitutionally provided protection of the Writ of *Habeas Corpus* of an American citizen, it refuses to do its duty when it applies to other than American citizens.

Given those in power in the U.S. Government must be cognizant of these facts they are willfully not acting under the Constitution for the interests of Americans. It is obvious they are not working for Americans but "*the Establishment*" that put them in power.

They are demonstrably willing to sacrifice America to fulfill the plans of a higher power. And that "power" has nothing to do with religion. It is the same power Jimmy Carter was satisfying by giving away the Panama Canal. They are all stealth *New World Order* worker bees. There is no other logical explanation.

***

If the intent of seekers of refuge from capitalism populating the U.S. Government is stealthily fulfilling *New World Order*, One World Government plans to stay in power in the U.S. Executive, Don Meredith will be needed sooner rather than later to sing "America's" new theme song, "*Turn Out the Lights, the Party's Over.*"

The Latino population will reach the critical mass of population to take over parts of the U.S. and representation in Congress to the extent they will redefine whole areas of America with their Latin culture, turning it into a replication of Mexico, poverty and all.

Their population is already reaching a point in some states wherein Latino "*pride*" is affecting business and politics in that the Spanish language, Latin culture and politics are displacing English, American culture and values. They do not have to speak English because their population is such a large percentage of the population they mostly speak only to one another, and they are too uneducated to understand the value of English to them.

There has already been a case, in 2002, in Florida, of a white, native born, English speaking American citizen being fired from her state government job because of her failure to speak Spanish. God help us because it seems earthly intervention is not available!

"*The Establishment*" media nonsense about Mexican contribution of cheap immigrant labor being necessary to the American farming industry is another negative.

European farming is being modernized to be technically superior while the U.S., which has been the superior producer for over one hundred years, is relying on cheap, Third World labor.

Again, this will result in the U.S. heading directly for Third World status in an industry it dominated for over a century.

What's wrong with those who support illegal immigration and make comments that they *"don't agree with"* those who have a position against "illegal" immigration? What kind of a mind does it take to disagree with being against something "illegal"? Wonder whether they disagree trespassing is illegal.

Don't they understand something that is "illegal" is against the law, and *"laws"* are one of the *"main foundations of every state,"* including the United States?

"Useful Idiot, liberal progressives" also like the idea of their position the U.S. is an *"immigrant nation"* therefore Mexican immigration is an American tradition and is *"good."*

This overlooks the fact that America's immigrant success has been the result of legal immigration and assimilation wherein the immigrants and their children have joined American mainstream culture and learned to speak the English language without the necessity to forget their Irish, Italian, or other heritages.

But they were mostly European with the same values that built first world Europe and North America, not Third World steeped in their religion and language because they have done nothing to be proud of during the past six hundred years the western world has passed them by. Don't believe this? Spend some time around a cathedral in Mexico.

This is what is wrong with the Mexicans. They are displacing advanced American culture and more efficient language with their own, backward culture and language out of *"pride"* that is being encouraged by the *"the Establishment liberal, progressives"* to further the success of the Brzezinski *"divide and conquer"* plan to change the nature of the U.S. population.

This does not bode well for the future of America. It indicates the new, Latin immigrant population, unlike the European immigrant population, is unaware of the benefits of the culture and language to which they are coming to escape the bonds of their own culture with which they ignorantly desire to displace ours. They are bringing their culture and language with them to the detriment of all Americans and their country.

That the Mexicans immigrating to the U.S. even have *"pride"* in Latin, or Mexican culture, when compared to Western culture, and desire to speak Spanish, rather than English, is further demonstration of an ignorance that does not hold a promising future for an America with a large Latino immigrant population.

A pragmatic look at the world at the beginning of the 21st Century should cause anyone intelligent to have something less than *"pride"* in the Spanish language, or Mexican or Latin cultures.

***

A realistic look at the world of the Spanish language versus English and the Protestant world versus the world of the Latin Church would provide an objective, intelligent person with all the necessary information required to show the benefits of English and Western culture over Spanish and Latin culture.

Twenty-five years before 2018 average annual per capita GDP of three hundred million Spanish-speaking people of the world was twelve hundred U.S. dollars, while the average per capita GDP of three hundred sixty million people whose first language was English was twenty-three thousand dollars, twenty times greater.

Thus, the Spanish language is demonstrably the language of poverty, whereas the English language is the language of wealth.

The average per capita GDP of the four hundred million members of the Latin Church, including the populations of Spain and Italy, was sixty-four hundred dollars, while the average per capita GDP of the nine hundred million members of Protestant churches, including Russia and the Ukraine which were under the constraints of Communism for seventy years, and South Africa, was seventeen thousand dollars.

If Russia, the Ukraine and South Africa were excluded the per capita GDP of Western Protestants was twenty-two thousand dollars. Therefore, given either the best, or the worst case, the per capita GDP of Protestants was between three and four times greater.

Thus, the culture of the Latin Church is also demonstrably a culture of poverty relative to the culture of the Protestant Church that is a culture of wealth.

However, it is not necessary for anyone to change his religion to become a participant in the benefits of Western culture. There are many Catholics and practitioners of other religions in America who are very successful. But English is mandatory for anyone to contribute to the American economy and realize the American dream benefits thereof.

There are more people in the world whose first language is English than whose first language is Spanish. But more important is the fact English has the most widespread use of any language.

Almost six hundred million people have elected to share English as a second language, resulting in a total worldwide English-speaking population of almost one billion people, almost three times as many people as the number that communicate in Spanish.

For Mexican immigrants to persist in speaking Spanish out of *"pride"* is ludicrous, especially when those people from much more successful cultures and countries such as Germans, Italians, Scandinavians, and others who having immigrated to the U.S. adopted English in order to be more successful.

"When in Rome" is a concept with which the most intelligent abide, showing just who are the Mexicans coming to America since most successful and educated Mexicans from the higher socioeconomic groups residing in Mexico are fluent in English.

Continuing to indulge in the characteristics of their Latin culture and speak Spanish, thereby depriving themselves of full participation in the superior benefits of America's Western culture out of *"pride"* represents a Third World ignorance that cannot be enhancing to America. And given their proclivities, their increasing numbers, and their failure to adapt, it is perfectly fair to define their invasion of the U.S. in terms of a threat to the American system, American culture, and the American economy.

***

Note in the prior paragraph Latin and Western cultures are addressed...two different cultures inhabiting approximately the same spaces in America. But the fact is there are also African and Asian cultures represented in significant numbers.

But do we hear about this in the media? No. We hear every day about the *"community"* when media and Government representatives are addressing these two major groups that have reached critical mass. In each case what we are seeing, and hearing is political correctness at work.

Both groups have cultural differences between one another, as well as differences with "Western culture" in values regarding education, work ethic, religion, languages, women versus men, etc., etc. because when any group becomes sufficiently large the members always seek the comfort of their culture.

Next time you hear about the *"community,"* realize this means culture... as differentiated from America's majority western culture by political correctness.

It is probably with this knowledge the *New World Order* and *"the Establishment"* are extremely happy with the success of their pro-illegal Mexican immigration policies, and that successive U.S. Governments have continued the policies that were so successful under them by ignoring their duties under the U.S. Constitution to stop this alien invasion

If the American public were not being deprived of knowledge of what is really going on at the Mexican border by the One World Government pro-weakening of the U.S. elements of the media, they would probably be in full concurrence with the Mexican southern border policy, and demand the U.S. Government to act in accord with the U.S. Constitution to respond to the Mexican military incursions, and repel the invasion of illegal Mexican immigrants by suspending the Writ of *Habeas Corpus* as authorized in Article I of the U.S. Constitution, detaining and deporting them to secure the future of a non-Latin, democratic and prosperous United States.

After all, President Bush unconstitutionally suspended *Habeas Corpus* for the American citizen his Administration held in jail without counsel by declaring, *"He is where he ought to be."* Why not do it, legally, to protect Americans, as he and all U.S. Presidents swear to do at their Inaugurations, by putting the illegal Mexican immigrants back in Mexico where they *"ought to be"*?

***

The foregoing addresses "*the Establishment*" deliberately importing thousands of people from Third World countries, Cuba, Vietnam, Cambodia, Laos as well as encouraging and facilitating illegal immigration of millions from Mexico, and the organized distribution of these people around the country to ensure their *"divide and conquer"* program of *"diversity"* is established throughout America.

They also imported thousands from Somalia, Ethiopia and other Third World Countries, and did the same distribution of them as part of this plan over the last two and one-half decades.

Obama even blatantly did this... because the inflow from Mexico had recently been insufficient to keep their destruction plan on schedule.

"Blatantly" because this importation of tens of thousands of young children from Honduras, the only Central America country in which the U.S. Government has a large presence, including the military, was very well organized.

They were bussed across Mexico, ushered through immigration and disbursed in a way that demonstrated prior planning.

In addition to the tightly knit structure of Latin families never permitting their children to be exported from their country alone in this way, neither the children nor their families would have been able to organize or finance this operation that has the fingerprints of U.S. planning all over it.

Of course, for each of the children at least two parents and other family members were not too far behind. So, this brought hundreds of thousands more dependents of the same culture as Mexico into the country at a cost of billions of dollars to American taxpayers to have their communities and towns further, more diversified culturally for the benefit of "*the Establishment"* Brzezinski Plan to *"change the nature of the population into one more accepting of more government control like those of Third World countries."*

Obama being the then titular head of the operational arm of the cabal of destruction we should understand why he did this. But it is impossible to fathom why he then began importing thousands of potential radical Islamic terrorists, or why the choice of "*the Establishment*" to replace him vowed to increase this by over five hundred percent. Hopes of creating "*another Pearl Harbor-like event*" as they stated in advance of "9/11"?

This bringing into the U.S. by Obama of thousands of Muslim refugees from Syria and other Mid East locales from which radical Islamic terrorism was being spread after every one of his military and security advisors informed him these refugees would be infiltrated by potential terrorists was an unconscionably heinous act on the part of this President whose multiplicity of Alinsky inspired and Brzezinski guided anti-American immigration and racially divisive acts over eight years had already done irreparable damage to the peace and harmony, and safety of all Americans.

And note: he brought almost five hundred of these potential terrorists into the U.S. during the week after the weekend terrorism in Orlando wherein fifty Americans were slaughtered by an Islamic Terrorist, and since his departure from the Oval Office he really had zero experience to occupy... except four years of Brzezinski ensuring he would fulfill his desired evil plans for America... many more innocent Americans have needlessly died at the hands of those he refused for eight years, as also did Bush II, to call "*Radical Islamist Terrorists.*"

It is the writer's opinion we are too far past the time when he could mentally justify this with his mentor, Brzezinski's comment, "*There isn't a global Islam.*" There is too much "*global*" evidence to negate this from any sane, rational, or honest mind.

So, we will have to leave this with the thought; immigration to "*diversify*" to "*divide and conquer*" is one thing, but aiding and abetting murder is quite another.

Therefore, whoever was responsible for bringing into the U.S. after the Orlando attack anyone who commits another attack resulting in the death of anyone should suffer the full extent of the law possible for aiding and abetting murder.

***

We should be aware by now President Trump is doing everything within his power to empower and enrich all Americans and protect us from terrorism and cultural and economic destruction the previous four Presidents, Carter and Brzezinski did everything within their power to cause through their "*New World Order Globalization*" efforts to "*divide and conquer*" us.

But in endeavoring to do this that is morally and fiscally right for Americans he is meeting tremendous resistance from "*the Establishment*" Goebbels-like minions in the media and many elected and non-elected Obama Government holdovers, plus many veneer Republican whores whose allegiance is also not to the American public but to those responsible for their American destroying political careers.

But these elements are not his, or our, only powerful enemies.

Obama is still assiduously pursuing a well-financed effort to *"disrupt everything our current President's Administration is trying to do."* So, not only was he given the Nobel Peace Prize without having ever done anything for anyone's *"peace,"* which put one million U.S. dollars in his pocket, and he left Office with a disclosed net worth equal to five times his eight year after tax income, he is still being financed to continue implementation of his mentor and puppeteer Brzezinski's plans to destroy America's sovereignty and make it just another member of his envisaged borderless, totalitarian *New World Order* One World Government.

If after reading the foregoing pages explaining the facts of this destructive conduct it is still not clear to you please read and reread the letter below making its way around the Internet in February of 2018 until you understand the truth of the foregoing. And while reading it please consider the writer to whom it is attributed was not an outspoken Trump supporter but was a decades long well respected unbiased political commentator.

"I do not understand how living in a country with its democracy established over 200 years ago, and now, for the first time in history, suddenly we have one of our former presidents set up a group called 'Organizing for Action."

"OFA is 30,000+ strong and working to disrupt everything our current president's administration is trying to do. This organization goes against our democracy, and it is an operation that will destroy our way of governing. It goes against our Constitution, our laws, and the processes established over 200 years ago. If it is allowed to proceed then we will be living in chaos very much like third world countries are run. What good is it to have an established government if it is not going to be respected and allowed to follow our laws?

"If you had an army some 30,000 strong and a court system stacked over the decades with judges who would allow you to break the laws, how much damage could you do to a country? We are about to find out in America.

"Our ex-president said he was going to stay involved through community organizing and speak out on the issues and that appears

to be one post- administration promise he intends to keep. He has moved many of his administration's top dogs over to Organizing for Action.

"OFA is behind the strategic and tactical implementation of the resistance to the Trump Administration that we are seeing across America, and politically active courts are providing the leverage for this revolution.

"OFA is dedicated to organizing communities for "progressive" change. Its issues are gun control, socialist healthcare, abortion, sexual equality, climate change, and of course, immigration reform.

"OFA members were propped up by the ex-president's message from the shadows: 'Organizing is the building block of everything great we have accomplished Organizers around the country are fighting for change in their communities and OFA is one of the groups on the front lines. Commit to this work in 2017 and beyond'

"OFA's website says it obtained its 'digital' assets from the ex-president's re-election effort and that he inspired the movement. In short, it is the shadow government organization aimed at resisting and tearing down the Constitutional Republic we know as AMERICA.

"Paul Sperry, writing for the New York Post, says, The OFA will fight President Donald Trump at every turn of his presidency and the ex-president will command them from a bunker less than two miles from the White House.

"Sperry writes that, 'The ex-president is setting up a shadow government to sabotage the Trump administration through a network of non-profits led by OFA, which is growing its war chest (more than $40 million) and has some 250 offices nationwide. The OFA IRS filings, according to Sperry, indicate that the OFA has 32,525 (and growing) volunteers nationwide. The ex-president and his wife will oversee the operation from their home/office in Washington DC.

"Think about how this works. For example: Trump issues an immigration executive order, the OFA signals for protests and statements from pro-immigrant groups; volunteers are called to protest at airports and Congressional town hall meetings; the leftist media springs into action in support of these activities; the twitter sphere lights up with social media; and violence follows. All of this happens from the ex-president's signal that he is heartened by the protests.

"If Barrack Obama did not do enough to destroy this country in the 8 years he was in office, it appears his future plans are to destroy the foundation on which this country has operated for the last 241 years.

"If this does not scare you, then we are in worse trouble than you know.

"So, do your part. You have read it, so at least pass this on so others will know what we are up against. WE are losing our country and we are so compliant. We are becoming the 'PERFEECT TARGET' for our enemy!

Attributed to,

Charles Krauthammer

Hopefully this will reinforce what is presented in this book to explain what is being done, and by whom, to Americans and our country that is terminal unless it is stopped now!

You should now understand also that what the previous *"Establishment"* Presidents were laying the groundwork for was the foundation... single political party, indoctrination, changing the nature of the electorate through immigration, and deliberately impoverishing us... for the final totalitarian nails to be driven into the coffin of our free and democratic America, and that Obama was as un-American a whore for *"the Establishment"* as they could have found except for Hillary Clinton who was intended to willingly provide the lid and the final nail for the coffin of our AMERICA.

But the fact she was not elected is likely the genesis of Obama's OFA. They are frantic not to permit *"outsider"* President Trump reverse their four decades of "progress," and divert America from their intended end for it as part of a doomed to failure *New World Order* One World Government in which Brzezinski and his ignorant, actually nut case, acolytes do not possess sufficient intellectual acuity to understand what they are pursuing is nothing but a worldwide version of the failed USSR that would also fail for the same reasons this earlier communist vision failed.

Therefore, if we are to survive we cannot permit them to stop Trump as the foregoing states they plan. He absolutely must survive and be successful!
Trump is our last hope!

If he is not successful there is no one else. Most of the powerful in the U.S. Government and in power elsewhere in America have tasted the rewards of membership in the cabal destroying America for personal gain and will not be diverted from their *NWO* course unless Trump is sufficiently successful to cause them to be rewarded via traditional values and work ethic that Made America Great from its beginning.

Also, the two oldest of the younger generations of Americans that will provide governance and corporate management as the current generation is replaced by them were schooled via the Brzezinski indoctrination model and will therefore not have the knowledge or will to redirect America to its previous course because they have been indoctrinated that is not the proper course.

They are "educated" communists like the Facebook founder advocating lower income groups be given money to increase their income like the hundreds of thousands of "*millennials*" marching and supporting Communist Bernie Sanders because he also advocates they receive so much free without working for it.

So, consider all this and what happened to Greece, Egypt and Rome that like other great civilizations literally disappeared, taking much accumulated knowledge, advancement and history with them, most of which was not... like something as simple as concrete in Rome... recovered for hundreds of years.

No one should be so complacent as to be a member of the *"It can't happen here"* group of non-thinkers. It can, and we are well on our way via loss of our history and culture being imposed by blacks, Latins and ignorant indoctrinated youth destroying historic symbols of American history and attacking our foundation: our culture.

Immigration is the planned final nail in the lid of the coffin of the America that was. Therefore, IT MUST BE STOPPED!

"Lose your history lose your culture and lose your country."

CHAPTER TEN
HEALTHCARE

IMPLEMENTING CONTROLS ON HEALTHCARE TO CONTROL THE PEOPLE AND CREATE A TOTALITARIAN STATE

1992, the year Bill Clinton was elected President, was almost two decades after Rockefeller and Brzezinski formalized their organization to enhance the power of the corporate/government *"Establishment"* to lead America to its planned destruction.

During this time their plans were being implemented and expanded to the detriment of ninety-nine percent of Americans and their country, as proven by the cost of housing being four times greater, private transportation three and one-third times greater, food three and one-half times greater, and the cost of healthcare more than five and one-half times greater.

The healthcare system during that time, and since, has been seriously, adversely affected and become exorbitantly expensive primarily as a result of the success of their plans to *"divide and conquer"* the population through immigration, as well as the success of Lyndon Johnson's *"Great Society."*

The explosion of Mexican immigration after Carter's signing of the Refugee Act of 1980, adding millions more to the population who could not afford to pay for their healthcare, and the planned breakup of black families through welfare legislation that turned a majority of the black population into welfare dependent single parent families added tremendously to the total cost of healthcare for all Americans.

The cost of providing this free healthcare to millions of non-paying, mostly impoverished recipients who procreate at a higher rate and require more healthcare than most citizens of America, has been laid off on average, responsible, working, asset owning, taxpaying Americans, driving up their costs while fewer of them were employed, and those who were have been losing purchasing power as a direct result of this and other actions of *"the Establishment"* in charge of the Government.

Though not politically correct to talk about, the procreation rate of Mexican immigrants is two to three times that of Protestant white America, the seventy percent of black babies born out of wedlock, the cost of gang warfare gunshot victims, the quarter million dollars for each crack baby before they leave the hospital, etc. by people who are demonstrably less personally, socially and economically responsible are all costs laid on the backs of average, working, taxpaying Americans of all ethnic groups.

For example: before Johnson's *"Great Society"* average working, taxpaying Americans could go to the hospital to add a new member to their family for a cost of less than one thousand dollars. But by 1992 they were charged an amount equal to the cost of seven babies to cover the cost of the non-payers, or about $7,000 even though their incomes during the same time increased maybe three times.

But let's not forget this was not monetary inflation. It was largely population "inflation."

While the subject is healthcare let's put something to rest. That would be the years' long rhetorical debate about not having... and the non-desirability of..."socialized medicine" in the U.S.

How would healthcare provided for free to tens of millions of people by the Government, but paid for with funds taken from others be classified? What would this form of Government provided healthcare be called if not "socialized?

The answer should be obvious to rational, intelligent, objective minds. So....

***

In 1993, Bill Clinton's first year in office, presumably because of this unsustainable healthcare situation providing cover, Hillary Clinton attempted to impose ostensibly her own version of a stealth healthcare system on America she created illegally, secretly, out of public view.

It would have nationalized fifteen percent of the U.S. economy, rationed healthcare and turned over to U.S. Government bureaucrats the decisions about who would receive what care.

This would have added to the size of the Government tremendously, in addition to removing the legal protection under the law of *"physician/patient privilege,"* thus actually changing the law, and reaching into the private lives of people as probably never done before... at least not in America.

Remember: Hillary was a lawyer at the time she proposed this. But she became a lawyer after passing the bar in Arkansas after failing the District of Columbia bar exam. So maybe in addition to not being licensed (unless she passed the D.C. bar exam later) she might not have been fully cognizant of the law.

But, as she has proven over and over since, "making false statements" to Federal Government investigators in 1996 and as Secretary of State she treated like a worldwide traveling fellowship, visiting one hundred and twenty countries, breaking laws regarding handling classified documents, committing perjury by lying to Congress and obstruction of justice in destroying evidence, she does not think laws apply to her.

So, additionally, she planned to criminalize the conduct of any Americans over the age of sixty-five who sought unapproved healthcare, or healthcare providers who provided this care to them.

She also planned to reduce the number of doctors by twenty-five percent and the number of specialists by fifty percent, virtually eliminating medical science advancement in the U.S.

Presumably this was to provide funding for the massive increase in Government employment required to intervene in every doctor/patient decision in America.

Her plan included a card be provided to each person that would be required for access to healthcare. This is reasonable and normal except for one little addition: her cards would be geographically limited, thus limiting people's movements unless they were willing to risk not having access to healthcare or getting Government approval for their planned trip *a la* totalitarian communist China.

This was not different from Mao's China wherein Chinese citizens and everyone else in the country was limited geographically by their "papers" it was necessary for everyone to have with them at all times, which brings to mind the subject of immigration again.

How many Americans are aware they cannot be in Mexico unless they have Mexican Government issued "papers" proving they are in the country with the approval of the Mexican Government, and if they are found there without these papers they will be arrested because it is a crime to be there illegally without documentation proving the government approved their presence in Mexico?

This is a fair question at this point because we are discussing a major problem created to a very great extent by Mexicans entering the U.S. without "papers" or the ability to support themselves, just as Brzezinski planned to change the nature of the U.S. electorate.

After all, Bill Clinton and George Bush I and II were friends with the President of Mexico because he was also a member of their *"New World Order,"* and familiar, as they were, with the fact Americans caught in that country without proper "papers" would be treated like Central Americans crossing Mexico's southern border: sent directly to jail!

Presumably they have very different views than most Americans of what friendship is. But back to Hillary and her planned healthcare for America's also planned growing masses of illegal residents who cannot support themselves.

Why would she have desired to limit travel of American citizens within their own country on the ostensible basis of healthcare, yet… at the same time… be a *bona fide* member of *"the Establishment,"* supporting the mass *"migration"* of literally millions of Mexicans traveling freely into, and presumably within the U.S?

How would she have handled their healthcare? Would they have been given a pass on needing cards for their free healthcare, or assigned geographically limiting cards also? So many questions about an illogical plan that failed to address the cause and effect of the problems at hand: too many people not paying for their healthcare and how to pay for it?

It seems she was just too "hung up" on making America a non-sovereign member of the Socialist Totalitarian *New World Order* to be bothered or concerned with the actual problems of ordinary citizens, or even her desired illegal residents, a position she was supported in from the very top of "*the* [deliberately destructive] *Establishment.*"

During the process of endeavoring to impose this destructive totalitarian program that would have been prohibitively expensive, as well as destroy much of what was "America" at that time even before Obama, or before her husband, Bill the new President, was fully informed of her plans.

In a press interview about the proposed program Bill suggested some of it might be flexible, or subject to change. Subsequent to this West Virginia Senator Jay Rockefeller, nephew of THE *New World Order* co-conspirator of Brzezinski, David Rockefeller, was informed of Bill's comment by another member of the press.

His response, "*Well, he* (the President) *should ask his wife about that,*" tells us all we need to know. Hillary was a *bona fide* member of "*the* [America destroying] *Establishment*" as far back as when she was at Yale in the early 1970s, as confirmed by her, since she claims to have met Bill at Yale.

As previously stated: after she was in the White House, in response to a reporter's question, she stated, "*My! I have known Vernon Jordan even longer than I have known my husband.*"

This Jordan person is a powerful early member of the "*Establishment,*" organization, close to its two founders, who like Brzezinski the media never mentions, but has played a large role in many Government decisions over the years since 1973, and possibly before, as well as being a member of the boards of numerous major corporations in the list of *Members of the Club.* Want to confirm this? Just Google his name to see all the corporate boards and other "connected" positions he has held.

Hillary is the best example alive in America today of the phrase "*Power corrupts, absolute power corrupts absolutely!*" She has been protected by the very powerful behind the U.S. Government for so long she has no problem lying under oath or breaking any laws she thinks do not apply to her.

The Director and very top "management" of the F.B.I. along with the directors of the C.I.A. and National Security Agency, and the Attorney General of the U.S. proved she was correct in this assessment in 2016 by refusing to indict her for proven criminal acts, totaling seventeen at last count, including risking national security of the U.S.

So, don't expect her to change. She won't. Why would she when all her co-conspirator members of the Brzezinski *"Deep State"* broke so many laws endeavoring to ensure she would be the next Obama, and Donald Trump would never be the *"outsider President"* they knew he would be because he is not a member of their vast formal conspiratorial club engaged in the deliberate destruction of a free, democratic, capitalistic America.

Had Hillary won the Presidency it would definitely have been *"Turn out the Lights"* time for the America so many elected President Trump to save from the continuing destruction they could see was being wrought. But we are far from out of the woods on this yet. Hillary, Obama and all the above listed criminals with the help of their complicit media are still assiduously pursuing removing him from office, illegally.

***

But thankfully, all those years before, she was not successful in this, her first official totalitarian effort, of imposing a "healthcare" program to control them on unsuspecting Americans at that time.

They would have to wait a generation for a Bush appointed *New World Order* Supreme Court Chief Justice willing to ignore the Constitution and rule the un-Constitutional act of Government forcing citizens to pay corporations for something they might not desire to purchase a criminal act if they elected not to comply.

Just this first act by a supposedly, but demonstrably not impartial Supreme Court should have informed Americans their historically reasonably free, fair and just Government, and the country they knew was no longer. And they would have had this happened at the time Hillary endeavored to impose her plan.

But Brzezinski/Carter imposition of Government indoctrination to dumb down the population proved its worth in this case, especially where the indoctrinated young were concerned.

Few people, especially these subjected to the public-school system since Hillary's "healthcare" effort had a clue what was being done to them by taking away their right to choose whether they wanted to buy something they did not need or desire to pay for.

Since Hillary's effort the inflation in costs of living continued to become much worse, especially in the case of healthcare, in which the Government has the most hand.

The increases in salary, wages and retirement benefits have not even come close to keeping up with the increases in living costs. Clearly, the programs of Brzezinski have served only to impoverish Americans, as planned. But it was going to get worse! The next *"Establishment"* whore to address the "healthcare" care problems at least had a plan that solved the problem of "how to pay for this?"

***

LYING ABOUT "HEALTH" INSURANCE AND FORCING THOSE WITH ASSETS TO FATTEN INSURANCE COMPANY COFFERS

In 2008, it was time for someone else to take a shot at doing to the American people what Hillary failed to do on behalf of the Rockefeller/Brzezinski *"Establishment"* in 1993.

That person was Muslim sounding named Barrack Hussein Obama II who has never provided qualified proof, only a Certificate of Live Birth that is not proof, he is a natural born American and qualified to be President.

Never mind that though because he was not qualified in any other way either. His only experience before Zbigniew Brzezinski, according to Brzezinski himself who spent four years grooming him to be President, was as a "community organizer" on the South Side of Chicago. This was a position that involved informing welfare recipients about and helping them obtain maximum Government benefits... a work he continued as President

He did this as an acolyte of avowed communist totalitarian advocate Saul Alinsky in addition to following Brzezinski guidance in wreaking as much damage on America as humanly possible in eight years, endeavoring to get it ready to be the impoverished, racked by racial divide, and predominately non-Eurocentric non-sovereign member of the borderless *New World Order*, rivaling if not exceeding Carter's damage, eventually sending it into history's dustbin of failed Socialist states.

He did so much damage to America, and continues to do so through his anti-America OFA organization many have asked the pertinent question, *"How could a real America loving American deliberately do this much damage to his fellow citizens and their shared country, obviously attempting to destroy it?"*

There are a couple of possible answers: 1.) he really, as his actions indicate, does not even like, let alone "love" the America so many of us *"Deplorables"* do, 2.) he was promised so much, and obviously received it, anyone as unprincipled as he could not refuse.

But whichever, at this point we should remember the influence of both Alinsky and Brzezinski on him. So, not surprisingly, having liked Alinsky's anti-American ideas for years, and seeing many of them already imposed on us, the good little groomed and surely to be rewarded enormously puppet followed Brzezinski guidance, as if he had a choice, endeavoring to accomplish what Hillary could not.

Obama pushed his vision of "healthcare" reform that satisfied Rockefeller and Brzezinski's desires through Congress a decade and a half after Hillary's effort.

He did this with knowledge it has "squat" to do with healthcare, and he was lying to Americans all the time he was further impoverishing them while enriching insurance company executives.

He deliberately increased the costs of already insured working, taxpaying, asset holding Americans, increasing by fifty to one hundred percent their cost of "health" insurance and getting young Americans who do not need it to pay for it through unconstitutional penalties complements of "*the Establishment*" Chief Justice of the Supreme Court described above.

Why would he do this only so these billions and billions of dollars eventually amounting to trillions if America can stand that long after what Obama and his three predecessors have done... can be unnecessarily taken from working, taxpaying Americans and passed through insurance companies when he is fully aware there is no such thing as "health" insurance?

We should, by now, know the answer to that, but to ensure everyone understands the *"Why?"* part of it, let's explain what Obama knew about "there is no such thing as 'health' insurance."

He knew insurance was not required for people who could not afford it to obtain healthcare because it is legislated hospitals cannot turn away those in need of care if they cannot pay.

He also knew because he was a community organizer; all the costs of uninsured care for inner city gunshot, and accident victims and any other healthcare, including births of the exploding populations of illegal immigrants and other inner-city populations were already covered by working Americans and companies through income tax payments.

He had to know this because informing his inner-city clients of this was part of his only pre-political paying employment as a "community organizer."

He also knew, as do the non-paying recipients; "health insurance" is not required for them to receive care because they do not possess assets against which providers can place liens to collect their exorbitant fees, which are primarily the result of their having to "eat" the cost of providing for the non-payers that is not reimbursed by the Government.

He was probably also aware the major cause of bankruptcy filings of most retired Americans is they have only as much insurance as they can afford, which is frequently insufficient to cover the exorbitant costs of their healthcare that is a result of the non-paying minority patients like his community organizer clients. But that was obviously not a concern for him. Other Americans were not his clients, even as President.

He proved this in many ways, but especially when he provided free cell phones and free usage time to inner city residents but did not provide them to any other Americans.

Obama and all others in the Government are well aware of its inability to cover the cost of all those who do not pay. Its current and anticipated taxation revenue stream covers barely half of the current cost of his greatly expanded Government.

As well as this tremendous current cost, he deliberately increased costs through *"the Establishment divide and conquer"* plans by planning for those already here illegally to become voters and planning even more to follow to further enhance Government power and increase costs further impoverishing his non-client citizens.

He was also aware taxes on corporations already highest in the industrialized world could not be increased nor would further tax increases on the working be politically acceptable even though that is from whence he and his socialist Government cronies knew the money must come, as did Rockefeller and Brzezinski years before.

Therefore, although Obama knew "there is no such thing as health insurance" because he knows **it is only asset protection insurance** he could not refer to it by this true name without informing the masses they do not require what he, a modern sort of snake oil salesman, desired to sell to them that they did not need without informing them of what he was really doing.

He knew Obamacare, AKA the Affordable Care Act, was nothing but socialist redistribution of wealth through further taxation on those with assets already paying more than they can afford. So, rather than a tax, he and his co-conspirators presented it in a non-Constitutional format of forced payments to "health" insurance companies who are now stripping out a further unnecessary share of the dwindling wealth of working Americans.

This is for being the middlemen to provide "insurance" coverage to welfare receiving members of the population who will continue to receive care free via subsidies provided at the expense of the now further burdened taxpayers through increases in the cost of their asset protection, "health" insurance.

Now, hopefully, every reader understands Obama was nothing

but a "community organizer" head of a national corporate/socialist regime who was working to equalize the wealth of his constituency base of non-working dependents with that of those who work and contribute, while diverting as much as he could from contributors into coffers of his second constituency of corporations and their executives who in turn rewarded him and other seekers of refuge from capitalism, its risk and work requirements by hiding out in Government, or as lobbyists.

He was doing the same as all his predecessors since Carter, except Reagan; pursuing conversion of the U.S. from an ostensibly representative democracy to a plutocratic, centrally controlled, corporate/government, Fascist/Socialist by definition totalitarian State as promulgated by his "*outstanding thinker*" mentor, creator and puppet master, Zbigniew Brzezinski.

He also rewarded international corporations that already benefit from not paying taxes on foreign income kept overseas with even more profits potentially to be kept tax free through accounting treatments involving overseas divisions while being rewarded lavishly for this and keeping Americans hoodwinked about all this being at their expense, not knowing what is being done to them and unaware to thwart their demise what they need do is follow and stop the M-O-N-E-Y they should be aware is the problem, considering Obama like the Clintons had very little before entering the Presidency but after almost eight years of earning less than four hundred thousand a year had a reported net worth of over nine million dollars when left office.

He probably also knew his "health" insurance plan would also assist him in lies about the economy. The way GDP, Gross Domestic Product, is calculated the massive increased costs of his plan paid by taxpaying Americans increased the reported GDP although it did nothing to enhance the real economy.

Meanwhile, not a damned thing about actual physical healthcare has changed, except it seems to have become more limited, especially for older, retired Americans on that "entitlement" called Medicare they paid into for fifty years, and do not have the choice to cease paying more into each month until they die.

Obviously, we now know Hillary's and Obama's Totalitarian programs were structured not to solve any problems plaguing Americans because they were deliberately created to change America as Obama promised at the beginning of his reign. He just failed to reveal his changes would worsen the plight of America!

***

But if Americans keep Trump in office two terms we can be saved from changes like what Obama wrought on us and future Supreme

Court decisions like enabling Obamacare because, in addition to replacing Justice Kennedy, he may have two more opportunities by replacing Ginsberg and Breyer, thereby ensuring solid Constitutionalists will comprise a majority in the Court to the benefit of all Americans for a generation.

CHAPTER ELEVEN
"GUN CONTROL"
The final Nail

REMOVE THE ABILITY OF THE PEOPLE TO DEFEND THEMSELVES FROM THE GOVERNMENT TO CREATE A POLICE STATE.

Note: the members of the Brzezinski *"Establishment"* cabal have been working assiduously since 1973 *"TO CREATE A POLICE STATE"* in America.

However, before we proceed let's address facts relating to this that those in the *"It can't happen here"* crowd of believers that all of this about Brzezinski and his formal organization cabal to do what is previously presented in this book is nada but *"conspiracy theory."*

In 1975 the Trilateral Commission cofounded by Brzezinski and Rockefeller in 1973 released a book length report entitled The Crisis of Democracy that was concerned with the *"governability of the democracies."* One of the authors was Samuel Huntington a U.S. Government advisor and former chairman of the Department of Government at the alma mater of Brzezinski and Kissinger the Author of this work has previously designated *"the epicenter of the destruction of America"*- Harvard University.

This appellation is based on its contribution to exactly that through many of its graduates, especially PhDs like Brzezinski and Kissinger, and so many others who have been senior participants is so much of what has been detrimental to the survival of a free, democratic and capitalist America for at least half a century.

In that report is stated what is needed in the industrial democracies, like the United States, *"is a greater degree of moderation in democracy."*

For any who might be confused by the subtleties of the English language this is just another way of saying what Rockefeller stated; *"Americans have too much democracy."*

Readers interested in knowing what these people intend for America can Google "Trilateral Commission" and read the propaganda purveyed by it in language of obfuscation to endeavor to conceal its actual nefarious purpose and facts of it, some of which are included in Brzezinski's statements presented in this book.

Should one care sufficiently to do that he or she would find tidbits about the views of Commission hierarchy like human rights are non-extant in their desired world that would be more like the feudal systems of Medieval Europe ruled by autocratic kings and queens, and the media like we have witnessed since Trump became President that is *"properly submissive"* to the state propaganda system, like Hitler's Goebbels system.

These are frightening but true facts about desires and plans of the anti-Trump media and so many others we know Hillary Clinton and Barrack Obama have assiduously followed since they were students.

Both were adherents of ideas that were the guidepost for *"leftist counter-culture"*... meaning opposed to the culture of America ... radicals in their young adulthood, as proved by their being acolytes of communist Saul Alinsky.

Then throughout their adult political lives both have proven through actions and statements they have endeavored to implement totalitarian policies of population control advocated by him and secretly pursued by Brzezinski and his *"Establishment."*

If members of the electorate were aware in the 1980s and 1990s what Hillary, then Obama in the first decade of the new century were interested in doing to America neither would have had political careers unless they immigrated to Eastern Europe.

Thus, the dishonest, *"leftist Establishment"* controlled U.S. media in which many had to have known about these two could have saved America from their destruction.

But what is more frightening is what the major players in *"the Establishment"* media who continue to tirelessly support and promote these two informs us those in control of our Government are still pursuing for Americans on this subject of gun control.

It is obvious what Hillary, Barrack and *"the Establishment"* in control of the U.S. Government and all the *"leftist"* media advocates for *"gun control"* really want to do:

They definitely want to remove our ability to protect ourselves from them as they work to turn America into a non-sovereign, borderless, *"leftist"* Police State member of their *New World Order* modeled on Stalin's USSR.

This is pure evil, like most of Brzezinski's written words clearly define it. There is no other word for it.

Hillary Clinton, Barrack Obama and all the others in *"the Establishment,"* their controlled media and the Government advocating and working to implement this and the other, previous five steps to destroy America are pure evil incarnate, as was Zbigniew Brzezinski as the instigator of much of this with Rockefeller backing and money.

Hillary Clinton and Barrack Obama have been prominent faces of the evil assiduously pursuing the destruction of the America most

Americans and the world loved. <u>It is time they were uncovered and shown to the electorate for what they really are.</u>

***

Since Hillary raised the issue of Trump's tax returns in 2016 and she has continued to nauseously complain about the election results there should be a big push to get her to unseal and grant public access to her college thesis, all her speeches to *"the Establishment"* plutocracy and all others, in addition to all her Emails, including those her State and Justice Department co-conspirators were still withholding in 2018 for reasons that should be obvious.

Given she insisted all these contain *"no "Classified" information"* and the State Department concurred, stating they will release them since they are defined public information, and must be released sometime... we know not when... unless this country is already under control of a *de facto* totalitarian regime.

She is already disliked. If the public is made aware of her thinking and what she has been working to do to America for forty years she would be "toast" to more than the half she decried as *"deplorables,"* and maybe she would finally disappear.

"Crooked Hillary" is one thing, but *"**America destroying Hillary"*** is another.

Most people think there are crooks everywhere, especially in government. But they don't associate this with any adverse effect on them personally. However, they do relate to America and understand what destroying it would do to them personally, which is important. Thus, *"America destroying"* is a truth that would personalize it for everyone. So, this would be partisan for America.

***

Amendment II. of the Constitution of the United States states, *"... **the right of the people to keep and bear Arms, shall not be infringed."***

This is a complete thought, and it is obvious the first part of this Amendment, *"A well-regulated Militia, being necessary to the security of a free State..."* was intended to be made up of *"the people"* with *"Arms"* to maintain the *"security of a free State."*

Amendment IX. States, *"The enumeration in the Constitution, of certain rights, shall not be construed to deny or disparage others retained by the people."*

Therefore, *"A well-regulated Militia"* cannot, in any legitimate way, *"be construed to deny"* that *"the right of the people to keep and bear Arms"* is granted, or *"enumerated"* elsewhere in the Constitution.

In this year 2018, this *"right"* of individuals, *"the people,"* to own firearms, *"arms,"* is one with which legal scholars concur. It is still argued, however, by the *"liberal"* gun control advocates, especially in media such as THE NEW YORK TIMES Op Ed columns, that the Constitution confers the right to bear arms only upon a *"Militia,"* and not the citizens.

Constitutional "Right" Confirmed

To his credit, Attorney General, John Ashcroft stated during the Bush II Administration, *"**Let me state unequivocally my view that the text and the original intent of the Second Amendment clearly protect the right of individuals to keep and bear firearms. While some have argued that the Second Amendment guarantees only a 'collective right' of the states to maintain militias, I believe the amendment's plain meaning and original intent prove otherwise.**"*

Further, the Ashcroft Justice Department, unlike that of Obama, defended gun laws. It's stated position was, *"...the Second Amendment more broadly protects the right of individuals, including persons who are not members of any militia or engaged in active military service or training, to possess and bear their own firearms, subject to reasonable restrictions designed to prevent possession by unfit persons or to restrict the possession of types of firearms that are particularly suited to criminal misuse."*

Given Ashcroft's statement and that of his Justice Department, it would seem the Bush Administration was on the side of the people regarding the right to bear arms. But the problem is at least one in that administration, possibly to balance Ashcroft's position to maintain Bush family *"New World Order"* credentials declared by Bush I, appeared to be on the side of the Clinton and Obama Administrations that both assiduously pursued destruction of the people's rights.

Continuum of "Establishment" Control

Secretary of State, Colin Powell's office supported the position that could explain why he was advanced over many others to his high military position. That was the ridiculously anti-American sovereignty position that the United States should sign a United Nations gun control treaty.

Given the United Nations has a stated objective of disarming the entire world, especially the U.S., except for itself in the form of its military that would be the control element of its *New World Order* One World Government, why did not the Bush Administration disavow the Powell position and have a consistent policy for both domestic and foreign dissemination?

This lack of a clearly defined policy on this issue so important to the freedom of Americans is disconcerting, but not surprising because the little Bush was always a strictly *NWO* President, following in his father's footsteps in every way on every issue.

However, the knowledge that at least some members of that administration were on the side of the American public should give Americans a little comfort relative to the position of the previous, *"Leftist liberal,"* Clinton Administration and the even more so Obama Administration's consistent anti-gun policy on the issue.

The entire Clinton Administration was with Hillary on the side of the *NWO* United Nations in its desire to disarm honest, law-abiding, Americans… as she still is.

Notable among *"the Establishment"* members of the Clinton Administration in the anti-gun ownership corner was Vice President, Al Gore, who, it should be noted, did beat Bush in the popular vote of the American electorate.

This is important because if it were not for the citizens of Gore's home state of Tennessee voting for Bush, Gore would have been President, and the administration that would have been in power in 2001 would have, without ambiguity, aggressively moved the U.S. in the direction of the United Nations on this issue, as well as many others in conflict with the interests of Americans… as did Obama.

The people of Tennessee elected not to support their native son because they knew him and his position on the issues of gun control and others. Many likely voted for him because they really did not know him. Otherwise, the degree of concurrence with *"the liberal Establishment"* of the American electorate bodes very badly for the future of freedom, as does the fact that *"Establishment"* President Bush signed the Campaign Reform Act unconstitutionally restricting groups such as the National Rifle Association from running advertising sixty days prior to elections to inform and educate voters during the time it is really important to do so.

The fact Bush II chose not to support his Attorney General's position, but that of Clinton and Obama demonstrates the absolute fact of the "two party" sham perpetrated on Americans, as well as the pro United Nations, One World Government position of Bush.

"Gun Control Establishment"

The position of so-called *"liberals"* like Hillary and Obama regarding the right of citizens to bear arms has been well articulated for years. They have been strongly in favor of limiting through *"gun control"* the individual's right to bear arms.

This *"Establishment"* position has not changed. But rather than continuing to openly inform voters of their true intent, after Gore's loss in Tennessee, they... at least for a while, surely to Hillary's dismay... tempered their official policy to a more broadly acceptable *"sensible gun safety."* However, since Obama they flipped back to "control," which, thankfully, helped adversely affect Hillary's bid for the Presidency.

This will be more difficult to address from an opposition point of view should Republicans endeavor to support the positions of those members of the electorate they purport to represent.

The *"liberal"* position on gun control has never made sense. It seems illogical for anyone to desire to deprive himself of the right to protect his family by suppressing the rights of everyone to own a gun. Therefore, those who support this *"liberal"* position must believe they are in the same category as Hillary, exempt from laws of the land.

Surely, there cannot be many who count themselves in the *"liberal"* camp who do not understand the meaning of the term "outlaw" even if they don't, as evidenced by the Clinton Presidency and more recently by Hillary, Obama, the FBI Director and the Attorney General, fully understand the term "criminal."

Obviously, both terms describe those who choose not to abide by laws most members of society abide by. Thus, by definition, criminals choosing to ignore the law would still have guns, while the law-abiding would not have the means to protect against them.

Still, members of *"the Establishment"* its media and the Hollywood *"liberal"* contingent assiduously pursue the disarmament of American citizens. They do this while they must be aware of the large criminal element that would surely be a threat to many of them who have obvious wealth demonstrated in the size and locations of their homes and their expensive automobiles.

For example: The *"liberal"* Hollywood supporters of *"gun control"* (and Clinton/Obama) could not live in Los Angeles without being aware of the very large criminal element versus the meager police resources.

They could not be unaware of the estimated twenty thousand, armed gang members (outlaws and criminals) residing within an easy fifteen-minute drive of their large homes and families, or of the frequent home invasion robberies, car-jackings, and other crime in their city to which they are not immune. Why then would these people advocate a position that could clearly be potentially so detrimental to their own health and safety?

The answer to this question is like the answer to the query; why anyone would desire to be a Communist? The answer to that imponderable turned out to be quite simple: It is advocates of Communism like Hillary, Obama, *et al* who desire to be in charge and think they still would be even if everyone else had to live under communism.

The precepts of their desired *"leftist Establishment"* totalitarian society would not apply to them. Rather, they would be the enforcers of the precepts, just as in Hillary Clinton's Totalitarian Socialist scheme to ration healthcare of Americans wherein she was never concerned her healthcare would be rationed because she envisioned herself as the one who would be doing the rationing. Those at the top of communist regimes live very well.

The Clintonesque, *"liberal,"* advocates of *"gun control"* would never have their guns "controlled." Their positions would exempt them, and they would still have the means to protect themselves and their families. Only the majority, the proletariat of their utopian society, would be left to fend for themselves without the benefit of the right to bear arms.

Should anyone not believe this the case, consider the following: Sarah Brady who for decades has been one of the leading, most vociferous, politically connected and media supported, voices of the *"gun control"* movement preaching the evil of guns, and removal of them from the hands of Americans, gave her son a rifle for a Christmas present.

Further, television "personality" and avid anti-gun proponent, Rosie O'Donnell, frequently used her television program as a platform for spouting *"liberal, progressive Establishment"* agenda, including the elimination of guns, but had her personal body guard apply for a concealed weapon permit for her protection.

Let's not forget the Socialist (Democrat) veneer of the *faux* "two party" system. Even though their position is avid "gun control," their congressional members have had hunting fundraisers. Yes, that is "hunting" with a gun.

If anyone who is now aware of the true nature of the so-called *"liberal Establishment"* gun control movement cannot spell HYPOCRISY they better be able to know who and what the effete *"elitist"* are, and what they believe.

That is: *"It's OK for me, but not for everyone else. I am in charge,"* Totalitarian thinking, because this is the way the Gores, Clintons, O'Donnells, Bradys, Obamas, Bushes, "Hollywood," most of *"the Establishment"* and many others of their club who desire to deprive Americans of their rights and freedoms "think."

They are dangerous to the health, wealth and safety of all Americans!

Oxy"morons"!

As in their other positions, *"the liberal Establishment"* advocacy of *"gun control"* is void of common sense, or any reliance upon historical or contemporary evidence. In fact, their positions defy common sense and empirical evidence.

With complete disregard of the evidence of recidivism among sexual criminals, they promote leniency of incarceration. With one hundred percent of the evidence of human conduct to the contrary they promote *"diversity is strength."* With decades of evidence of the abysmal failure of wasteful Government programs such as the anti-poverty efforts, they continually seek more money for them. With the obvious disintegration of the fabric of American culture, and with it the productivity and standard of living of all Americans, they continue to insist on immigration programs that favor only those who cannot contribute to an increase in U.S. productivity. In fact, they work assiduously to inhibit immigration of those who could enhance technological advancement and productivity.

It is just not reasonable to assume so many, particularly those considered the effete *"elite"* clerics of the *"liberal"* side of politics, could be so unaware of the facts of quantifiable failures; criminal recidivism, the empirically evident conduct of humans, or the impact of Third World immigration. Thus, they are given much too much credit for much more intellectual acuity than their ridiculous positions indicate they possess.

The majority of *"liberals"* in the congregation are different. When one of them takes a position like *"You must have a license and register a car, so you should have to register a gun and have a license to own one,"* you should endeavor to show them the fallacy of their "thinking" by pointing out it is legal to own a car without registration or licensing. These are required only if the car is placed into operation on public streets.

Similar laws for guns already exist because licenses are required for hunting or should anyone want to actually carry a gun. If their eyes begin to glaze over, or there is some other indication they are incapable of coping with facts, or these simple concepts, you can be assured you are addressing a member of the congregation of *"liberal*ism" for whom *"gun control"* is just part of the dogma.

Since the *"liberal"* clerics like Hillary and Obama must be given credit for fully understanding the eventual ramifications upon America and its citizens of the positions with which they are indoctrinating the minds of their congregation and disseminating through the Government "school"/indoctrination system, their positions such as *"gun control"* deserve critical scrutiny.

Facts of Freedom

Machiavelli observed five hundred years ago *"The Swiss are strongly armed and completely free."*

This remains true in 2018. The Swiss are still strongly armed and completely free. And it was the Swiss who were the model for the American Democratic Representative Republic. The Swiss have not changed in over five hundred years.

All males in Switzerland are subject to military service and training until the age of forty-two, as they should be in the U.S., but aren't because "*the Establishment*" decided against a citizen military to avoid citizens having any "skin in the game" of their criminal military adventures, thus avoiding protests by the citizenry.

The Swiss citizen military also take their military weapons home with them, surely minimizing crimes we see in the U.S. like home invasions, robberies or MS 13 crimes in American neighborhoods.

Therefore, given the empirical evidence of Swiss success, it is intellectually difficult to cope with "reasoning" behind the persistence of supposedly intelligent people in their efforts to disarm honest, law-abiding American citizens. Thus, there must be some sinister "evil" afloat in these efforts. There is not another intellectually reasonable explanation.

All Americans should be cognizant of the fact the "*liberal*"' actually "*leftist Establishment*" do not acknowledge the existence of empirical evidence refuting their claims about guns, and they do so to prevent average Americans from being aware of such truths as the Swiss experience or the following:

- In some counties in the U.S., laws regarding the issuance of concealed weapon carrying permits have been loosened, making this privilege more readily available to the citizenry. The result: a decline in crime.

- In Australia, the government did what "*gun control*" advocates are endeavoring to do in America. They outlawed private ownership of guns: the crime rate soared.

- In the United Kingdom they have the most rigid gun restrictions in Europe, and, yes, you guessed it: they have the highest crime rates in Europe.

- Washington D.C. and Chicago have some of the strictest "*gun control*" laws in the U.S. They also have the highest murder rates. Surely there is some reason for this other than gun ownership. Possibly the demographic similarities between Washington and Chicago should be explored as a reason for the violence?

- In France, prior to the German invasion in World War II, gun owners were required to register their firearms with the local city government. The result: when the Germans invaded, they just went around collecting all of the registered guns, depriving the French of the opportunity to defend themselves.

It is this last point that is most salient in the minds of Hillary,

Obama and other *"Establishment gun control"* totalitarian nuts desiring to disarm Americans.

There is probably not a *"liberal"* alive who, in addition to being a *"gun control"* fanatic, is not also, either clerically consciously, or congregationally unconsciously, a strong supporter of Big Government, a United Nations led *New World Order* One World Government, the Paris Climate Accord, NAFTA, the myth of "free trade," Globalism, larger foreign "aid" packages, higher taxes on the working, more welfare, or the many other foolish, oxymoronic non-common sense, *"internationalist,"* utterly intellectually insulting and mostly intellectually impossible, Utopian schemes to which an armed American citizenry presents a potential deterrence.

Need for Vigilance

Even without declared *"Liberals"* in office Americans who cherish their freedoms and the "rights" granted to them under the *Constitution of the United States*, should be ever vigilant of *"the Establishment."*

President Bush II tied the hands of the National Rifle Association to prevent them from advertising to inform the public about those politicians who would deprive Americans of their *"right"* to bear arms during the last, important sixty days of election periods through his signing of the unconstitutional Campaign Reform Act. This emboldened *"Establishment gun control"* advocates like Hillary and Obama, and obviously Bush.

The Government, under the Bush II Administration, clearly stated it would not use profiling to protect American lives against terrorism from male Islamic, non-citizen terrorists of Middle Eastern heritage between the ages of eighteen and forty.

Obama actions, including censoring Government use of the term *"Radical Islamic terrorists"* and deliberately importing potential terrorists seems eerily consistent with the Bush mindset... apparently opposed to free speech.

Fact is; the entire Bush family, Hillary, Obama, Kristol, Romney, and so many others unknown to the public are top members of each of the "two parties" of the one big *"Establishment"* party that are nothing but two thin publicly presented veneers.

This is the Reason Romney, along with many other Republicans, did everything within his empty suit personage to prevent Trump from being the Republican Presidential nominee, and the Bushes refused to support him.

In fact, George H.W. proudly announced he was voting for Hillary. Could there be any more solid proof there is, in reality, only one big political "*Establishment*" party?

Those who do not understand this yet should have some kind of intellectual test.

<u>Trump and any other "*outsider*" non-"*Establishment*" person seeking any position of power is a threat to their many decades and generations of control that has enriched all of them... and not only do they not like it, will likely continue to do everything they can to keep their gravy train from being derailed. (Let's hope Trump is also "ever vigilant.")</u>

***

Americans can bank on their Government, in the event of potentially devastating attacks against citizens by persons like these above, taking every action in its power, whether legal or not, under cover of the "war," to prevent even the possibility of Americans possessing registered weapons from defending themselves.

Machiavelli was an astute observer of human nature and had a lot to say about the wisdom of people being armed. In the ensuing five hundred years, human nature has not changed, nor has the nature of those humans in positions of government power.

The nature of the source of conflicts also remains unchanged. Therefore, in the current atmosphere of the strong "*liberal Establishment*" opposition to President Trump, even among Republicans like McCain, the Bushes and other *Establishment*" insiders desirous of increasingly, larger, more powerful Government, and the Islamic Crusade against Western Culture, those who are interested in maintaining their Constitutional "*right*" to bear arms would be wise to seek pragmatic consultation:

"All armed prophets have conquered, and unarmed prophets have come to grief." - Machiavelli

"One should read history to discover the reasons for victories and defeats so he can avoid the latter and imitate the former." - William Cowper

CHAPTER TWELVE
WHAT HAVE WE LEARNED?

"The age of virtuous politics is past, and we are deep in that of cold pretense. Patriots are grown too shrewd to be sincere: And we are too wise to trust them." - William Cowper

Americans today are suffering "*The Establishment*" and Government *"leftist, liberal progressive evils"* and their political correctness intended to prevent discussion of them. These "evils" are, in part:

- Deliberately created racial division i.e., "*diversity*" created through immigration to provide a "*liberal progressive*" and dependent power base at the expense of <u>all</u> Americans, and create a need for a larger, more Socialist, Totalitarian Government.

- "*Gun Control*" efforts to disarm law-abiding honest Americans.

- A deplorable "education"/indoctrination system that, primarily because of "*diversity is strength*" multiculturalism, is the worst and most expensive in the Western world.

- An exorbitantly expensive healthcare system resulting primarily from the cost of providing free healthcare to all the Third World residents of America, and Mexican Nationals who do not pay for any of their U.S. provided healthcare.

- A U.S. Government, both Socialist Democrat and Republican, that pays taxpayer money to support a Socialist United Nations run by Third World, un-elected bureaucrats who have a plan to tax and disarm Americans, eliminate ownership of private property that is the cornerstone of democracy, and place everyone under a United Nations led, *New World Order,* One World Government.

AND many in "*the Establishment*" are also destroying many of American's freedoms, as well as endangering others.

Examples of this are:

- Drug "war" policies permitting unconstitutional invasions, and seizures of private property without proof of any crime.

- Continued conversion of the "education" system that was so important in providing America's prosperity, into the Government indoctrination system.

- The Bush U.S.A. Patriot's Act that deprived Americans, in one stroke of the pen under the dictates of political correctness and multiculturalism, of more rights and freedom than all previous administrations combined.

- The Transportation Safety Administration debacle with its thousands of federalized, unionized, non-terminatable employees.

- Further economic destruction under more destructive trade deals.

- More potential Islamic terrorism in the U.S.
- Creation of the Northern [military] Command for the United States, which signals the possibility of military on the streets of America.

This last one should be particularly troubling to all Americans given Presidential powers to declare a *"State of Emergency"* and rule by Executive Order.

Further, although it is not a pleasant thought, think what a U.S. President, as Commander in Chief, with the Totalitarian *"leftist"* One World Government leanings of Hillary Clinton or a couple of the veneer 2016 Republican Presidential candidates who displayed the same leanings striving to disarm Americans would be able to do to the people with this force.

Also, given U.S. commitments to NATO and the United Nations, could these forces be far behind in "policing" the streets, and the citizens, of America?

These potential democracy depriving actions have been implemented by *"the Establishment,"* Democrat and Republican alike, and because there is no opposition from American citizens they are banking on Americans being *"placidly governable"* and compliant. Based upon the evidence, it appears they are correct.

"Placidly governable," complacent Americans of 2018 appear to possess the same mental and physical characteristics: they seem as intellectually lazy as they are physically lazy. And since that which they can see and feel does not seem to concern them, the perception is; the stealthy stealing of their rights, freedom, and culture is also of no concern to them.

> *"...all experience hath shewn, that mankind are more disposed to suffer, while evils are sufferable, than to right themselves by abolishing the forms to which they are accustomed."*
> -Thomas Jefferson, -*Declaration of Independence,* 1776

This statement was just as true in 2018 as it was in 1776. But in 1776 the suffering *"mankind"* of the American colonies decided to *"right themselves"* by casting off the bonds of the King of England.

Today, the question is: when are present-day Americans going to choose to peacefully *"right themselves"* as their ancestors did?

Maybe never?

***

WHAT WILL HAPPEN IF TRUMP IS NOT PERMITTED TO FINSISH THE TASK OF SAVING AMERICA FROM THE BRZEZINSKI *"ESTABLISHMENT"* EVIL THAT HAS BEEN CONSUMING IT FOR OVER FOUR DECADES?

During the 2000 Republican Presidential Primaries Republican, non-"*Establishment*" black candidate Alan Keyes stated, regarding the state of America at the time: "*The house is burning down, and no one is yelling, fire!*"

Nero-like Americans who for at least two decades by that time were... as they still were two Presidents later in 2018... too busy "fiddling" with sports, movies, music, celebrities and recreating to even be aware what Mr. Keyes was really saying.

He was also shunned by many because he was not representative of the majority political voice of his race. Even his chosen Republican Party, shut him out of one of their televised primary debates though he was the most articulate of the candidates in stating what are supposed to be the values and ideals of his chosen veneer party. Why?

Well first, because he made bumbling Bush II who was already anointed to be the next President look so plain f***ing stupid "*the Establishment*" Republican hierarchy feared this "*outsider,*" like Trump sixteen years later, could possibly interrupt their twelve-year run of having a *New World Order* America destroying effete puppet in the White House.

Second, Mr. Keyes, also like Donald Trump sixteen years later in 2016, was not a member of "*the Establishment,*" and what he was defending that Republicans should have supported were the values that historically served as an example for the world by providing the most prosperous and free society humans have ever experienced.

But these values were inconsistent with those of the controlling, "*Establishment*" members of the veneer Republican party as most should have become aware by the beginning of 2018 because of the conduct of the Republican "leadership" in not too thinly veiled opposition to Donald Trump

The Republican party faithful, as well as the media and even black "leadership" permitted them to get away with this travesty, and squelch what would have been a much better outcome for them, the rest of America and the world with nary a protest because of the affiliation of all these with the America destroying "*Establishment.*"

The results of this pathetic display by the hierarchy and their demonstrably "*placidly governable*" sheep were: "9/11," another unnecessary criminal war that made the country five trillion dollars poorer, an American President known worldwide as an international war criminal because of his actual acts of that nature that have elicited most of the fifteen years of worldwide *Radical Islamic Terror* Bush, even before Obama, refused to acknowledge as that, and the democracy destroying Patriots Act.

Good job, Republicans!

***

As previously established, the "two party" system was created to appease, control and divide the electorate on the basis of its human, herd instincts of needing to belong and have leadership lead them where it desires they be led.

This enables *"the Establishment"* to *"divide and conquer"* them to accomplish what is desired for the benefit of its membership that actually represents only about one percent of the population.

This is to the detriment of the other ninety-nine percent of an increasingly... by design... disparate electorate unaware of what is being done to them for the sole benefit of *"the Establishment"* that consists of owners and the owned, neither of which are bound by traditional values, ethics, morals, or even laws.

This was proven 2016 to 2018 by the F.B.I. Director, Assistant Director, at least two other officials, the Attorney General, two Assistant Attorney Generals, the Head of the National Security Agency, C.I.A. Director, ex F.B.I. Director and Special Counsel, his staff, Hillary Clinton, Senior Democrat Party Officials, several members of Congress and probably many more, including, based on his post Presidential OFA activities, President Obama. This was a true, real, anti-Trump conspiracy by senior law enforcement and other Officials of the U.S. Government.

In short, the U.S. definitely was governed by criminals for the eight years prior to 2017, and although likely not as widely spread or consistent among so many of its high-ranking Officials for many decades prior to 2016 who were not working for the good of the nation and its citizens, but with M-O-N-E-Y and power as the driving forces.

But the "conspiracy" proved above proves something else. What is that? Well, how many times prior to Trump have any of us ever witnessed an effort by so many of both party stripes, especially from the same party, go so far as even breaking multiple laws to try to bring down either a Democrat or Republican President?

The answer is; never! And the answer to why is simple: these people are all members of *"the Establishment"* who do not care whether the President is veneer Republican or Democrat if he is an *"Establishment"* Republican or Democrat, as the Author was informed by Republican bigwigs in 1982.

We should now rest our case about there being only one big *"Establishment"* party with two veneers in the United States in 2018! Call it a conspiracy, *"Deep State,"* or whatever you choose, as long as you recognize there is only one, not two parties, no choice, in charge of the Government, and guiding the country to its demise.

***

Outside of Government, the owners are wealthy individuals,

corporations, especially global ones, insurance, healthcare and pharmaceutical companies, defense contractors, big banks, and others who have money and favors to pay for what they desire.

The owned…"*bought and paid for*"… are those in positions of power or seeking these positions such as members of Congress, heads of Government agencies, even the Presidency, i.e., positions that control Government decisions, actions and legislation that can enhance the finances of the owners without regard for the people or finances and future of the country… and let's not forget the media that covers up, misleads, and tells outright lies to enable the growth of this destruction.

Thus, the pro American citizens agenda Mr. Keyes was advocating in the year 2000, and Donald Trump in 2016 and 2018, is a threat to the entirety of "*the Establishment*," and its money and power because the stated agenda of both candidates provided knowledge to the people… knowledge of what "*the Establishment*" members have been doing, and how it has adversely affected Americans and their country, that if implemented would be the end of the money and power they enjoy.

Additionally, what both proposed is deemed politically incorrect, but not solely because of a conservative point of view. It is also deemed culturally improper because it threatens the "*divide and conquer*" element of "*the Establishment*" immigration program.

It is not acceptable to be a voice in favor of the opportunity afforded everyone by the culture and economic system "*the Establishment*" and its "*leftist, liberal progressive*" media like Mika Brzezinski despise and attack so vehemently.

From the point of view of what passes for main stream minority culture in America, as represented by the media, advocating being educated, promoting the economic system, democracy, lack of dependency, families and marriage, rather than illegitimacy, that are best for everyone is racist, politically incorrect and unacceptable.

Thus, Mr. Keyes and others like he and Mr. Trump who have achieved some success in the American Capitalist System are called racist with the tacit approval of "*the Establishment*," since they have not been heard to promote the economic system that is the hope for the future of all Americans, and everyone everywhere.

They are continuously working assiduously to convince minorities they are victims of a white, racist society that has deprived them of their fair share of America's economic success.

Why?

Because minorities, to a great extent, since beginning of the last half of the Twentieth Century, have been convinced by "*the Establishment*" and their co-conspirators in minority "leadership" they are victims, which they are. <u>However, they are not victims of a white, racist society. They are victims of their own "leadership."</u>

Minority "leadership," like all who desire to attain leadership positions of power, as opposed to working for the betterment of themselves and others through hard work, setting an example and helping others through their deeds, understands to be a leader it is necessary to have a constituency.

The easiest way to create a constituency is define those you would like to lead, as different from, being deprived by, or mistreated by others you can target as an obstruction to your constituency's ability to obtain their fair share of freedom, land, economic success, or opportunity. Then define yourself, via words and deeds, as one who can obtain for them what you have convinced them is unattainable without your leadership.

This is defined as classic "*divide and conquer.*"

However, minority "leadership" is not solely responsible for this victimization of minorities in America. Self-defined "*liberal progressives*" or whatever members of this contingent of "*the Establishment,*" like Hillary Clinton, choose to call themselves on any given day are as guilty, if not more so, in victimizing certain people for political power. But this is not true of all "liberals."

There are two kinds of these "liberals" just as there are two kinds of communists, or those of other political or religious affiliations; those who follow without questioning, or seeking answers and enlightenment, and those who seek positions of leadership and power by deliberately fostering those attitudes, beliefs, conflicts, untruths, opinions, or whatever they perceive will provide them the position and power they desire.

It is the latter, Clintonesque, not the former, "*liberal progressives*" who share responsibility with minority "leadership," for the victimization of minorities and the resultant denigration of American society in general through their agenda of multiculturalism "*diversity*" and political correctness intended to impede any improvement in the declining state of American society by inhibiting open discussion of the topics it is absolutely necessary to discuss if solutions are to be found and implemented. Why?

Knowledge is power, but uncommon knowledge superior to that of those over whom one desires to have power and control provides even greater power. Also, the more fearful people are to openly discuss anything that could possibly be disruptive to the power bases of those in power the less likely it is those who are subject to the desires of the powerful will be permitted the collective knowledge to be able to mount opposition to their power.

<u>A divided population is more susceptible to control by a strong</u>

central government and the self-interests of those in _"the Establishment"_ whose desire is to use segments of the divided population as their power base than is a population unified in language, customs, desires, goals, and objectives.

Thus, although short sighted, power is the answer. Strong central government power over a divided population, based upon their words, actions, deeds and legislation is the desire of _"leftist, liberal progressive"_ Democrats and many Republican members of _"the Establishment"_ whose plans are to ensure continuation of this.

Anyone who disagrees with the previous regarding _"the Establishment,"_ minorities, their leadership, _"liberalism,"_ political correctness, or any of the rest of it should reconsider the fact that the foundation of upward mobility to a better and more prosperous life is knowledge gained primarily through education.

Although there are individual exceptions, there are not any examples wherein _"diversity"_ of language, ethnicity, religion, culture, etc., promoted by _"the Establishment"_ media as _"strength"_ has resulted in the harmonious coexistence of the various groups required for an effective education system.

To the contrary; education in America has declined dramatically since creation of the Department of Education by President Carter when "teaching" what to think, i.e., indoctrination, not how, began.

Consider: why do _"liberal progressives"_ and minority "leadership," like the Congressional Black Caucus and other Democrats send their offspring to private schools, rather than public "school" holding pens of Washington D.C., yet oppose opportunity for inner city, predominately black, youth to attend better schools?

Are they afraid they might become educated, more knowledgeable, and thus able to ascertain how badly they are disadvantaged by their "leadership" and other _"Establishment"_ members who for power encourage disharmony throughout American society by continually promoting a racially divisive _"diversity"_ agenda to the detriment of all, especially minorities?

To have a relatively free and democratic society like America had before _"the Establishment"_ obtained _de facto_ control of its Government in the 1970s it is necessary to have an educated, informed and knowledgeable population.

An educated, knowledgeable population... not an indoctrinated one, as has been created through the Government "common core" program... would be much less susceptible to _"the Establishment"_ lies and propaganda promulgated by persons and groups who use the divided population as a base for personal power and enrichment.

Would an educated minority population in possession of the facts of upward mobility advantages of Western culture, education, and knowledge available to them as Americans, rather than being "taught" ancestral heritage and *faux* benefits of *"diversity,"* engendered with a spirit of harmony and the benefits of collective interests be as accepting of the deliberately divisive lies of their "leadership" over the informed articulation of an Alan Keyes, Thomas Sowell, or Clarence Thomas?

Would Mexican Americans continue to vote for those of their own ethnicity and the *"liberal progressives"* who promote bilingual education and cultural *"diversity"* if they were aware, as are the Chinese, Swiss, Dutch, and so many others, of the necessity of the English language for upward mobility and economic success on a worldwide basis, the divisiveness of *"diversity,"* and the fact children learn languages better at an early age?

The answer to these questions is, obviously, no. The reason: rarely do individuals choose that which is detrimental to them, or the future of their children.

Therefore, it would seem, since they have within their power the ability to educate, inform and help all Americans better their lot in life, and thus enhance America for everyone, that, at least, non-*"Establishment,"* truly conservative Republicans... if there are any left... would aggressively attack the programs and agenda of the *"liberal progressive, Establishment"* minority "leadership," and others working on their special interest power base programs, rather than pandering to them to the detriment of all Americans and the future of the nation.

***

Why do veneer Republicans insist on referring to them as *"my good friend"* and rarely ever confront those whose ideas they should be assiduously diametrically opposing? Has *"the Establishment"* grown so large and so all powerful it cannot be confronted?

This must be the case since it had become exceedingly rare to see a Republican demonstrate any backbone or testicular fortitude for anything of importance to the future of liberty and prosperity in America until Trump.

Maybe it is unfair to blame any veneer Republicans for their ineffectiveness. Maybe it is just a result of contemporary *"Establishment"* Republican culture in which anyone who does not toe the party line is not likely to last long in the party, achieve any success or be supported by the party in the next election, which may well be Trump's big problem in 2020, especially if Romney or others like him are elected.

If anyone actually endeavors to forestall gains of *"liberalism"* he or she would be out of step with *"the Establishment"* in control of the party. After all, the Republicans provided Americans with two recent Bush Presidents whose demonstrated *"liberalism"* on issues of illegal immigration and foreign trade would make Bill Clinton proud and could have likely resulted in a Hillary Clinton clone President, due to Bush engendered *"conservative"* disaffection, if not for Trump.

One would think so-called *"conservative"* Republicans would have naturally embraced the likes of Alan Keyes and Donald Trump who speak out and stand up for what Republicans historically represented, i.e., the successful growing America of lore.

But, no! *"The Brzezinski Establishment"* **Business Plan for America** of *"diversity"* imposed via illegal immigration, political correctness to avoid truths being told, even trade deals favoring corporate America and the workers of other countries prevails over everything unless Trump can continue on his winning streak of 2018, and the crooked *"Establishment"* media lies do not adversely affect him with his base or others who would otherwise favor him.

Proponents of true Republicanism have not been in control of the party since Ronald Reagan was succeeded by George Bush I who was a *bona fide* charter member of *"the Establishment"* in control of our economic decline since the early 1970s.

***

He, after having spent many *"Establishment"* Renaissance weekends at Hilton Head with Bill and Hillary Clinton and others who support a One World Government to the detriment of America and all other sovereign nations... never covered by the press... apparently forgot he was not supposed to tell everyone about the *New World Order* he proclaimed after becoming President. (Remember memory is a gauge of intellect.)

He also, like his son Bush II, demonstrated a strong affinity for ideals and leaders of other countries who do not have the best interests of America among their objectives, preeminent among them the Saudi 'Royal' family.

In addition to these medieval tyrants who supposedly supplied sixteen of the hijackers on "9/11," and paid each of their families $250,000, the son seemed too close to the President of Mexico who was a strong supporter of illegal immigration of Mexican Nationals into the United States he referred to as *"natural migration."*

The son also proposed, *a la* Jimmy Carter, the first *New World Order President,* granting amnesty to millions of criminal illegal aliens because, God help us, he either "thought" he was encouraging Latinos to vote for Republicans, or worse; he was fulfilling his obligations to *"the Establishment"* to continue implementing its *"diversity"* plans detrimental to taxpaying, asset owning Americans.

Smart money would be on the latter of these two choices. He is his father's son intellectually and politically. However, his mother stated what is *"wrong"* with him is she *"smoked and drank"* when she was pregnant.

But whichever. This he did, rather than fulfill his sworn Constitutional obligation as President to protect America's borders from invasion, which he shirked in allying himself with the Mexican President at the expense of American taxpayers, and a continued free and democratic America, rather than turning it into a northern version of Mexico.

***

The illegal alien problem amounts to, as encouraged by his friend, then President Fox of Mexico, a deliberate foreign government encouraged invasion of sovereign American territory by over one million illegal invaders per year that are not, as the junior Bush stated, *"Just good folks looking for a better life."*

They are mostly members of Mexico's population that are the least well educated and least productive who also, as a side benefit to Mexico's economy, send many of their U.S. earned dollars back to Mexico, augmenting the tremendous benefits bestowed upon Mexico through NAFTA, at the expense of the U.S. economy, by the elder Bush's *"New World Order"* weekend friends who preceded junior in the White House. It is, however, not in America's best interest.

It is only in the best interests of Mexico, as was NAFTA that moved massive numbers of highly paying American jobs to Mexico to enhance U.S. auto maker's profits at the expense of the destruction of much of the American Middle Class and Detroit.

In fact, NAFTA bestowed on Mexico so much massive new industrial might it created a new middle class there these illegal immigrants to the U.S. could be beneficiaries of, like hundreds of thousands, if not millions, of other Mexicans, if they were well enough educated or inclined to participate in Mexico's new booming, productive economy.

Remember: Aguascalientes, Mexico is like a new Detroit only safer. Asian and European auto manufactures along with American makers are in evidence in a big way, and these massive industrial facilities are surrounded by sprawling subdivisions of middle class homes with new autos in the drives. Forbes calls this *"America's new car capital."*

At another location in Mexico is another massive production facility... probably a quarter mile long... where most of the kitchen appliances sold in America, except the few smaller ones like microwave and toaster ovens made in Asia, are manufactured.

No! The Mexican illegals coming to the U.S. are not *"Just good folks."* They are poorly educated, economically disadvantaged, poor people from the backcountry farms and villages of third world Mexico where there is no welfare; food stamps, housing allowances, etc., and everyone has to work for his livelihood.

But, yes. They are coming to the U.S. *"looking for a better life"* solely because of these benefits provided at the monetary and jobs expense of American workers since Jimmy Carter and his *NWO* Brzezinski *"Establishment"* puppeteer implemented this *"divide and conquer"* step of the destruction of "America" as we knew it by initiating the provision of welfare and other benefits for them.

And remember: this was preceded by importation of the same socioeconomic level of large numbers from Vietnam and Cambodia in the 1960s under Democrat President Johnson and expanded by Bush II with Somalis from Africa and others from the Middle East, and further accelerated by Obama who greatly expanded this *"divide and conquer"* part of *"the Establishment"* plan by recruiting and importing thousands of Central Americans, and Muslims.

Veneer Republicans have been shooting themselves in the foot as willing participants in the Brzezinski Plan since Bush I because they are enhancing potential long-term Democrat control of *"the Establishment"* Government, unless Trump remains successful, which would not make the Bushes and other *NWO* whores happy.

Latinos, blacks and these others are not going to vote Republican in large numbers no matter how much they pander to *"leftist, liberal progressive"* minority "leaders" complicit in the plight of their constituencies growing beyond their ability to support their irresponsibly increasing numbers or contribute to the economic growth of the country.

The more illegal aliens granted amnesty, the faster Republicans are sealing the fate of their side of *"the Establishment,"* faux "two party" system, and of the America that was once the destination for those desiring to better themselves through assimilation and contribution rather than parasite on America's citizens and their dwindling resources.

The majority of these immigrants will vote for Democrats as long as it is the party that represents their values by offering the most Government largesse. This is the aspect of these cultures political correctness... also supported by some Republicans... has successfully inhibited Americans from discussing.

With some members of the Republican veneer of *"the Establishment"* being willing participants in the plans to destroy the America that once was by pandering to every special interest group, except its conservative political base Bush II's Karl Rove designated just *"another special interest group,"* and the complicit *"leftist, liberal Establishment*" media lying and misrepresenting through imposition of political correctness, what future is there for a united, prosperous America?

Even though *"the house is burning down,"* don't count on the Republican Party veneer of "*the Establishment*" to act as the firemen for America.

It is up to the American electorate to save America for themselves and their heirs. Americans, however, will not take the necessary action to accomplish this unless they become better educated about the "*the Establishment*" and issues confronting them.

Therefore, they need to begin to understand the seriousness of "*the Establishment, leftist, liberal progressive*" multicultural, politically correct, United Nations, One World Government threat to the future of a united, free and prosperous America.

And they need to ensure they elect only leaders who represent their values and have the testicular fortitude to act on their behalf, in the best interests of all Americans, not in the interest of the Bush *"New World Order."*

So, for Mr. Keyes, Donald Trump, and all Americans, in an effort to prevent Russian Prime Minister Krushev's threat to then Vice President, Richard Nixon at Glassboro New Jersey in 1960, *"We will bury you* [America] *from within,"* becoming reality, the preceding pages are an effort to alert the American electorate to the facts, and reasons, their wonderful *"house"* that took over three hundred years to build is now, seriously, burning, and all who really care should not only be figuratively screaming, *"FIRE!"* but doing everything they can to extinguish it.

But how do they do this in addition to reading the preceding pages of this book and learning the magnitude of the threat they are facing they will not likely find anywhere else?

Well, a few million of them have at least made a sort of "fire bucket brigade" start by rejecting another "*Establishment*" insider Bush and over a dozen others of his ilk, and electing a non-"*Establishment*" member, non-politician, "fireman" businessman as the new Republican President of the United States.

***

The Author of this work who has a background in business turnarounds and management has been writing for almost two decades the United States has been in serious need of a turnaround that no "professional" political hack, because of his chosen course in life, would have the knowledge, ability or incentive to accomplish.

It would take a businessman with financial, organizational structure, high level interpersonal and management skills to easily understand the massive financial and other problems of the country and its citizens, and how to solve them.

Had the country ever had successful international businessmen in the position of Chief Executive Officer instead of political hacks motivated by obtaining money and power by implementing the Brzezinski *"Establishment"* America destroying policies for their legacy or playing military leader without any military experience, the country would not have been, metaphorically; in the last few minutes of the last quarter of the last game of the season with fourth down and ten facing it, and a "quarterback" with nothing but a string of losses behind him, which is where America was until the election of Trump.

Fortunately, he is like an experienced "knight on a white horse" in possession of the experience and skills needed who arrived to take over and save the "game."

Also, fortunately the other "pretender to the throne" was a dubious candidate who was nada but another... although criminally dishonest... effete *"elite Establishment"* member with no experience other than being tenured in their club.

Even though the former had all the delineated experience required to win and rebuild the country for success in the future, almost half of those deciding which would be chosen preferred the pretender because they are largely Government dependents that have *"no skin in the game"* of America, and if she won they would continue to be taken care of even if they did not bother to get out of bed in the morning.

The choices were Donald Trump, a patriot who spent $50 million of his own money to endeavor to save America, and does not need additional money or power, or Hillary Clinton whose only loyalty was to *"the Establishment"* and those who *"bought and paid for"* her, and whose only desire was to continue *"the Establishment"* destruction of America for even more power and money.

Those in favor of the latter were resolute in their ignorance, and uninterested in facts. But again, fortunately, the educated, productive, asset holding, thinking members of the electorate realized what had been done to them, and Hillary as President would do nothing but continue the destruction whereas a President Trump really was their last and only chance to *"Make America Great Again."*

But please do not forget what we were seeing on the streets and campuses of America since 2016. This anarchy is the result of the success of the Brzezinski/Carter indoctrination program begun forty years before, and is still the only "education" available in America to the masses but has also migrated to the nation's most prestigious colleges and universities.

Therefore, if Trump does not eliminate the *New World Order* communist indoctrination in these institutions, in the end he will have failed America!

And he will have done so not only because he failed to save America from the internal destruction wrought by Brzezinski and his acolytes in the Oval Office over the four decades before his arrival there.

If he does not redirect "education" to teaching young Americans the real history of their country, the facts about the differences, strengths and weaknesses of its three cultures and how to analyze and think about the world and their place in it America will not have the internal unity and harmony required to effectively deal with its two major external threats.

CHAPTER THIRTEEN
THE EXTERNAL THREATS

To the chagrin of the New World Order closet communist Brzezinskites like the Bushes, Clintons, Obama, most Congressional Democrats, the Obama "Deep State," FBI, NSA, "Justice" and State Departments holdovers, et al, and their anti-Trump 'Fake News' media, one of these threats is not Russia and its less than two hundred million people. It is the combined two and one-half billion, over thirty-five percent of world population, people of the Islamic World and China that pose a potential threat to America, precisely because of what these NWO whores destroying America, have been planning for them also, as telegraphed by what they have done in the Middle East, North Africa, Vietnam, Indonesia, Cambodia and elsewhere for the last fifty years.

- The Author

ISLAM

The events of September 11, 2001 possibly proved Harvard Professor Huntington was prescient in his writings regarding *"Islamic intolerance."* If nothing, else it is likely a fact all the young men piloting the planes into the buildings that day were mostly Saudi Islamists possibly willing to give their lives for their religion.

It is too bad, however, this reflects poorly on *New World Order* President Bush II that he was either not sufficiently prescient, even with his three vast security agencies, the NSA, CIA and FBI, to prevent this event of the magnitude and results of Pearl Harbor in which each the deaths of American innocents were about three thousand, or he did not agree with the "9/11" Commission about who the perpetrators were.

The fact he continued, possibly under the guidance of his *New World Order* handlers, to speak favorably of, or lie to the American public about the Arab nations, especially the Saudis and the Islamic religion substantiate this.

If so, many others have since agreed with him, including the "9/11" Commission that found the FBI had no less than twenty-three prior warnings of the event. It has also been determined some of those said to have died in the planes were still alive in Saudi Arabia a decade later.

Given the fact the Justice Department, including the FBI, reports directly to the President, this also reflects poorly on President Bush

II and his Administration.

But whatever history eventually reveals about this terrible incident it will also record that as of 2018 the following statements were still mostly factual:

"They [the Arab nations] are literally making a play to take over the world with the combination of economically crippling high oil prices and oil embargos, terrorist attacks against the U.S. using weapons of mass destruction and war in the Middle East that spreads around the world. What has become painfully apparent is that Israel and the U.S. are fighting the same enemy. And despite what you may believe, we are losing the war.... Until we realize that our enemy is Islam and the Arab world, we will find no enemy to fight. Until we accept the cold, hard truth that our enemy is Islam, the religion that has sworn to destroy us, we will constantly be losing a defensive war."
-The Wall Street Underground May 2002

"The notion that we have been allies for 60 years is an absurdity. We have been protecting the Saudi regime, which is a repressive regime living in the Middle Ages. Their values, their policies, their attitudes are diametrically opposed to ours. They have oil, we need oil and that's why we protect them. That's the basis of the relationship... to say we share the same values I think is absurd. This a very clever P.R. trick..."
-Tom Lantos, Representative, CA

These quotes about the Arabs are fact, except two comments about the Saudis. The U.S. does not protect the Saudis because *"we need oil."* It is because Kissinger cut a deal with them, the largest Middle East producer, in the early seventies to accept only U.S. dollars for sales of their oil.

This created what is called *"the petrodollar"* because after this deal the dollar that was only a fiat currency before, i.e. had no physical backing, was then supported by the demand for oil that thereafter was priced only in U.S. dollars, creating a demand and concomitant value for dollars based on the demand for oil.

Also, the comment about *"crippling high oil prices"* is factually incorrect. Truth is; the Saudis manipulate the price of oil to their advantage; getting the highest price the market will bear when they can. But they have also reduced the price to endeavor to eliminate competition, as they did to attempt to drive the high cost U.S. fracking industry out of business in 2015.

But these facts aside, the truth is; the two quotes, rather than the statements from Bush and Obama, are the facts about "*Islam and the Arab world.*"

This would be substantiated by anyone willing to recognize the actions of Bush and Obama were inconsistent with their rhetoric on this subject. But maybe we should look elsewhere for more facts... possibly from someone who was much older, wiser and with more experience than these two combined, garnered before either of them was born:

"Islam is more dangerous in a man than rabies in a dog."
"Individual Moslems may show splendid qualities. Thousands become brave and loyal soldiers of the Queen! All know how to die: but the influence of the religion paralyses the social development of those who follow it. No stronger retrograde force exists in the world. Far from being moribund, Mohammedanism is a militant and proselytizing faith. It has already spread throughout Central Africa, raising fearless warriors at every step; and were it not that Christianity is sheltered in the strong arms of science, the science which it had vainly struggled the civilization of modern Europe might fall, as fell the civilization of ancient Rome." - Winston Churchill

This quote alone should raise the pertinent question: what the hell were Obama and Hillary thinking when they began bringing tens of thousands of Muslims from the Middle East and Africa into, and scattering them throughout, the U.S., then threatening to bring in tens of thousands more; creating another Pearl Harbor-like event for the purpose of creating terrorism and Government enhancing fear among the citizenry?

Could there possibly be any other reason?

Had not Merkel in Germany, the French and Swedes created sufficient terror, death and fear in their countries to scare the hell out of any rational person by even the thought of bringing thousands more of these people who will not assimilate into American culture, society, or any other anywhere outside a Muslim country?

Also, what the hell was wrong with Schumer, Pelosi, others in Congress, judges, the media, Mika, and other obviously intellectually challenged groups and individuals attacking Trump for endeavoring to save America from what happened in European countries just because they and their *New World Order* want to get rid of *"outsider"* Donald Trump?

Do they really hate America so much they are willing to destroy every aspect of it with Islamic terror, as well as destroying it economically with immigration from Mexico and Central America just because they and their *New World Order* want to get rid of *"outsider"* Donald Trump?

From Obama this was not surprising. But Trump better recognize very quickly the problem is educationally indoctrinated ignorance of other people, religions and cultures. The American people must be made aware via education and the media they are at war with Islam, and if they do not awaken quickly to this fact, their county is doomed because Islam and Christianity cannot reside in the same place at the same time peacefully.

The commentary and quotes above are all anyone really needs to know about Islam to act appropriately to protect their family, themselves, their home, their country, even eventually their lives from this actual other world.

But Americans, especially younger ones cannot just accept whatever anyone tells them because they tend to believe they are a lot smarter than they really are.

So, with this thought the following on this subject is presented to both prove we know of what we speak, and to add to American's seriously lacking knowledge on this subject with the objective a majority of Americans wise up, listen to Trump and vigorously support him in his endeavor to save your country from this very real Islamic threat.

***

Oil prices were raised by Arab producers from ten dollars per barrel in early 2001 to twenty-seven dollars by mid-2002 and have risen as high as over $140 per barrel since.

Also beginning in 2015 the Saudis reduced the price of oil to endeavor to destroy the emerging U.S. based oil production industry, successfully bankrupting many of the fracking oil production companies, although damaging their own economy

This was all-out economic war against the U.S. intended to damage its economy to their advantage in oil production just as the U.S. has done to Russia and others to have their way. Yet many in the U.S. Government *"Establishment"* continue to argue the Medieval Saudis are U.S. allies because of the need for a Mid-East balance to Iran that has been a designated enemy of the U.S. military/industrial complex for decades, since the departure of their Iranian puppet, the Shah, almost four decades ago under Carter.

This is yet another example of world trouble directly caused by actions of the cabal in control of the U.S. Government that are never disclosed to the American public.

Remember "*the Establishment*" in charge of the U.S. war-based economy, in addition to endeavoring to take control of the entire world along with their *New World Order* accomplices in the European Union, is also focused on endeavoring to control the world's natural resources in several choke points around the world, as well as going "all out," as they did in Indonesia in the 1960s and 70s to control that country's resources.

But regardless of who did what to whom first, attacks against Americans… who are mostly unaware what their Government has been doing around the world in their name… and American interests had been perpetrated by Saudi, Palestinian, Libyan, Lebanese, and Egyptian Islamic terrorists for over forty years in Africa, the Middle East, America, and Europe, as of 2018.

The Bush Administration talked up the potential threat of weapons of "*mass destruction*" in Iraq, and began pursuing a diminution of radical Islamic teachings in Muslim Indonesia and the Middle East through aid and other means while they had the U.S. military engaged all over the world in Muslim countries including, Iraq, Afghanistan, the Philippines, former Soviet Muslim republics, and who knows where else, ostensibly and probably to some extent in reality fighting terrorism, but also actually creating through their actions much of the terrorism aimed at Americans.

This was not just continued by Obama and Hillary. It was expanded into Libya, other parts of North Africa and Syria, creating more terrorism, including, as Donald Trump pointed out, another major terrorist threat, ISIS, which although spread worldwide by 2016, Obama began, for no logical reason, bringing thousands of refugees from countries in which it was operating into the U.S. against the advice of all his Government national security advisors.

Then Hillary, during her Presidential campaign without explaining why, stated she would expand that program 550%, also greatly increasing the probability of terrorism in America.

Although both were members of the America destroying "*Establishment*" for most of their adult lives, the benefit of its plutocracy enriching itself at the expense of Americans explained most of what they did to those aware of this fact, but doing this that actually threatened the lives of Americans???

Their Saudi allies were known to be funding Palestinian terrorists, and Israeli, Benjamin Netanyahu, was telling Americans, over and over, the enemy was the same, funded by the same Arabs.

But that fell on deaf ears directed elsewhere for reasons unrelated to the security and well-being of American citizens and

Borders their borders they were sworn to protect.

The *New World Order* so-called efforts to maintain peace for the benefit of big global businesses and trade profits have failed miserably in the Middle East, as they continue to fail elsewhere, because they were never there to maintain peace. They are there to secure, maintain and control, as well as protect American business interests like oil companies operating in those countries, as is known only too well by the citizens of those countries under the thumb of the U.S. military.

But these failing policies and actions in the Middle East *"have come home to roost"* in the form of expanded terrorism in America and Europe. Therefore, it is time to recognize the cause of the problem is *"the Establishment"* member's personal greed, and lack of common sense and sensitivity to others in the combined Islamic nations, AND begin to solve the problem, rather than continuing to officially refuse to recognize its genesis.

The conduct of Bush lying to Americans continued by Obama, about their *"Arab allies,"* the *"great religion,"* the *"peaceful religion"* of Islam and the media's complicity in this has irresponsibly potentially damaged America because this is exactly the type of national *"head in the sand"* conduct of its political class that wrought America's involvement in World War II.

In addition to substantiating examples of the Islamic problem cited above are; pro-Palestinian poetry of the Saudi Ambassador to the U.K., the Saudi's refusal to permit U.S. use of its bases in its Afghan endeavor, Iran shipping weapons to Palestinians, and Nation of Islam leader, Farrakhan, refusing to acknowledge Islamic terrorists as the perpetrators on the planes in the "9/11" attacks.

But the Obama and Hillary refusal to acknowledge *"Radical Islamic Terrorism"* is what wrought terrorism deaths in San Bernardino, Orlando and elsewhere really was the height of either stupidity, deliberate covering up for political purposes, or political correctness run amuck…to the detriment of Americans.

There is more than sufficient smoke here to cause any rational, thinking, objective, reasonably intelligent, non-politically correct, or politically motivated person to be yelling: *"Fire!"*

Not to do so is the equivalent of national suicide. And suicide is exactly what the Bush, Clinton, Obama *New World Order* policies represented for America.

Radical Islam is not just an enemy. In 2018 it was THE rapidly growing enemy that was producing a prodigiously large army of anti-Western, anti-Israel and anti-American cannon fodder in many parts of the world, including in the U.S.

"the 22 Arab states... soaring birthrates indicate that by 2020 they will have 410 to 459 million... the Arab world is falling off the globe. (The GDP of Spain is greater than that of all 22 Arab states combined.) ... it's due to a shortage of freedom to speak, innovate and affect political life...of quality education... the milieu that produced bin Ladenism, and will reproduce it if nothing changes..." -Thomas Friedman, "Arabs at the Crossroads," *THE NEW YORK TIMES,* July 08, 2002

"Islam already has 1.3 billion adherents and is spreading rapidly; particularly in Africa ... it's reasonable to worry about the implications of the spread of Islam for the status of women and for the genital mutilation of girls.... Islam is troubled in ways no one can ignore... the Islamic world has 'bloody borders,' ... Of the 26 countries torn by conflict in the year 2000, 14 have large Muslim populations. And on average, Muslim countries mobilize twice as large a share of the population in armed forces as do predominately Christian countries." -Nicholas Kristof, "Bigotry in Islam - And Here," *THE NEW YORK TIMES,* July 09, 2002

Then Mr. Kristof stated, *"focusing on the moral deficiencies of other peoples simply underscores our own,"* indicating, as usual, THE NEW YORK TIMES either did not get it, or like Brzezinski, his co-conspirators and acolytes, the Bushes, Clintons and Obama, they are so blinded by political correctness and support of all things U.N. and *New World Order* they desire America to be submerged into their One World Government no matter the cost to Americans.

It should take no more than one reading of the above, published in, of all places, the *"leftist Establishment"* NEW YORK TIMES, for anyone to realize the danger to America posed by those people who have been attacking Americans for almost forty years, and if some of the evidence presented is to be believed, were involved in an attack *"on American soil"* equaling or exceeding the attack on Pearl Harbor in the number of Americans killed.

And, it should also be noted; these Americans were non-combatant, innocent citizens in their workplaces.

No! Focusing on the *"deficiencies"* of these *"other peoples"* has nothing to do with *"our own."* It only represents a desire for self-preservation on our part.

But had Mr. Kristof been writing for THE NEW YORK TIMES in 1941, consistency would insist he would have, after having pointed out all of the problems of the Japanese atrocities in Asia, and German atrocities in Europe, also stated "*focusing on the moral deficiencies of other peoples simply underscores our own.*"

Also, commenting on consistency and what might have been requires addressing the conduct of Mr. Kristof's publication's contemporary compatriots in the Bush, Clinton, and Obama Administrations. Had these *New World Order* compatriots been in charge in 1941, the results would have been the same as those Mr. Kristof's mindset would have yielded.

Any one of these Presidents would have commented on the "*day of infamy*," declared "*war*" on the concepts of Shintoism and Fascism, federalized U.S. airport security workers, and using this opportunity like the Bush Administration that actually forecast "9/11" twelve months in advance did.

Push through Congress a previously prepared multi-hundred-page piece of legislation suppressing rights and freedoms of Americans, treating them exactly as these *NWO* co-conspirators view them: as their real enemy because so many of them are those "*deplorables*" who would eventually put Donald Trump in the Oval Office to protect them from the actions of future anti-American *NWO* Presidents like these four.

"One should read history to discover the reasons for victories and defeats, so he can avoid the latter and imitate the former."

Human nature has not changed since Mr. Machiavelli wrote these words five hundred years ago. Civilizations, religions, people have clashed since the beginning of history, and religions have been notoriously responsible for those conflicts.

Reason: religions are visceral and emotional. They are not intellectual or based on reason. The more religious and less well-educated or enlightened with real world knowledge adherents of religion are the more easily leaders of their faith can manipulate them. Thus, they are more easily molded into soldiers for their faith... like "Christian Soldiers" or *radical Islamic terrorists.*

The words above from THE NEW YORK TIMES should be adequate to inform Americans what they are up against. And Mr. Machiavelli's words should be sufficient to provide insight about the potential outcome if *"the Establishment"* puppets persist in their ways. But, if those are not enough, further insight may be gained by looking at the irreconcilable differences between Christian America and its Islamic enemy. Yes, "enemy."

In America, Government indoctrination centers are training children to be pacifist, compliant and accepting of others, especially the Third World. Some "schools" and universities are even promoting the study, understanding and acceptance of Islam in their culturally and nationally destructive "*diversity*" programs.

In the Islamic world, children are being taught all non-Islamic persons are infidels. They are being taught to hate infidels. Some are being taught to kill infidels by sacrificing themselves to do so because Christianity is a crime to them.

There is a rapidly growing Islamic population already exceeding the population of the U.S. by a factor of over five hundred percent, and the combined U.S. and Western European populations by over two hundred percent.

U.S. and European Christian populations are declining while the populations of the poverty stricken Islamic world are exploding, expanding in places where some of them either choose to or are indoctrinated with what to do for *Allah,* like killing infidels.

America and Western countries, including Israel, negotiate *for* peace while the Arabs negotiate only for time and more power.

The concept of "truth" has no meaning in the Arab world... nor, quite frankly, in the Christian world either in 2018, especially in "*the Establishment*" world of lies, deceit and crime left over from the Clinton, Bush and Obama administrations.

In the West, Christian countries other than the U.S. promote peace. Islamic leaders in the Arab countries and Africa promote aggression. They respect strength and power, disrespect weakness, and perceive those with power who do not use it to be weak.

The Christian Western world has created wealth, freedom and advancement while the Islamic world has created poverty, destruction, repression, and keeps its citizens from advancing.

"...the modern streets of Tehran... are bustling not with industry but with hysteria; where ...rage was what I saw...the holy city was also a city of rage... [in Pakistan] an Islamizing military government unresponsive to the populace; the fundamentalists...fomenting a fever of faith. [Malaysia] ...a new generation of Muslims crazed by their confused faith, awaiting the emergence of a homebred Ayatollah Khomeini to lead the entire country into Islamic purity."
- V.S. Naipaul, *AMONG THE BELIEVERS*

Meanwhile, American Christians continue to employ their moral and ethical values in attempting to understand happenings in the Islamic world while the Islamic world does not concern itself with the moral or ethical values of the Christian world.

Islamists have a simpler, more lucid world view everyone should be aware of. They are Islamic. Everyone else is an infidel, and infidels are to be eliminated.

Some Americans, even after dishonest simpleton Bush II and corrupt Obama are already out of the picture, continue to talk about democracy in the Islamic Middle East.

There will not be "democracy" in the Middle East, including the phony one peddled by Bush II from the barrels of guns as the excuse for starting another unnecessary war.

The Western version of democracy is out of the question in the Islamic world because their religion and government are not separate. This is simply another *New World Order* lie that will remain unfulfilled.

Muslim leaders will continue to rally their faithful in response to continued American meddling, peddling Christianity and attacking them on their soil, which are major problems for the West.

Democracy requires an educated populous, as its decline concomitant with the deliberately contrived for this reason Brzezinski/Carter American "education" system products on the streets and campuses of America in 2016 to 2018 proved.

Real education, not indoctrination as we have in both the Middle East and America, equals advancement, unlike unrest among populations indoctrinated with beliefs of communist theory or with repressive governments represented by youthful demonstrators in both areas of the world.

Education and prosperity are declining, rather than increasing, in the Middle East, as in America and Europe. Thus, Radical Islam is increasing in strength, as is Christianity.

And, as in the Seventh Century AD, Muslims are making a second attempt to expand the Islamic world, as it also appears the *New World Order Establishment* in the U.S. and some of its allies in their relatively new European Union did at the beginning of the 21st century in Iraq, and continuing to other Islamic countries, including those in North Africa.

Much of the Western world needs Middle East oil for its prosperity, or as Henry Kissinger stated in a white paper to President Nixon in the early 1970s *"to maintain our standard of living"* to which he added less than tactfully a comment about this also requiring a *"reduction"* in the non-white world's population.

***

How does this comport with *"the Establishment"* media line of we are the *"good guys"*?

Think the non-white population of the world that includes most Muslims might have a dim view of this that could elicit their less than friendly attitude toward the West?

Ditto: even here in the USA where those who could be affected by these remarks would not be able to separate one of the *"the Establishment Bad Guys"* like Kissinger or Brzezinski from most Americans who really are among the world's *"good guys."*

The Middle Eastern countries have nothing of value for trade other than oil. Their oil reserves are finite. The West is pursuing alternative sources of fuel. At some point, the Middle East will lose its oil income stream and its bargaining chip.

But more importantly; within the time between 2002 and 2022, Arab populations were expected to double. So as of 2018 there were more than 50% more Muslims in the Middle East than in 2002. But there was not an increase in proven reserves of oil we refer to as the "lifeblood" of civilization that is truly that for them.

So Islamic leaders seemed to have little to lose in 2018 compared to what their future losses may be. Therefore, armies of radical Islamic terrorists who could see little hope in their futures were beginning unleashing more terror on Western Christian and Jewish worlds without any effort of Middle Eastern "leadership" to cause a cessation of it for obvious reasons.

Therefore, Donald Trump was correct in calling for destruction of ISIS on the ground in the Middle East in sort of a Crusades-like response a thousand years after the first Crusades.

But Hillary Clinton and Barrack Obama had another solution to help. Clinton possibly because Arab regimes were paying her tens of millions to help reduce their oil dependent populations by shipping them to the U.S., and letting its taxpayers take some economic stress off their Arab regime buddies.

Maybe this is what Kissinger was thinking over four decades before, rather than the actual nasty, inhumane implication of what he meant by *"reduction"* that was what anyone would infer given his genocide in Cambodia and one-off action in Chile, and possibly elsewhere, but probably not based on these other bad acts that put him right up there with the worst 20th century war criminals.

However, whether this is what Kissinger meant, it is consistent with what these two, Hillary and Obama, and their *New World Order* co-conspirators were doing for Mexico for at least three decades by 2018. So why not a few million more to help *"level the playing field"* by reducing the circumstances of Americans and increasing those of Mid-East regimes some of whom seemed to have Hillary on their payroll, as was already being done for Mexican "leadership"?

***

2018 was beyond time for *NWO* dreamers of world domination and destruction of the America that was, like these two, to *"Leave aside imaginary things,"* realize the time had come for the common sense to accept; like their plans for Japan domination of Asia, their Middle East plans were also coming apart at the seams.

It was time for all these political hacks who have been screwing up the Middle East along with the rest of the world since 1973 to get out of the way, shut up and let businessman Donald Trump take care of this, as he was so many more of the disasters left behind for him by the effete and incompetent Obama under *New World Order* counseling of Zbigniew Brzezinski he said *"is one of our country's most outstanding scholars who has done a lot for our country."*

Given what Brzezinski had already done TO *"our country,"* while doing not a damned thing *"for"* it, for those who might have even an infinitesimal urge to continue any of his destruction, *"Get out of the way"* is necessary because of his guidance to *"divide and conquer"* even with Muslims, ignoring the reality of Islam as stated by Winston Churchill in his quote above.

***

For fourteen hundred years it has been proven it is not possible to deal with Islamists. From their point of view everything, religion, culture, lifestyle, laws, etc., is entirely, to put it in an oft used American phrase, *"my way or the highway!"*

So, in the interest of self-preservation of Americans, our lifestyle and a positive future for our country the only intelligent way to deal with the Muslim problem is like the way they deal with Christians in their Middle Eastern native lands.

They do not permit any evidence of Christianity, bibles, churches or worship, and in some of their countries certain acts of Christianity result in severe criminal punishment.

Therefore, we should require they assimilate by accepting U.S. law and customs or hit *"the highway"* back home. Or as President Trump stated so eloquently: ***"the hell out of our country!"***

And while on this subject; the same should be the attitude and actions toward Mexicans and other Latin immigrants. Treat them exactly as the Mexicans do anyone, including Americans, entering their country illegally. They go directly to jail. Period! No judges. No hearings. No nothing, but jail.

All Americans should demand RECIPROCITY; the *reciprocal state or relationship, mutual action, or exchange between two countries to the advantage of both as is the historically accepted conduct between nations.*

There is absolutely zero reason for Americans to tolerate having their country and culture destroyed by a small cabal of Brzezinski acolytes solely for their personal gains in power and wealth!

They should all get solidly behind President Trump and demand nothing less than reciprocity in trade, immigration/emigration, tariffs and all matters of state and business for the United States of America. Nothing less should be acceptable anywhere, especially with the following where the President and all others should ensure no one will *"prevail over"* the United States no matter which way any *"wind"* is blowing.

China
"The East Wind shall prevail over the West Wind."
- Mao Tse-Tung

The entire world should be praying, dancing to their Gods, or whatever their faith guides them to do to seek intervention to ensure Professor Huntington will not fare as well in his prescience regarding *"Sinic assertiveness"* as he did regarding *"Islamic intolerance."*

In *RED DRAGON RISING*, Edward Timberlake and William Triplett II addressed the reality of the People's Republic of China, the PRC, and its continued adherence to the philosophy of Mao Tse-Tung. They pointed to the military achievements of the PRC that in 2018 is a Communist superpower, possessing advanced nuclear technology, which is of greater strength and harboring darker ambitions than the former Soviet Union.

According to them, the Chinese People's Liberation Army is well on its way, thanks to financing by the West, especially America, through trade, to developing its Twenty-first Century war-machine, including its *"East Wind"* series of long-range nuclear missiles.

"Without a people's army the people have nothing."
- Mao Tse-Tung

This quote should put to bed debate in the U.S. about the right to bear arms. But even if aware of it, the *"liberal"* set would still cast aside the wisdom of those who have gone before and persist in their misguided attempts to create their vision of a perfect Utopian world with total disregard of human nature and its history.

Mao was a practicing pragmatist. He, like Machiavelli, did not view the world through the <u>rose-colored lenses of those who choose to believe the world to be the way they desire it to be, rather than accept it the way it really is.</u>

The economic success of the PRC over the three decades before 2018 is primarily attributable to their employing pragmatic economic, trade and birth control policies, following Mao doctrine and ignoring "*New World Order faux free trade*" philosophy that has almost destroyed American economic vitality and its Middle Class.

The Chinese ignored "*New World Order*" policies that would have been detrimental to them and availed themselves of only those detrimental to the U.S. to their advantage.

Primarily, they have taken advantage of America's self-destructive "*New World Order free trade*" policies designed to enhance American corporate and political coffers, and of their competitive advantage of cheap labor by manufacturing everything possible and shipping it to the West while keeping their own markets pretty much closed to imports, as well as ignoring Western patents, trademarks and copyrights. They also ignored financial guidance of *New World Order* "geniuses."

The Chinese are one exception where the Trilateral program of shipping production to Third World countries to enhance them worked. Problem is they did not benefit from it.

While most Third World nations in Latin America, Africa and the Asian Sub-Continent were engaged with "*New World Order*" flawed policies of its *"first rate"* minds, and failing economically, the Chinese were "making hay" at the expense of the West.

They outsmarted the Western "geniuses" attempting to remake the world to comport with the Brzezinski Utopian vision of a world of human equality and economic "equilibrium" proven to fail in the USSR and China in the last century, i.e., communism.

But what is truly frightening about this is the same people with the same policies are still in charge in China AND America!

The winners are still in charge in China, and the losers in America fighting to stop President Trump's America saving agenda to cease shipping production, jobs and money offshore, and pursuing their other policies detrimental to Americans, including ignoring the growing economic and military strength of China and its relationship with Islamic nations, while continuing to pursue Brzezinski's *faux* Russia story as the first step to their envisaged world domination Hillary would have pursued.

***

The Chinese have already given sufficient indication of their view of their position *vis-à-vis* the U.S. and the rest of the West. They have a complete industry of hundreds of thousands of people engaged in funneling nuclear technology, missile delivery systems and weapons of mass destruction to fanatic Islamic regimes.

Yet, even though this has been going on for years with knowledge of the U.S. Government, the Clinton/Gore Administration was instrumental in assisting the PRC obtain U.S.

intelligence and technology, and even a complete missile production assembly line from a U.S. defense contractor.

Additionally, the Clinton administration that took the Brzezinski "*one giant step*" against American workers and the U.S. economy with NAFTA is responsible, with Republican assistance, for granting permanent most favored nation trading status to China. Yep! One Clinton Presidency was "great" for America.

"Too bad" we did not have another, as at least half of the Obama Administration "top brass" and Obama himself assiduously pursued, even through criminal acts.

Given the Chinese Government provided hundreds of thousands of dollars of financial aid to the Democrats during the Clinton Administration, this gives new meaning to politics being about money, and, raises the question of who has done more damage to the security of Americans: a spy who for tens of thousands of dollars sold secrets to the Soviets and Israelis, or the President and his wife who, for untold hundreds of thousands, or even millions of dollars, sold out the country to its greatest potential enemy?

Clinton, like Carter or the Bushes, would not have taken any actions or made any policy decisions without full support of his Brzezinski "*Establishment*" mentors and handlers who put him in the White House.

Therefore, it is fair to question: just how far into their Totalitarian Socialist "*New World Order*" One World Government do members of the official Rockefeller/Brzezinski organization desire to take America? What is the ultimate objective of their quixotic, doomed to fail Socialist One World Government? Just what do they desire; a world like that of their flailing European Union the Brits have possibly opted out of, or the significantly less than successful United Nations after over seventy years of its failure to fulfill the objectives for which it was ostensibly created?

Again, these are fair questions to ask because their entire conspiratorial scheme is hair brained in ignoring, or ignorance of the impossibility of having all the different cultures, races and languages of most of the world function in relative harmony to create "*economic equilibrium*" with other world economies to achieve Brzezinski's "*New International Economic Order,*" i.e., *New World Order*... without consideration of cultural or other empirical differences dooming any such scheme to failure.

Or is their plan like what they planned in the U.S., just on a larger scale?

That would be that a divided population would empower their world government over all the people. But the empirical evidence of the destruction this has already wrought in the United States and half a dozen European countries should prove to even the relatively not so smart the implausibility of this.

But this insipidness of endeavoring to empower oneself and his cabal by dividing and weakening his own base should be of grave concern to Americans because the only country that is a threat to U.S. economic and military superiority is a result of the planning of these same people whose intellects are demonstrably inferior to the relatively simplistic brilliance of the leadership of this threat.

***

"The unification of our country, the unity of our people... these are the basic guarantee of the sure triumph of our cause." - Mao Tse-Tung

Thus, unlike the intellectually doltish *New World Order*, One World Government Utopia seekers in the U.S. represented by people like Nancy Pelosi and Chuck Schumer assiduously, consciously pursuing internal disunity of America through immigration policies, including the U.S. Government State Department *"Immigration Diversity Program"* in pursuit of a multicultural America, Mao understood, as did Machiavelli, the cold hard empirically demonstrated facts of the need for *"internal unity of the people"*

But both *"the Establishment"* veneer Democrats and Republicans are pursuing destruction of *"internal unity of the people"* of America through a *"divide and conquer"* program in an effort to attain more political empowerment at the expense of a prosperous and unified America. **These people are just plain DUMB!**

Bush abandoned a proposal to grant amnesty to nine million illegal Latin immigrants after "9/11," but in the 2002 congressional election, Dick Gephardt stepped up to the plate to try to knock one out of the park for the Democrats by proposing legal residency (citizenship and voting rights to follow) for the same illegal aliens.

Thus, it should be obvious to anyone with a partially functional brain both veneers of the *faux* two-party system are interested in only one thing: a larger voting base that will expand the power of the Government over all Americans at the expense of a more prosperous future for the country.

The executive director of the Federation for American Immigration stated, *"These guys just want to give away green cards for votes basically without any kind of preventative strategy."*

Latino "leaders" in the U.S. speak freely about the *de facto* return of a large chunk of the Southwestern U.S. to Mexican control, Mexican Presidents implicitly support this, while many Mexican politicians explicitly support it, and about sixty percent of Mexican citizens believe Mexico should have it back.

Yet the intellectually challenged "leadership" in Washington is intent on accomplishing this by displacing American culture and the English language with Latin culture and the Spanish language to sate their hunger for increased power.

While these "brilliant" ones in Washington fight for votes of people who are not yet citizens of the U.S. and should not be because they have broken U.S. laws, the Chinese continue to outsmart them.

While these U.S. political whores for votes, are consciously promoting disunity and divisiveness within America, the Chinese are resolutely following the empirically proven, common sense philosophy of Mao Tse-Tung and Machiavelli.

The Chinese Government wisely continues to *"Stress Unity, Stress Stability."*

Meanwhile the internal unity of America has been disintegrating for years through racial conflict, political correctness and hate crimes legislation, which are a direct result of multiculturalism.

But this disintegration was increased, seemingly deliberately, by Obama through his obviously pro-black versus police interference by jumping into cases wherein blacks were killed by police without getting the facts, and inappropriately acting based only on the color of his skin, nothing else, just like Maxine Waters.

His administration even chose not to protect Americans from potential terrorists, or even define the real enemy, but import more of them, and even be more lenient on those who commit crimes than on American citizens because of political correctness.

Many Americans, including American Muslims and the Black, Nation of Islam leader even refused to acknowledge the source of the "9/11" terrorist strikes in the face of overwhelming evidence of the Middle East ethnicity and Muslim religion of all of the terrorists.

***

The promoting of Spanish and public discussion of return of the Southwestern U.S. to Mexico is racial, religious and ethnically based thinking with total disregard of reality, or any thought about unity. It is the demonstrated human nature of *"birds of a feather flock together"* which is real world reality.

The empirical evidence of this disintegration is available to everyone, every day, on the cable television news channels.

While the unity of America is crumbling, the U.S. "education" system continues its decline further into the status of Third World Socialist indoctrination centers, and the means of production continue to be shipped offshore, the Chinese are "on a roll."

They are making tremendous financial and political gains, and educating their people, in addition to imbuing them with a capitalist, prosperity enhancing drive to the future.

They are also consolidating economic and political ties in Asia and Africa (Which was one of the two major reasons for the Hillary/Obama attack on Libya and the murder of Gadhafi. The other was he was not a member of the International Monetary Fund with billions in physical gold who was going to begin selling his oil in something other than U.S. dollars... likely Chinese Yuan.)

They are at least ninety-five percent ethnically homogenous, and culturally and philosophically cohesive. They are mostly one country, one people, and one government.

After the "9/11" attack on America they banned visas to citizens of Arab countries.

And, it might be worth considering: whereas the population density of the U.S. is seventy-two people per square mile, with its European ethnicity population declining, the density of the PRC that is only two percent larger in land area is three hundred and twenty-six mostly unified souls per square mile and growing.

It is also worth noting *"unity of our people"* has another meaning for the Chinese. It means the reunification of Taiwan with the People's Republic of [mainland] China.

Just as Israel is the American, and the world's powder keg in the Middle East, Taiwan amounts to the same in the Pacific.

According to subscription publication, *HUMAN EVENTS, June 2001;* January 24, 1996, *THE NEW YORK TIMES* ran a story wherein senior Chinese officials were quoted stating China would sacrifice *"millions of men"* to reunite Taiwan with the People's Republic of China, a position anyone who has ever been to Taiwan could never begin to understand. But most wars have begun based on what most could not understand either. But it should be noted; territory reclamation has been a cause.

Then, three days after the *NYT* story, the *LOS ANGELES TIMES* published one quoting the second highest ranking officer in the Chinese People's Liberation Army who reportedly said, *"America would not be willing to sacrifice Los Angeles on Taiwan's behalf."*

Also, sometime during this decade of craziness in which he more than played his part by starting another unnecessary war that was probably the greatest and most expensive blunder in American history, Bush II stated *"the Establishment"* party line the U.S. would provide *"whatever it took to help Taiwan defend herself,"* which if it meant another war indicates he would have been happy to oblige.

Does not the Chinese supplying military technology to terrorists, their seeking U.S. military technology during the Clinton Administration, their totally ethnically driven designs on Taiwan and the implicit threat against Los Angeles present a *Clear and Present Danger* to America?

Didn't the Bush comment regarding Taiwan put America squarely in the path of conflict with the People's Republic of China? And, since the U.S. has admitted it does not have the capability to engage in battle in two theaters, or on two fronts, simultaneously... as Bush proved in Iraq... could not this irresponsible statement by this already proven irresponsible member of the cabal of people addressed above whose intellects are demonstrably inferior have potentially put the U.S. in a terribly vulnerable situation?

The answer is yes, but thankfully, the Chinese were more intelligent and more interested in improving the prosperity of China than this U.S. President was in not acting in the best interest of his country and his people.

But China is more than a military threat to the U.S. As previously discussed; it has displaced U.S. ally Japan... which we should note; the U.S. also has a defense agreement with... as the Asian economic powerhouse. This has greatly adversely affected U.S. power in Asia that has always been problematic.

According to *THE NEW YORK TIMES, June 28, 2002 "China replacing the United States as the dominant power in Asia... is already an economic and political threat to Japan... is forcing its Asian neighbors to adjust... to hedge their position with the United States. Asian leaders are choosing to praise China's rapid development as a benefit to their economies... a mutual courtship has emerged... [Indonesia] is taking a more independent stance regarding the United States... [according to Malaysia] China... is going to be a very prosperous, very big and economically powerful China. Singapore... lost more than 42,000 jobs* [between 1998 and 2002], *most of them to China..."*

In the following fourteen years preceding the 2016 U.S. election year China's continued growth and prosperity financed by the West, especially America, was accomplished without adopting, or having forced on them via the barrel of a gun, as Bush claimed to be doing in Iraq, the democracy promoted for the entire world by the America and world destroying *New World Order*.

The PRC remains a Communist country with only one political party, and incredible government supported capitalistic success.

While the *New World Order* "geniuses" went *"hog wild"* over their one-sided *"free trade"* that is the primary fuel for Chinese economic success as the result of their policies permitting China to ship any and everything into the U.S., the U.S. shipped practically nothing to China except jobs also because of them. Additionally, because of them the U.S. didn't manufacture much of anything anymore until Trump became President.

The Kissinger and Brzezinski-like *"first rate"* minds of the *New*

World Order singlehandedly deliberately helped the Chinese create the *"biggest and baddest"* threat in the entire world to their One World Government plans, and the future of America.

Is this probably not the greatest demonstration of pure "brilliance" ever?

The growing Chinese economy caused it to be a growing consumer of energy at the same time its relatively small domestic oil reserves were being depleted. So, the "brilliant" *New World Order* bunch, in addition to having created an economic and political powerhouse (Remember: Politics are about money.) growing at four times... during Obama's term, more... the rate of the U.S. also created a competitor for the world supply of oil, a very large percent of which belongs to the Arabs.

Now, since the U.S. and China compete for Arab Islamic oil, and the Chinese are providing the Arabs with weapons and technology for their Jihad against the West, doesn't common sense suggest that, maybe, the Chinese are going to have a repeat of their being granted "most favored nation" trading status? And, no: not by the U.S. Can everyone say SYNERGY and PROXIMITY?

In addition to the Chinese having the basis for a very good trading relationship with Middle Eastern Arab oil nations, the increased demand for limited supplies resulted in upward pressure on the price of oil that has been much more detrimental to the U.S. economy than to that of China because the U.S. consumes more oil.

The fact oil that was around $10 a barrel at the beginning of Bush II's Presidency has fluctuated to as high as over $140 since and was just under $50 in 2016 is proof of that which would be more dramatic had not U.S. "ally," the Saudis, deliberately reduced the price of oil trying to bankrupt the nascent U.S. fracking industry threat to their hold on pricing and supply in the world market.

Granted the near-term pressure on the price of oil from Chinese demand was limited due to smaller demand of the Chinese economy when the "geniuses" began destroying the U.S. economy to enhance their *"Establishment"* co-conspirators wealth via "crimes" against America's economy for their personal benefit. But it was negative for the U.S. economy near term, which the "geniuses" they are should have been able to foresee.

Also, the relationship of China as arms supplier to America's enemies at the time was known, and the growth of that continues to be very negative for America.

So, what were the "brilliant" *New World Order* strategists who controlled the U.S. Government and created policy then doing about the situation regarding China, Japan, the Middle East and the U.S?

"So far, the Bush administration is loath to talk publicly

about China as an economic challenger in Asia."
-THE NEW YORK TIMES, June 30, 2002

Wouldn't anyone intelligent have been? Maybe that was the problem? Still is!

If one's policies were failing worldwide, and even generating a negative effect in some parts of the world... especially their "Homeland"... who would want to admit to it?

But this *"head in the sand,"* combined with their foreign aid and other actions representing "business as usual," continued to confirm the previously stated theory; their inbred, multi-generation culture and determination for world domination would not permit the *New World Order* cabal, who have never had to deal with it, to deal with reality until along came Trump. Thankfully!

While the U.S. continued to lose economic strength and influence in the productive, Asian part of the developing world and almost everywhere else to China, Americans continued to have their economic and political influence reduced by the numbskulls in their own Government because they were continuing to squander these on their doomed to failure Third World policies that are suicidal for the U.S... until Trump arrived.

As Bush continued the misguided policies of the prior Clinton *New World Order* Administration at an accelerated rate, Obama accelerated even that. It's almost like the Enron management model for failure wherein much more of the same bad policy was supposed to cover up past policy mistakes until Trump began to change them.

The continuing efforts to *"make the weak strong by making the strong weak"* that would ultimately result in destruction of a free and prosperous America would not have ceased until a pragmatic management displaced the inbred, generational destructive culture of *"the Establishment"* of the U.S. Government, as Donald Trump began endeavoring to do in 2017, which is the reason there is a full court press by all Democrats, many Republicans and the Goebbels-like U.S. media to oust him from office.

There was no collusion, which is not a crime anyway, no obstruction of justice in firing incompetent *NWO* whore Comey, as confirmed by the Assistant A.G. and Inspector General, nothing to justify *"the Establishment"* hit-man's efforts to oust Trump except his *bona fide "Establishment"* enforcer credentials.

If those responsible for U.S. Government policy cannot accept reality-based observations of human nature by Machiavelli, possibly it is because he passed out of this world almost five hundred years ago, and they really believe human nature has changed sufficiently to permit them to engage in their inherent stupidity to the detriment of the rest of America without protest.

If that is the case they should listen to the driving force behind their challenger Chinese economic and military power with which America is faced, who passed on over 40 years prior to 2018.

"The people, and the people alone, are the motive force in the making of world history... The enemy will not perish of himself... nor...will [they] step down from the stage of history of their own accord."   - Mao Tse-Tung

Then, look at the relative success of the twenty-five years prior to 2018 of those following this reality-based guidance of Mao, and applying Machiavellian pragmatism.

"Men nearly always follow in the tracks made by others and proceed in their affairs by imitation. So, one should always follow in the footsteps of great men."

It will have been a shame and a disaster for the people of the world if when the history of the Twenty First Century is written it will have been Mao Tse-Tung and his followers who were perceived the *"great men"* of our time because of their successes. But the fact is; it is the winners who get to write history.

So, for the sake of a better future, and history, for Americans and their country it is important the Conservative electoral revolution of Trump survives through the 2018, 2020, 2022 and 2024 elections and many decades beyond. If not, it could be either the Maoists or *"first rate"* minds of the *New World Order* Globalist One World Government acolytes who write the history of a failed United States of America. We cannot let that happen, can we?

CHAPTER FOURTEEN
THE ELECTORAL COLLEGE

In the year 1787, the founders of the United States of America included in the Constitution thereof a provision for the process governing the election of the President of the United States.

"Each state shall appoint, in such manner as the Legislature thereof may direct, a number of electors, equal to the whole number of Senators and Representatives to which the state may be entitled in the Congress: ...The electors shall meet in their respective states, and vote by ballot...make a list of all the persons voted for, and of the number of votes for each; which list they shall sign and certify, and transmit sealed to the seat of the government of the United States... President of the Senate shall, in the present of the Senate and the House of Representatives, open all the certificates, and the votes shall then be counted. The person having the greatest number of votes shall be the President"
- <u>Constitution of the United States</u> Article II

This process worked very well for over two hundred and thirty years as of 2018, as have the other processes of the Government established by the creators of this document. In fact, because of their brilliance and their foresight the United States of America has enjoyed greater stability and prosperity during this time than any other nation, possibly except for Switzerland which was the model for the U.S. Government.

Their idea evident in this document is the election of the President is consistent with the way the country is governed. Simply stated, this means each of the individual states is represented in the election of the Chief Executive Officer of the country by the same numbers as their representation in the Congress of the United States.

The number of electors appointed in each of the individual states is equal to the total number of Senators and Congressional representatives from each state. Then based on popular votes cast for the President within each of the states these electors send their certified representative votes to Washington D.C. just as the states send their Congressional and Senatorial representatives to represent the interests of the people in the states from which they are elected.

Thus, the President is elected by popular vote of the people of each state just as are the Senators and Congressional representatives. As a result, each state is represented in the election of the President as it is represented in the Government.

And the central Government of the United States represents the will of most of the people, tempered by the represented interests of each of the states that, collectively, are the United States of America.

In this simple way, the states are bound together by treaty with a central Government in which they have a proportionate representative voice without giving up power of self-government.

Brilliant? Yes!

Yet, because of their loss in the close 2000 Presidential Election the Democrats spearheaded by the Clintons attacked this system of governance that has provided so much for so many for so long.

Then again, sixteen years later in 2016, in those intervening years nothing changed for the Clintons, at least for Hillary.

She was at it again. Even though she was defeated in her bid for the Presidency in a landslide victory by Trump, rather than accept her loss in this two hundred and thirty-year old system she blamed the system and began again to campaign against it, and for discontinuation of it,

This proves Hillary and *"the Establishment"* do not only desire to change the "nature" of the U.S. population in accord with the Brzezinski plan, but also desire to change the system of governance of the United States to ensure the success of their desired *"New World Order"* at the expense of a sovereign America.

***

Yes! This is an attack on "the system" of governance of the U.S. because an attack on the Electoral College is a direct attack on the *Constitution of the United States,* and the Constitution that IS the basis of the system of government of the United States of America.

In 2000 the Clintons were joined in this attack by their American Socialist (Democrat) Party comrade Al Gore, the sore loser, college professors, lawyers, the leftist People for the American Way, which should be renamed The Peoples Communist Way, the usual assortment of *"liberal progressives,"* and *"the Establishment"* media, *et al* who hate America and desire to remake it into Brzezinski's ideal Socialist Utopia in which they would be in charge of a system of government for the government, as demonstrated by the refuge seekers from capitalism populating the "Justice" Department, FBI and State Department who tried so desperately to prevent Trump becoming President.

In 2017 Hillary and her 2000 mob of anti-American characters was expanded to include the pro-illegal immigration/sanctuary city, open borders, indoctrinated souls mob, most of whom are ignorant of what they are doing and never heard of Brzezinski whose *NWO* America destroying guidance they are following.

But this is ironic, as is the fact Al Gore could easily have been elected President of the United States in 2000 just as Hillary Clinton could in 2016 under the extant wonderful system we have had they been sufficiently intelligent to work within it, rather than spending most of their lives endeavoring to destroy it.

All Gore had to do was get a majority of the people in his home state of Tennessee who once sent him to Congress to vote for him. But he did not primarily because of his *NWO* stance on gun ownership, and his hypocrisy on the environment.

All Hillary had do was spend some time and money courting voters in states other than those dominated by her chosen voter base in the *"liberal"* and minority populated large urban areas while arrogantly ignoring working, tax-paying Middle America.

The voting population of American residing in Mr. Gore's home state of Tennessee who knew him best clearly stated with their votes they did not desire to have Gore as their President because his views of governing them were not representative of their ideas. Ditto: the rest of America versus Hillary.

Thus, the reason Hillary Clinton and her *"Establishment"* co-conspirators, including Mr. Gore, desire to get rid of the Electoral College is to silence the people's voice in their Government to the extent they are able, especially that of the citizens of Tennessee and any other states who do not agree with their idea of a Utopian Socialist state with a strong central government that does not represent either the combined or unique interests, of the people of each of the United States.

Their desire is to have the President elected by the disproportionate number of citizens of the ten or twelve most populous states whose populations are made up of more people of minorities and Government dependents who agree with their idea of a strong central, socialist welfare dependent Government. To accomplish this, they need get rid of the Electoral College.

***

States like California, New York, Michigan, Illinois, Ohio, Virginia, North Carolina, Pennsylvania, Wisconsin and Florida offer a couple of advantages that states like Kansas, Tennessee, Oklahoma, Iowa, Wyoming, North Dakota and other "Middle America" states do not.

They have large populations concentrated in small geographic areas, and these populations are increasingly, disproportionately Third World and Government dependent in character.

Metropolitan areas like New York City, Los Angeles, Detroit, Chicago and Miami have populations exceeding the populations of most states, and in many cases the populations of several states.

These large populations concentrated in small geographic areas are more accessible and cause the cost of advertising per person to be more cost effective than in the less densely populated states.

Since elections of the peoples' representatives in the Government are dependent on the ability of those desiring to be elected to "reach" voters through electronic media, television, and in person, the cost effectiveness, and relative ease of access of the voters in the large, densely populated areas is obvious.

But even though this is obvious, what might not be readily apparent to the average person is the magnitude of what a direct popular vote would mean in terms of the potential disenfranchisement of tens of millions, even a hundred million, Americans. New York provides a good example of this.

Hillary Clinton was elected Senator of New York by the disproportionately large population of New York City relative to the population of the rest of the state. Thus, Hillary did not represent the interests of all the people of New York State. She primarily represented the interests of citizens of New York City that is disproportionately non-representative of the demographics and interests of the rest of the state.

To extrapolate this New York example to the entire country, consider: the populations of only five states, California, New York, Texas, Florida and Pennsylvania represent over one-third of the population of the entire country. Yet, the populations of the four smallest states, Wyoming, Vermont, Alaska and North Dakota represent less than one percent of the population of the country.

For an idea of the relative population density of some of the states to some of the metropolitan areas, consider: the population of the Dallas metropolitan area is twice that of the four smallest states mentioned above, but the population of the Dallas area is only one-fifth that of New York City.

The population of the City of New York metro area exceeds that of each of four of the five largest states. Only California exceeds the population of the city of New York metro area. The population of the ten largest metropolitan areas represents over thirty per cent of the population of the country.

These statistics combined with the fact the majority of "minority" voters amounting to about forty percent of voters reside in the metropolitan areas of the largest states and vote Democrat should provide ample evidence of the reason Socialist Democrats like Gore and Hillary desire to relieve citizens of the United States of their representative democracy enhancing Electoral College.

Another factor that also may not be readily apparent to average citizens or voters is the *de facto* separation of the Office of the President from the rest of the Government should the President be elected directly by popular vote of the people rather than through the Electoral College process.

"If the will of the people is seen as an independent force, separate and apart from the rest of our constitutional structure, how shall we constrain a President who invokes the 'moral mandate' of popular will as his reason for ignoring that structure once in office?" - Michael Uhlmann, *Claremont Review*

It is frequently said the President of the United States is the most powerful person in the world. Most American citizens have heard this many times, but it is doubtful they have a complete understanding of the real power of the President.

Forget the *"most powerful person in the world."* It is Presidential domestic power citizens should be most concerned about.

The ability of the President to affect the lives and fortunes of average citizens without control of the legislative branch of the Government is tremendous, as every American should have witnessed with Obama in his non-Constitutional Executive Actions on immigration and other America destroying actions.

The power of "Executive Order," or of the President to engage in military action, set aside hundreds of millions of acres of land, determine energy policy, unilaterally decide whether, or not to protect the borders and citizens of the country, or many other decisions within his, or her tremendous, unilateral power should have become obvious to the people of the United States during the twenty-four years of Bill Clinton, Bush II and Barrack Obama.

Every citizen should contemplate what might happen if the President were to be elected by a simple majority popular vote of citizens residing in a very small percentage of the geographic area of the country with very narrowly defined interests relative to the rest of the country, and that person should decide to disregard the larger geographic and culturally diverse interests of the people of the total country.

But since Obama it is not necessary to "contemplate" that. All we need do is look at the statistics of how he was elected according to Professor Joseph Olsen of the University School of Law in Saint Paul Minnesota:

- **Of the fifty states, the number won by President Obama was 19 - only 38%**
- **Of 3,007,000 square miles of land that won by Obama was 580,000 - 19.3%**
- **Murder rate per 100 thousand in counties won by Obama – 13.2 versus 2.1 in others.**

In aggregate, territory NOT won by Obama "*was mostly the land owned by the taxpaying citizens of the country.* Whereas, the territory won by Obama was that wherein the population is largely composed of "*citizens living in low income tenements and living off various forms of Government welfare,*" i.e., inner city urban areas, which is about "*forty percent of the nation's population*" that has already "*reached the total Government dependency phase,* yet they continue to complain and riot because they are "oppressed." (If they are many in the rest of the world would love to also be "oppressed" in America, as illegal immigrants demonstrate daily.)

***

Now that we have seen who Obama catered to in actions and words for eight years... including free cell phones... we should be aware Presidents elected by a relatively small slice of America will most certainly pander economically to those who put them in the office, through favoritism, even ignoring laws and in every other way to the disadvantage of the rest of America and the country's future.

Thus, the prospect of a Hillary Clinton who vowed to replicate Obama's terms, as well as abolish the Electoral College, being a candidate for President either with or without the Electoral College being part of the process, should cause every freedom-loving American to think seriously about the national suicide a President Hillary would have represented for this and many other reasons.

She may seem "*smartest woman in the world*" to some who are not too smart themselves, or they would not believe this. But she is certainly not as smart as the collective brains behind the Constitution of the United States. This should be apparent to even those imbecilic advocates of the "*smartest woman*" theory.

Therefore, the truly intelligent person might ask: why does Hillary Clinton think her idea of eliminating the Electoral College is better than that of the collective brains who designed it?

The simple answer is she never thought about that. Her only thought was of becoming the first female President of the United States, and now that she is not nor ever will be, her desire is to disenfranchise all the people in "Middle America" she knows would rather die than have her or another Obama as President.

She was the prime candidate of the so-called "*liberal progressive*" element of Stalinist "*Useful idiots*" who insipidly promote nationally destructive "*multiculturalism*" and "*diversity*" in the ostensible interest of the United States being more culturally and ethnically diverse. But their actions confirm they "*quite frankly...don't really give a damn*" about cultural "*diversity.*"

In the same way they use other religions to attack Christianity to achieve their ultimate goal of a non-religious, Socialist Utopian society, they use "minorities" and the *"multicultural, diversity"* concept only to attack, divide and conquer the larger population of the country for their own interests and power.

Their attack on the Electoral College is proof of this. It is the only mechanism providing the best, but fading, chance the President of the United States will be elected by the diverse interests of the larger population of all fifty states of the entire country.

Their attack on the Electoral College exposes their real agenda is only power, and they will do anything to obtain that power, including division of the population of the country and destruction of the Constitution of the United States.

This attack, or any attack, on any part of the Constitution, is an attack on America, its people and the freedoms and Constitutional rights upon which the representative democratic Government of the United States of America is based.

But discounting the insipid suggestion loser Hillary is the *"smartest"* anything, remember: Stalin, Mao, Lenin, Marx, Engels, and Hitler were smart people, and the legacy of their smartness.

Then consider this could have been... or could still be... the legacy of the Constitution of the United States and the country based on it if placed in the hands of another President Obama or one some think is the *"smartest woman in the world,"* but has proven her entire adult life, in actions and words, she like Obama is an acolyte of Lenin, Marx, Engels, Alinsky and Brzezinski and their desired form of government.

Do you think if this were to happen the following would be the legacy of America?

'The greatest glory of a freeborn people is to transmit that freedom to their children." - William Harvard, *Regulus*

If not, retaining the Electoral College and all the other components of the Government of the United States as envisaged by those who founded the country and created its Constitution should be one of yours and all American's highest priority because the alternative is not a pleasant thought.

At the time of this writing Trump was able to appoint two Justices. But if he is in office another six years he will also likely have an opportunity to replace Ginsburg and Breyer with Justices who would be loyal to the Constitution, thus saving America from the ravages of *"the Establishment"* for at least forty more years.

This is a must do priority to direct America back on the course to its Greatness envisaged by our Founders!

EPILOGUE
WHAT ONE WORLD GOVERNMENT?

"...in shaping the future of the world. Will the global institutions, the distribution of power, and the politics and economies of nations in the 21st Century primarily reflect Western values and interests or will they be shaped primarily by those of Islam and China?" -Samuel P. Huntington

The United Nations desires to control the world through African style Socialism by pillaging the prosperity of the West and handing it out to the non-productive, growing populations of Africa the U.N. bureaucrats envisage as their power base.

The Bush I, Brzezinski *"New World Order"* of the industrialized countries desire to remake the world into a global "democracy," under their Socialist tutelage, because they envision six billion more consumers bathing with their soap, being cooled by their air conditioners, while using their computers or watching their televisions, and their dishes being cleaned by their dishwashers, before they get into their cars to go watch one of their movies.

And they also believe Western prosperity has to pay a price for their vision because it will not happen unless some of the prosperity of Western countries, primarily America, is shifted to the Third World to provide them with the needed financial foundation.

Islam desires to control the world by imposing its ideology upon everyone or eliminating those upon whom it cannot be imposed. It is succeeding in the Third World, and within segments of the Third World populations in Western countries, because it is not materialistic, and not demanding.

Those who have relatively little, and not educated, are easily seduced by tenets of this religion that offers an ideology they know they can possess, while "preaching" against those things perceived possessed by those they resent, and do not believe they will ever be able to obtain.

It cannot, however, succeed among educated, productive populations of most industrialized nations. Therefore, Islam can become dominant only through destruction of Western prosperity, and its overwhelming numbers of adherents, which are rapidly increasing primarily due to actions of the West begun in the Middle East by Bush II and extrapolated by Obama and Hillary Clinton.

The Chinese are in the game for the Chinese. And, justly so. With about twenty percent of world population they are a force to be reckoned with. They are pragmatic and non-religious, and their ideology has been employed to effect internal harmony and productivity. They understand the use of power is the only effective means of imposing one's will or system upon others.

The Chinese desire to surpass the West in economic and military strength. They have a multi-pronged approach to accomplish this. They are using the West to increase their economic strength by participating in the prosperity of the West to increase their own prosperity. And they are chipping away at the West here and there in the world while they are building allies and loyalty.

In the Middle East they are assisting enemies of the West. In Asia, they are helping build the prosperity of their neighbors, those with whom they have cultural and ethnic ties, those who have more natural affinity for the Chinese than for the West, especially Americans. And they are also making inroads to supplanting U.S. relations and power in the Americas via economic enhancement.

No rose-colored lenses, or idealistic world vision here. They are pragmatic, inventive, mostly homogeneous, and smart. They are the ones to watch!

All four plans for potential ultimate world domination require the demise of Western prosperity, military and political superiority, particularly that of the U.S. And all are dependent for their success on the populations they are using for their power base. Therefore, it is easy to predict which is going to be successful if current policies and courses of action are adhered to.

As Mao said, *"The people are the motive force in the making of world history."* They are also, for the most part, including the nature of their governments, determiners of their own fate, which seems to be beyond the intellectual capability of the average American.

It is not possible for anyone, any group, or power, to remake the different people of the world into their own image. Lasting change can occur only gradually, and from within. Therefore, all attempts to impose upon the people of the world, or to coerce them into accepting, a homogenized One World Government are doomed to failure, just as are all attempts to bring prosperity to those who do not choose to create it for themselves.

China, Africa, Europe, North and Latin America are all reasonably equally physically endowed. All have forests, rivers, arable land, ocean access, minerals, some oil, etc.

The Middle East has relatively less, but it has the bulk of the world's oil supplies. Yet, although endowed with pretty much an equal start, the history and the successes of the people of each has been vastly different.

Africa, cradle of mankind, is credited with the genesis of humans, but has produced very little else except more humans and human suffering since. Sub-Saharan Africa was Stone Age at the time of Nineteenth Century European colonization. No advancements of mankind can be attributed to the denizens of Sub-Saharan Africa... and since the Europeans departed Africa has mostly declined.

History shows attempts to help Africa will only deplete those basing their strategy on Africa because Africans have demonstrated an amazing ability to self-destruct no matter where they are. Africa where slavery and tribal warfare are still alive and well, inner city America and Europe, and Haiti are examples of this.

Therefore, unless the culture is changed, or displaced by one that is productive and would let the indigenous people benefit from their labor, forget it. Africa's future and the future of those whose strategy rest on it, is decline, as proven in inner city America.

Latin America is much more advanced than Africa in almost every way. It, however, is a long way from catching up to the industrialized First World. Many parts of it had advanced cultures prior to the European invasions. But unfortunately for it, the Europeans who invaded and colonized it were more opportunists than builders and creators.

Thus today, Latin America is lacking homogeneity in culture, prosperity, or ethnicity. Its populations consist of indigenous inhabitants, those of African and European heritage, and mixtures of all. As a result, Latin America does not provide the perception of need that Africa provides to those seeking an exploitable base, and its "*multicultural diversity*" prohibits mass exploitation.

Therefore, Latin America is pretty much on its own, left to finding its own way, neither "here nor there" as far as the play for world domination is concerned.

The Middle East had flourishing civilizations prior to the five hundred AD advent of Islam. They can be credited with inventing and discovering, first to domesticate animals, cultivate soil, use soap, the wheel, smelt metal, make bricks, and write. They also used mathematics and had a legal code.

But the introduction of the Islamic religion was the beginning of the decline of their advancement and their prosperity. After the introduction of Islam, their history is more one of war and conquest than of advancement, which is not uncommon to other cultures wherein pursuit of extra worldly, after life Utopias supersedes the pursuit of earthly successes except by those who use the religious piety of their religious masses to achieve their own earthly successes without concern for their afterlife.

So, if not for oil, Western advancement and prosperity creating the need for it, and the technology to get it out of the ground, the nations of Islam would be a very small blip on the world screen.

This is attested to by the fact of their recent decline in education with focus on religion, not prosperity and progress, even with oil.

Therefore, the only way any nations of Islam are a threat or contender, in any way, on the world stage, is due to Western tolerance, compassion, and political correctness, or their support of *Radical Islamic Terrorism,* which is a long term loser for them.

Asia and China in particular, have a history of power, strength and civilization. A millennium and a half ago China dominated Asia, beginning its rise about the time the Middle East world began its decline.

Japan modeled its government on China's over fourteen hundred years ago. The Great Wall was finished almost eighteen hundred years ago after over two hundred years of work. The Chinese created paper, gunpowder and even military rockets, and they were accomplished in mathematics hundreds of years ago. Now, they have been resurgent for at least four decades which coincides with the decline of America thanks only to the greed for expanded power and money of its "*Establishment*" political class.

***

Times change but people and human nature do not. Thus, there was never a time when the concept of the Rockefeller/Brzezinski Trilateral *New World Order* One World Government made any sense to the intelligent, thinking person. Common sense tells us that.

Islam and China also prove the concept flawed from its beginning. It was flawed because it ignored basic human nature, culture and history. It was truly the concept of those with *"weak people talents."* So, it should have died with the death of its founder, but it did not, as Mika discloses five days a week.

Neither China, nor Islam, was ever going to acquiesce to any One World Government unless they controlled it. And neither is tolerant, nor compassionate. China has a strategy called *"go global,"* and desires to advance.

Islam desires to take the world backward with it. China is using Islam and Western tolerance and idealism to its advantage.

The *faux New World Order* idea of endeavoring to avoid conflict at all costs was a good idea had it been sincere and honest. But it was not and is not because attempting to expand, or impose, prosperity and *faux* democracy in Africa and the Middle East militarily in pursuit of financial gain was a losing proposition for America and the West from the "*get go.*"

When the USSR was designated a threat, primarily for economic and expansion of power reasons the U.S. Government spent additional billions of dollars building a strong military deterrent ostensibly, as advertised, to prevent World War III. But now that China is a real, larger threat why are Americans not being told this by their Government?

The entire U.S. population was constantly bombarded with the USSR potential threat, and many were involved in construction of tools of deterrence; nuclear submarines, missiles, silos, planes, weapons, etc., etc. So, what is the reason Americans are not being told about the potential Chinese threat and that we are engaged in building deterrence to it, not Russia?

Also should not America be in the business of near term and long-term survival and perpetuation of its culture, rather than continued depletion of its prosperity through *New World Order*, doomed to fail schemes to deliberately shift a portion of its wealth to the Third World for enrichment of the one percent?

Right now, the West and America are only capable of being destroyed internally by their own "leadership," and this is happening now. This is a truly AMAZING world's first cultural suicide!

The only possible long-term results of Brzezinski *NWO* policies causing this, including the *faux* Russia threat, are either a slow agonizing suicide through prosperity depletion, or a relatively sudden death at some future date during World War III that will end questions about future prosperity increases of any non-Asian countries, or a non-Asian dominated One World Government.

***

As addressed in the Government Chapter, nations fail because of their government, military, and people. History clearly demonstrates this and contrary to popular opinion, it can happen in America!

Therefore, without a change in the orientation of United States Government policies in accord with President Trump's and a continuing Trump Conservative electoral and Supreme Court revolution to ensure the proper direction of the country for its survival the history of the Twenty-First Century is more likely to be shaped not by the West, but by the values of the People's Republic of China... possibly supported by Russian energy and technology entirely because of Brzezinski misguided anti-Russia policies... or much less likely by Islam, but also due to *"the Establishment"* media lies like Brzezinski's lie of ***"There isn't a global Islam."***

"People of the world, unite and defeat the U.S. aggressors and all their running dogs! ...Then the world will belong to the people. ...We are not only good at destroying the old world, we are also good at building the new." – Mao Tse-Tung
***

Above all else presented in this book Americans must be aware the biggest immediate threats to them within their control are indoctrination and immigration.

If President Trump does not remove education from control of *"Establishment"* indoctrinators youth support of communist Bernie Sanders proves there is little chance America will remain a democratic, capitalist country.

The placard carrying indoctrinated white kids among blacks, Latinos and Muslims protesting against borders and demanding elimination of Immigration and Customs Enforcement to open U.S. borders to everyone are evidence of this.

It proves they do not have a clue **there are differences in cultures and religions that cause the differences between American freedom and prosperity, and the others' poverty and lack of freedom.** This is proof of the success of Brzezinski's indoctrination program.

It also proves the more imminent threat is immigration promoted by the media and the veneer Democrat party following Brzezinski's plan to change the *"nature"* of the electorate to a Government dependent one to empower his socialist totalitarian Government.

Keeping in mind all opposed to open immigration are falsely painted *"racist"* by pro-open borders America destroyers, and numbers are not racist, but facts demonstrated by the immigrants and their cultures prove if this immigration is not stopped the nature of America will change to that of Mexico due to Brzezinski engendered replacement of homogeneity with proven divisive multicultural *"diversity."*

Then because of the proven tendency of the immigrants not to assimilate but replicate their cultures in "communities" concentrated in large urban areas, if Hillary, Obama and their acolytes are successful in eliminating the Electoral College there will be no stopping the turning of America into a multicultural dystrophic "swamp" hole of disunity, concomitant strife and poverty.

This not a racist comment. It is a fact cultures are different, and the nature of their home countries reflect the nature of the cultures of the immigrants, and therein lies the problem for Americans.

America is America because of its northern European Protestant cultural heritage just as Mexico is Mexico because of its Southern European Catholic heritage mixed with the indigenous Indian culture. The former has a history of laws, high regard for education, productivity, progress, organization and advancement, whereas the latter does not. The church is the center of its culture, and it has subjugated real education and advancement to maintenance of its control over life in all countries it occupies this dominant position.

Therefore, if America becomes a majority Spanish speaking population country it will naturally, eventually become a replication of Third World Latin America. It's in the numbers of majority rule.

Thus, America as we have known it will be gone unless voters stop this immigration! They are the only determinants. The future of their country is in their hands – not Trump's.

Whether America continues to not only be *"Great"* but even survive is entirely up to them – not Trump!

Hopefully, this book provided the knowledge we Americans have a serious problem, and what that problem is, so we can set about eliminating it via the ballot box in order to help *"Make* **[and keep]** *America Great Again!"*

So, please do not forget this book is about the single most serious threat to Americans and the future of their country, and that threat is not Russia.

THE INTERNAL THREAT posed by *"The Establishment"* NWO political whores inhabiting the U.S. Government and their *"fake news media"* is the only real threat to us, our country and its very existence. The evidence of this is presented every day on FOX NEWS if not anywhere else.

It is the threat posed by these people bought and paid for to destroy President Trump's Presidency and the good he is doing for all of us because they have become relatively so much richer and powerful under the Brzezinski Business Plan for America they cannot tolerate the rest of our country and us reverting back to the course of success we, our country and ancestors were on before it.

The ex-Directors of the FBI, NSA, CIA, many members of Congress, media pundits and commentators, appearing daily in opposition to Trump trade deals, tariffs, tax cuts, roll back of economy destroying regulations, yet in favor of open borders and more immigration are obvious examples.

But it is the not so obvious of those who have benefited most who are behind the slow-moving coup of President Trump.

It is the behind the scenes actions of Robert Mueller and his cabal, President Obama, the three previous Presidents and those loyal to them who are the real movers and shakers behind this.

BEWARE!